VIDEO DAYS

VIDEO DAYS

HOW STREET VIDEO WENT FROM
A DEEP UNDERGROUND PHENOM
TO A ZILLION DOLLAR BUSINESS.
FROM PIRATE TV TO YOUTUBE,
WHAT WAS GAINED
AND LOST ALONG THE WAY
AND WHAT WE SAW
THROUGH THE VIEWFINDER.
A MEMOIR BY

NANCY CAIN

EVENT HORIZON PRESS · PALM SPRINGS, CALIFORNIA

VIDEO DAYS
A Memoir By
NANCY CAIN

For Thunderheart

Contents

The Function of a Video Tape Recorder . . . overleaf

Chapter One: Subject to Change . . . 1

Chapter Two: Freex in Soho 1970 . . . 29

Chapter Three: Probably America's Smallest TV Station . . . 39

Chapter Four: TVTV . . . 64

Chapter Five: Perhaps it was the Fermi Fast Breeder Reactor . . . 77

Chapter Six: Something Entirely Different . . . 85

Chapter Seven: Free Speech and Dangerous Television . . . 90

Photos and Images . . . 99-126

Chapter Eight: Art and Life . . . 127

Chapter Nine: L.A. 1984 . . . 135

Chapter Ten: Love . . . 146

Chapter Eleven: Jobs and Money . . . 154

Chapter Twelve: I am the Nielsens . . . 169

Chapter Thirteen: Aunt Betty's Secret and the New Right . . . 172

Chapter Fourteen: The Wilton North Report . . . 181

Chapter Fifteen: Ian . . . 185

Chapter Sixteen: The Nineties . . . 190

Chapter Seventeen: Camnet, the Camcorder Network . . . 198

Chapter Eighteen: How to File for Bankruptcy . . . 219

Chapter Nineteen: Chicago Revisited . . . 221

Chapter Twenty: Quick Gig with the Greatest . . . 223

Chapter Twenty-one: Whee! . . . 225

Chapter Twenty-two: Greetings from Cracktown . . . 230

Afterword . . . 236

Index . . . 238

THE FUNCTION OF A VIDEO TAPE RECORDER (VTR) is to store or record the video signal. When a VTR receives a video signal from a camera, it converts that electrical signal to magnetism. This magnetism can be transferred onto video tape during the recording process. The process of changing the magnetism on the tape back into a video signal is called playback. The full process of making a videotape recording is: light is changed to a video signal in the camera; that signal is sent to the VTR where it is changed to magnetism; the magnetism is stored on the tape. To play back the recording: the magnetism on the tape is reconverted to a video signal in the VTR. This signal is then sent to a TV set or monitor where it is changed back into a representation of the light that struck the camera.

The Spaghetti City Video Manual
Videofreex 1973

Chapter One:
Subject to Change

IN THE BEGINNING there was video and it was good. Back then video technology was still virtually unknown. A portable video camera was an oddity. The only people who had them were cops, hippies, and conceptual artist Nam June Paik, who recorded the Pope's visit to New York in 1965 using one. The cops recorded the faces of the hippies at events and political actions and the hippies loved to shoot video of the cops shooting video of them. When I would overhear the word "video" being spoken on the street or in a restaurant somewhere, I would assume people were talking about me. It was logical. And if I turned to look, I would often see people pointing at me and my camera and they would be smiling and waving. They'd want to know how much it cost, was it heavy, and what was it for. It cost about fifteen hundred dollars, the deck and camera together weighed about twenty pounds, and it was for adventure and freedom and possibilities and truth. It wasn't movies or television, it was video. Video was a rover. Video came along for the ride. Video was immediate. It was participatory.

IT WAS EARLY AFTERNOON. It was hot. It was New York in the summer of 1969. Crossing 52nd Street at Sixth Avenue I tugged on my bra in the sticky weather. Alone in the elevator, I pulled it off quickly and stuffed it into my bag. At the 34th floor I stepped silently out onto the carpet, real art on the walls. A beautiful receptionist looked up at me through her dark eyelashes and in a hushed tone asked my name. I told her and said I had a lunch appointment with Don West. Don was the executive assistant to the president of the CBS network, and the producer of a new pilot presentation for prime time television. I was the lapsed actress still dizzy from a yearlong road trip across the country. I had worked in television and theater, but had given up acting while at an audition at Grey Advertising a year ago. One year since my soap

1

commercial epiphany and subsequent escape from New York. Now I was back, but changed.

LOOKING ACROSS THE TABLE at Don, he didn't fit the mold of television producers I'd met in the past. Don appeared to be sweet, soft-spoken, and almost actually shy. It is my way to allow the other person to begin a conversation on first meeting, but after a long moment I broke the initial silence saying, "Where are you from?"

"Virginia," he said. "I was an editor at Broadcasting magazine in Washington D.C. when I met Dr. Stanton (the President of the CBS network) and he gave me this opportunity to learn the television industry from the top down, so to speak. He liked the cut of my jib," Don said. "I rented a house in Connecticut and brought the whole family up. Where are you from?"

"Detroit. My dad's in the advertising business and produces a lot of TV. That's how I got into it." We nodded and looked at each other for a while, then checked the menu.

"This is my first experience as a television producer," Don said. "I've hired a couple of TV writers from *Second City* in Chicago, because the network would like me to come up with a show that could replace The Smothers Brothers," said Don.

"The Smothers Brothers? They're such a big hit."

"Yes, but they're being cancelled."

"Really? I've been away. I must have missed that. What happened? Were they too controversial?" I speculated.

"What do you mean?"

"I suppose I mean too anti-Vietnam war. Was that it?" Don didn't know. "The network wants a Smothers Brothers replacement variety show, but to tell the truth I'd like to try my hand at film documentary," he confessed, "even experimental."

"That sounds interesting," I said. I ordered the club sandwich. Don got an omelet.

"But if I do the variety show, I'd like to have three hosts," Don said. "An older man, like Kurt Vonnegut the novelist, a younger man, I'm not sure who, and of course, a girl." He smiled at me. "You were

2

highly recommended as a possible television personality, like a storyteller who could sing. Are you working now? Can I see you anywhere?"

"Well, I was working at the *Upstairs at the Downstairs* in a musical revue, but no, not now. I've been traveling. Now that I'm back I'm thinking about opening a small coffeehouse with a friend of mine. We're looking at store fronts to rent up near Columbia University."

"Oh, a coffeehouse, that sounds interesting. I wonder if we could do a TV show originating from a coffeehouse?"

"Why not?"

"Right, why not?" Don nodded in agreement. I dug into my sandwich. Don ate slowly.

"You were saying you'd been away," he said. Would I tell him? He seemed so sincere, and interested, I was tempted. "I drove across the country with my husband," I began.

"Oh?"

"Yes. We were in Aspen, on the return trip, when he disappeared," I said. Oops, now it was too late. I would have to continue. There was no going back and somehow I loved to tell the story.

"Disappeared?" Don asked. "That sounds serious. I don't understand."

"Have you ever heard of Gurdjieff, the Russian philosopher?" Don shook his head no. "Well, he had a cult back around the turn of the century in Eastern Europe. He and his students would take road trips and try different exotic drugs to induce altered states."

"What for?" Don asked.

"For self study, and to look ahead, to see beforehand, in advance." Don was silent. "I'm sorry Don, I seem to be way off topic. I'm not sure what any of this has to do with television," I said. "It's not something I particularly believe in, it's just that we happened to run into a few of Gurdjieff's so-called disciples in Aspen. I think my husband took off with them. It was a shock. I never understood my husband."

"Yes, well. Can you start right away?"

"What?"

3

"Oh, I'm getting ahead of myself. You know, the story you're telling would be an interesting documentary film. The counterculture, a nomadic lifestyle, mind expansion—."

"Acid?" I asked.

"Oh, yes, LSD," Don said. "All I know about that is what I read in Life magazine. I'm supposing you've tried it."

"Yes. I think it changed my perspective," I told him.

"What made you do it?"

"The first time I was curious, I guess. I didn't really plan it. It arrived in the mail. My husband's brother in San Francisco sent it to us as a wedding gift. Two tiny squares of ink blotter. If you weren't looking for them, you'd toss them out with the envelope."

"Oh?"

"So I just took one, popped it into my mouth, and let it dissolve on my tongue, and then, you know, we laughed and I forgot about it, and a couple of hours later it came on strong. Everything, I mean everything, like all of civilization was decomposing before my eyes. There are a lot more living things than we think there are zooming around us in the air, you know, microscopic. So there I was, having attained this new super-magnified vision, dealing with a new reality, when suddenly, from somewhere deep inside of me, I remembered that my agent had gotten me an audition at Grey Advertising for a soap commercial that very afternoon and I had to be uptown in an hour. Landing a commercial like that could pay the rent for a year." Don listened.

"Well, the subway was swirling in acid trails but I got on it. My car was filled with barnyard animals all snorting and huffing, but I rode it to my stop."

The waitress cleared the table. I ordered the chocolate mousse. Don ordered a coffee and motioned for me to continue.

"I stepped up to the receptionist, who had little sparks flying off of her, but was otherwise intact, and said I was there to read for Dial soap. She handed me the script and said it would be a few minutes. I took the script and executed my descent into the cushy sofa. At that point I noticed there was another actress sitting beside me. It was eerie.

4

She could have been my twin right down to the dark eyes and brown curls. She was holding an identical script. I gestured toward her to make sure it wasn't a mirror. The other actress nodded. Did she see the pinwheels in my eyes? I looked back down at the script. I scanned the text. From what I could understand, in this scene, the actress is supposed be feeling tired and sluggish as she steps into the shower with a bar of Dial soap. Maybe you remember seeing it? She turns on the water, and begins to lather herself up. Now she is supposed be transformed, ecstatic, getting very turned on. By the time she's all soaped up, she's supposed to be enraptured," I explained to Don. "Because the soap is so great, see?" He nodded silently. "They wanted me to come in the shower with a bar of soap!" Don's eyes bugged out a little. "So then the casting director appeared in the reception area and said something like, 'Suzanne, it's great to see you.' I watched her slip her arm around the other actress's waist saying, 'I hope you're feeling sexy today.' As they walked down the hall, that was it. That was my epiphany."

"It was?"

"Yes. It was like that trick your eyes can play on you when you stare at an image for a while and suddenly the subject and the ground reverse positions and an entirely different picture emerges. For example, it was a vase and then it was two faces in profile—like that. It was the same world, but now I saw it the other way. So I handed the script back to the receptionist and left the building. I stepped out onto 3rd Avenue weightless." Don nodded. I spooned up a big helping of pudding. "I guess what I'm trying to say is, that I don't feel right performing on television anymore. I hope I haven't wasted your time."

"Well, maybe you could be my assistant," said Don. "You wouldn't have to be on camera. Can you start right away?" I told him I'd have to think about it. We hadn't had a very professional meeting, but apparently that didn't matter to him. And, he had absolutely no interest in my résumé. I liked that.

CAROL AND I USED TO DASH across the West Side Highway for the fun of it that summer. We had that much energy. In the headlines men were walking on the moon, there were cult murders in California, and a terrible accident on the Chappaquiddick Bridge. There was a kind of black excitement in the air. People had even stopped hitchhiking. But still, we were water-skiing in the famously polluted Hudson River. We would wait until we got up to the Tapanzee Bridge, where the water was a paler shade of yellow before we jumped in.

"I knew you'd be back," Carol said one morning at breakfast.

"Because—?" I prompted her.

"Because hooking up with exactly the wrong person, driving off in that horrible Volkswagen van, with the little curtains?" She shook her head. She never did like Alan. "No. I knew you'd be back."

Carol imagined my road trip as a total nightmare, but when I thought of it, I saw the tranquil empty highway at sunset, the wind-swept flats of Montana, camped out, squatting unseen, hidden behind a railroad berm, cooking potatoes on a Bunsen burner, the two of us alone on a strange barren planet, thumbing through our tattered little library of paperbacks and comic books, written by obscure philosophers and R. Crumb. "How can we have peace in the world?" I would ask an unseen deity as a test question. I would close my eyes, and flip through the pages to a random spot and jab my finger onto a line of type.

"Everything is dependent on everything else, everything is connected, nothing is separate. Therefore everything is going in the only way it can go. If people were different everything would be different. They are what they are, so everything is as it is." That was Gurdjieff. Then I would try R. Crumb using the same method. "The universe is completely insane," said Mr. Natural. "But t-t-that's crazy," said Flakey Foont, and Mr. Natural said, "Yes, isn't it?"

MY AGENT RICK fixed me up with Alan Cain. It was a blind date and we made plans to meet in front of Radio City Music Hall. He told me on the phone that he was my age, a graduate of Temple University and that he grew up in the Catskills, where his dad had a job at the Concord Hotel running maintenance crews. He had been working in New York in the mail room at William Morris Agency, but quit after six months and went

6

into textile sales. When I caught sight of Alan in front of Radio City, he was wearing a shimmery goldish-green double-breasted suit and a large diamond pinky ring. I was coming home from an audition for a television commercial and was wearing a black mini-dress, boots, a London Fog trench coat belted tight, and a brown beret. I felt immediately that he was definitely not my type but, as the evening progressed, I noticed his eyes were blue and later he seemed sweet and his teeth were so white, then at some point he became extremely sexy and really pretty amusing and lovable even. Later that evening he pressed his cheek to mine.

Alan moved out of his place in Queens and into my apartment on Washington Street and my roommate Carol Vontobel moved to her boyfriend's place on 15th Street. I married Alan. We drove in a borrowed car to Elkton, Maryland and soon we were on our first acid trip as man and wife. His pinky ring was gone (he gave it to his dad) and so was his job. In place of his suit, Alan now preferred flowing robes. And he didn't want to laugh with me at the obvious absurdity of life.

I WATCHED CAROL rifling through the cupboard looking for the Muesli. I told her "Yes okay you were right and I'm back. Of course the note Alan left tacked to the screen door on the morning of his disappearance had a lot to do with my decision."

"What did it say?"

"Think of me as dead.'" We both began to laugh. "It was on my birthday, too! Can you believe it? I was coming back from the laundromat on the morning of my birthday with a big pillowcase filled with his clean underwear slung over my shoulder, and there it was on the outside of the door. I just stood there. He had taken the van and vanished. He was gone."

"You're better off."

"For sure."

DURING MY STAY at Carol's apartment on West End Avenue, her cats Puck and Timma begat twins, Peaches and John. Carol, who was

7

teaching elementary school in Harlem, had just broken off her engagement to a pale serious fellow from the Communist Workers party. He was gone, but his cats remained. It was a small apartment for so many cats. You had to be careful at night because if you got up in the dark and you were barefoot, you could easily step on a slimy chicken heart that had been batted around the room and abandoned at changing locations on the parquet floor.

Over the next few days Don sent gifts. Flowers and candy and ultimately, a sterling silver subway token holder from Tiffany was delivered by messenger. As it happened I would never know why Don wanted to hire me, but those were strange times and I was down to my last forty dollars, and three subway tokens.

"What are you waiting for?" asked Carol. "Be realistic. If we had an investor we could go ahead with the coffeehouse, but we don't. You've got to get a job! The rent must be paid. Never forget that." So I called Don and told him I would do it, even though I had little idea what it would actually entail. "Don't worry, "said Carol. "It's going to be fine. I'd take the job myself."

"What? And give up elementary school? You would?"

I introduced Don to Carol and he hired her too, as the production office manager, and the next day he hired Carol's friend, Skip Blumberg. Skip had been going to business school at Cornell but dropped out when Nixon took away the grad school deferments and had gotten a job teaching at P.S. 80 with Carol. He'd spent the summer traveling around Mexico and letting his hair grow. Our new venture sounded great to Skip and he quickly decided television production was for him. I felt good having Carol and Skip along on the project. We all had a warm feeling for Don and wanted his show to be a big success.

OUR FIRST OFFICE at the network was in a large boardroom on the 14th floor of the dazzling CBS headquarters, known in the industry as Black Rock. My salary was measly because I took less than Don offered because I was stridently uninterested in money because somewhere in the Rockies I had held money in my hands and examined it closely, slowly, turning it over in bright moonlight and again under the sun and concluded that money was of no value. The idea of working for it seemed insane. I now wanted freedom more than employment. Consequently, there were no contracts, no provisions, nothing promised or implied. I just began to show up.

The boardroom, our temporary home while the large third floor suite was being completed for us, was on the same floor as the New York Yankees office. CBS owned the Yankees that summer of 1969. I won't forget the day the New York Mets won the World Series. I watched the utter pandemonium on the streets as miles of toilet paper, confetti and shredded documents fluttered from the windows along the Avenue, all played against the dead silence from the Yankee's office down the hall.

IN 1949 THE TEN INCH Admiral TV in the blonde console arrived in our home. I was just a little kid but we were instantly inseparable. TV had an extra appeal for me because my dad, Leon Wayburn, produced a lot of the TV shows in Detroit. He was in the advertising business and was no fool about the potential of television. He had some big accounts including Velvet Peanut Butter, Twin Pines Milk, and Restocraft Mattresses. Of course he advised his clients to advertise on television. So they said that sounded like a good idea but there were no programs to advertise on, so that's how he started producing the programs for his clients to put their ads on.

His most popular show was *Milky's Movie Party,* sponsored by Twin Pines Milk every Saturday afternoon live. Milky the Clown was a magician and had a bunch of kids in the studio, like the peanut gallery on Howdy Doody, and there were games and contests and magic tricks and some kids got to plunge their hands into a huge fishbowl filled with pennies and they could keep as many as they could hold. Then there was a puppet show, and a movie, and the Twin Pines Milk "Smile of Sunshine" photo contest where the winners got their pictures put on television.

It was all produced live from WJBK-TV, and later moved to WWJ-TV. My sister Linda and I got to go anytime we wanted to. I would sit in the control room with the director. I would watch him sitting at the big console next to his technician, while he called out which camera to

9

switch to. I was amazed at his skill and calmness. And, when Milky the Clown was telling the kids about Twin Pines Milk, I felt proud because Twin Pines was obviously better than Sealtest. I felt glad that my dad had found the best milk and was telling people about it. I felt the same about Velvet Peanut Butter. We all knew that Velvet tasted better than Skippy. And who would buy a Sealy mattress when there was Restocraft? And so I loved TV, which I understood was completely generated by advertisers.

FOR THE FIRST TWO WEEKS at CBS I sat in the 14th floor boardroom rolling fat joints in long strips of the New York Times and meeting with a steady stream of peculiar and amazing people who we hoped might be fun to see on television, or who wanted to be on television, or had something to say about what they thought should be on television.

Word had gotten around that we were looking for contemporary themes for documentaries, so now we were being wooed by the counterculture, lefty college politicos, drop-out rock and rollers, maverick rabbis, and any and every group with an agenda for the revolution. For example, the politically radical married-to-each-other couple who were university professors from Long Island and had me cornered in the conference room for over an hour. I was straining their patience. Why was it so difficult to explain to me what was wrong with television? It was so simple. It was my politics! Why couldn't I see how uninformed and backward I was compared to them? "You can't have advertisers if you want to be politically correct," the woman professor wailed at me. "I agree with you. Myself, I wouldn't say that stuff," I said, always remembering the soap commercial, "but that won't change anything. I have no control over the advertising policy of the network." Now they were furious. "You just don't get it do you? We came all the way over here to explain it to you but you just don't get it," the professor shouted. "It's selling out! *Selling out!*"

"Well, how about this?" I suggested. "Suppose we told our advertisers that in order to buy time on our show they would have to tell the truth in their commercials. Would that be a compromise?"

"No!" they wailed. "That's even worse!"

"What do you want from me? You want me to quit my job? What good will that do?" They just shook their heads. "Visualize your product for a moment. What is your product?"

"Our show is our product, I would think."

"Do you think your program is your product? Think again. Your audience is your product. You are selling your product, your audience, to the advertiser! Don't you see?" Ultimately they gave up. "Take some responsibility for what you're doing!" said the professor as the door closed behind them. "Let's try to get the Beatles!" I said to Carol.

YOU COULD FEEL THE PULSE and hear the beat of our new corner suite on the third floor the moment you stepped out of the elevator. This was obviously something very different than the corporate culture that surrounded us. At Black Rock, the management was enormously fussy. The building, designed by Eero Saarinen, had windows that were sealed and latchless. The air was a uniform temperature and, along with everything else, regulated centrally. Nothing was left to chance at CBS. It was all the grand plan of Dr. Frank Stanton, whose power had been bestowed upon him by the Chairman William S. Paley himself. From the first blueprint Dr. Stanton had the final say on each detail at Black Rock, including all the art on every wall. The art was doled out to each floor from a central art room. You went down there to the central art room and chose from artwork that Dr. Stanton had pre-selected as being suitable. And then the art-hanging crew would bring it to your office and make sure it was hung properly. So, I knew the scotch-taped Mao posters and psychedelic head shop designs that were being thumb-tacked on the walls and the constant thump of rock and roll were not going to go over well.

Don was rapidly cutting back on the comedy writers' input and becoming more seriously interested in looking for stories that would work as documentaries. He had just returned from a quick trip to Boston and he was excited. He was onto something. Don had found Mel Lyman. Or perhaps Mel Lyman had found Don. It was never quite clear which. Don thought Mel Lyman and his followers in their Roxbury

11

Massachusetts commune would be a fascinating story for his first documentary film.

"Mel Lyman," Don announced. "Have you heard of him?" I hadn't. "Mel writes for the *Avatar*. It's an alternative publication out of Boston. And they all live together in this big house in Roxbury."

In the first issue of *Avatar*, June 9-22 1967, Mel Lyman wrote a piece titled "To All Who Would Know." It began, "To those of you who are unfamiliar with me let me introduce myself by saying that I am not a man, not a personality, not a tormented struggling individual. I am all those things but much much more. I am the truth and I speak the truth. I do not express ideas, opinions, personal views. I speak truth. My understanding is tinged by no prejudice, no unconscious motivation, no confusion. I speak clearly, simply, openly and I speak only to reveal, to teach, to guide. I have no delusions about what I am, who I am, why I am. I have no pride to contend with, no hopes, no fears, In all humility I tell you that I am the greatest man in the world and it doesn't trouble me in the least … ." In the same issue, Mel advertises: "Mel Lyman is Unhappy. Why? Because he has no film to make movies. Make Mel Happy by sending money … Please hurry, I can't stand to hear him cry."

"Is he a folk singer?" asked Skip.

"He's a banjo player, I think," said Carol, "in Jim Kweskin's Jug Band. My brother has their album."

"Yes I think you're right," said Skip. "And the Jug Band is part of this larger commune. There was an article about them in *Fusion* magazine."

We did a little research and discovered the apparently power-hungry Roxbury commune members hadn't liked the way they had been portrayed in *Fusion* and had actually kidnapped Robert Somma, the magazine's editor. He had gone with them without a struggle and was ultimately unharmed, but he was quoted as saying "I will forewarn you, they really don't joke around. They're as malicious and malevolent as any group I've met."

"Mel is an amazing person," said Don, unimpressed with the

scary stories about the pseudo hippie, Nazi commune. Don had just spent the weekend living at Mel Lyman's commune and had participated in their daily routine, even pulling "guard duty" one night.

"Why do they need guards?" I asked.

"I want to go back there with a film crew," Don answered, ignoring my question. Don was beginning to form his vision of film vérité based on two little movies Mel Lyman had shown him during his visit. One, a film Lyman made of the children in the commune waking up in the morning, Don found very moving. He was quite interested in the way the scenes had been edited in the camera. Then Lyman showed Don his movie of Jim Kweskin on acid. "Kweskin completely changed his personality right on film," Don said excitedly. "I think something like that happened to you, didn't it, Nancy?"

"Not exactly," I said.

Memo
To: Don
From: Nancy (clipped onto recent articles we'd found)
Did you see these? I don't get it. What do they want?
What's going on?

Memo
To: Nancy
From: Don
Let's get a crew from WGBH in Boston
and go out there right away.

Don was going to go back to Roxbury with a video crew from WGBH in Boston and frankly I was afraid for him. Aside from being a powerful subject, Don wanted Mel Lyman himself to make some films for the program. In *Rolling Stone* magazine two years later Don was quoted as saying: "For me this was a completely mind-blowing experience. I came right out of the 34th floor of CBS, I was approaching middle age, and I just fell in love with the Hill. And, I thought, they with me. I guess they thought I was the route to taking

13

over CBS. They probably found me a very pliable instrument. I suspended most of my critical judgment and just let it happen, if you know what I mean."

Don was enthusiastic about the possibilities of having Mel Lyman make documentaries for the show. He asked Mel if he thought he would be able to follow a shooting script if they gave him one, and Mel said, "No! Absolutely not!" Then according to Don, he flew into a rage which lasted for several hours. I was feeling frantic to find an alternative to going with this story—but what?

BEFORE THERE WAS A WORD FOR NERD, there was Louis Brill. He had the glasses held together with gaffer's tape, the pocket-protector, the pens, and the high-top sneakers. He wore a colored cloth bandana which partially obscured a strange eczemic stigmata on his forehead, while simultaneously drawing attention to his wild eyes gleaming. Louis's job, it seemed, was to hand-deliver memos from office to office at Black Rock but I don't know for sure what he was doing. I would occasionally catch sight of him whizzing down the hallway. Sometimes he'd pop his head in and say hello.

"Nancy! Did you miss me? I've been to the Woodstock Festival of Peace and Love, and I think I've found what you're looking for."

"Is that right?"

"That's right. I met some hippies who call themselves the Videofreex. They had these little portable video cameras and they were videotaping all around the tents and the campsites and the medics and the kitchen and the long lines of people waiting to use the port-o-potties. That's where I met them."

"Sit down, Louis."

"I told the Videofreex that I worked at CBS and could get them a television series," he said, "so I'd like you and Don to come downtown with me to meet them."

Louis and Don and I went down to Rivington Street on the lower east side on a beautiful quiet Saturday morning. In the stillness we shouted up from the street to the Videofreex loft and David Cort came down to let us in. David was a wild-haired, jovial and flamboyant man with an immense laugh and tremendous energy. In his mid-thirties, David was one of the first members of the video underground in New York and had recently held a job where he introduced video to the Brooklyn Children's Museum. He did the talking. He told us he had gone to Brandeis University with Abbie Hoffman, the political activist who was about to go on trial as a member of the Chicago Eight for conspiracy to incite riot at the 1968 Democratic Convention. "It's going to be the trial of the century," David said enthusiastically. "It's very high-profile due to the theatricality of the defendants." As David went on about the possibility of going out to Chicago with a video camera, Curtis Ratcliff watched him through the viewfinder of their video camera, smiling silently as she recorded him.

Curtis was an artist and this was her loft where she had been happily painting and sculpting until she met David, and he had moved in with his video gear. Her long light brown hair was parted in the middle and fell straight down past her shoulders in the preferred fashion of the day. Her pale blue eyes and rosy cheeks contrasted David's black eyes and bushy beard.

At the loft with them that morning was Parry Teasdale. Parry, a long lanky kid with just above shoulder-length hair, wearing a sleeveless, purple undershirt with VIDEOTRIPS stenciled on the front, was setting up the video monitor on the table in front of us. Parry, who was about twenty, had met David at the Woodstock Festival the previous week where they had probably been the only two people carrying portable video cameras at the entire festival (and Parry's camera was only a Panasonic surveillance type without even a view finder). Parry had dropped out of Colgate, let his hair grow, much to the dismay of his mother and father in Poughkeepsie, and seemed to prefer living in his van to their suburban home.

At the Woodstock Festival, David had a small booth in the Hog Farm/Movement City neighborhood and Parry happened by and they agreed to pool their resources. David had electrical power and a Sony Porta-pak, and Parry had what amounted to a stationary system which they set up at their booth where they used it to tape reactions of people seeing themselves on a video screen for the first time. At the end of the

15

festival David and Parry agreed that Parry would come to New York where they would try to edit the Woodstock tapes together.

PARRY HAD TO SPEND a good deal of his time that summer dealing with the Army. Everyone at the Selective Service Board thought Parry was very sweet, and more than a little spaced. They always sincerely hoped he would find his way home when he would leave their office. "Are you going to be all right?" the motherly recruiter would ask. Parry had only recently moved out of his van and into the loft on Rivington Street with David and Curtis. "Three makes a group," David had proclaimed, so one of the guys in Buzzy Linhart's band in the loft above them dubbed them the Videofreex! Everyone liked the name. It had "video" and it had "free," it had "freaks," and it had the popular letter "X," making it play on some of the hippest words and symbols of the day.

The Videofreex sat us down in front of a nine-inch monitor and David showed us his tapes, "First Aid #1" and "First Aid #2." It was information he'd videotaped to play back in the field at the festival to help people with medical emergencies. Then he played "Latrine," affectionately known as "The Shit House Tapes," showing endless lines of stoned hippies waiting for the port-o-potties. I was riveted. It was like being there without actually having to be there. The people, the atmosphere, the drama. I liked it. A lot.

Don hired the Videofreex right away and we started searching for stories and events to videotape. There was major excitement. We had a new way of seeing. Whatever was happening during the fall of 1969, we wanted to videotape it. We wanted to show it. At this point, the writers from Second City left the project with the clock ticking at three months until Don's show for the network, which was scheduled for presentation on December 17.

By early September the Videofreex project had become known as *Subject to Change,* and/or "The Now Project." I was assigned to go to Chicago with the Videofreex, David, Curtis, and Parry. The revolution had begun in the streets of Chicago during the Democratic convention the previous year, and David's college pal Abbie Hoffman was now on trial for planning it (the revolution) with other radicals. The govern-

16

ment had defined their actions as "conspiracy to incite a riot." From August 19 to August 25, 1968, there had been a major confrontation between the Chicago police and the anti-war protesters. The protesters had been brought together by the Mobilization to End the War in Vietnam (the Mobe), and the Youth International Party (the Yippies), who planned a Festival of Life to counteract the Democratic Convention of Death. The Yippies papered cities across the country with their invitation.

"People, Get Ready," it screamed. "Free people, free pot, free music, free theatre, a whole new culture will manifest itself to the world, rising from the ashes of America. Rock groups will be performing in the parks, newspapers will be printed in the streets, provos and police will play cops and robbers in the department stores, Democrats and dope fiends will chase each other through hotel corridors. Long boats filled with Vikings will land on the shores of Lake Michigan, and discover America! Chicago will become a river of wild onions!"

It hadn't quite worked out that way. Now, a year later, the Videofreex and I were headed for Chicago. The trial of the *Chicago 8* had begun. We took off from New York in Don's family station wagon in the late afternoon. We spent the night in a motel off the Pennsylvania turnpike, and rolled into Chicago in the gray early morning past long stretches of smoke-belching factories and industrial landscapes. "Wouldn't it be great to make this our opening shot like, you know, "America!" I said. And Parry hooked up the video right there in the car and started videotaping. We videotaped the ride into Chicago. In a flash I understood that we were able to record video anytime and anyplace we wanted to. I realized that, battery permitting, all we had to do was keep shooting. Tape was cheap. We left the camera running.

We got pulled over by the Chicago police the moment we arrived in town. I showed the officer our letter of introduction from Don West at CBS, all the time with our camera running, and they allowed us to proceed. We kept the camera running, shooting the raucous throngs and playing back the video for the protesters right there in the streets.

17

"VENCEREMOS!"

"Ho Ho, Ho Chi Minh, the NLF is gonna win!"

It was about that and it was about a lot of things. It was about ending the war. It was about equal rights. It was about all kinds of freedom. We played back the video we shot right there for the people in the streets, which was unheard of back then. The news media would never do it. But that made the difference. People loved it. We all loved it. Now we were all in it together.

We connected the long Sennheiser microphone the engineers at CBS gave us to make sure we got good sound, and fell into the roiling river of protesters. David, holding the microphone, walked over to a group of people in the neighborhood watching from the curb. "No comment," said a fifty-ish white woman wearing a babushka, speaking carefully into the microphone.

"No comment? Why not?" asked David.

"Because we don't know nothin'."

"You don't know anything at all? Do you know what this is about?"

"No, no," she answered. A young pale boy about fourteen who was standing next to her shyly asked, "Is it stop the war or somethin' in Vietnam?"

"Yeah," said David. "What do you think about that?"

"It's crazy," said the boy.

"What's crazy about it?"

"All these people out here."

"What's crazy about it?" David said. "What do you think about stopping the war, man, you think there's anything crazy about it?"

The woman in the babushka piped up again. "I think it should be stopped but I don't think you're the person to do it."

"Who is?" David asked.

"The government," said the woman.

"Aren't we the government?"

"Yes, but this is not our job. We have other people to make the decisions."

"Oh, I learned to make decisions myself," said David.

18

"Well good for you," said the woman, "but you can't make everyone's decision. That's only your opinion when you say you make the decision."

"Do you want to stop the war?" David asked.

"I can't stop it by myself, no sir," said the woman.

"Do you want to personally stop the war?"

"Would I like it stopped? Yes," she said.

I called Don in New York and told him excitedly that we were in the streets and we were having a dialogue. We were barreling along, swept up with the protesters. David was being aggressive with the microphone. The crowd chanted "Hey, hey, LBJ, how many kids did you kill today?"

A young male protester asked David: "What station you with?"

"We have our own. It's an underground media thing. You know, it's like we play closed circuit television," said David.

"Oh yeah?" said the protester.

"Yeah, we're gonna try to play it on Sunday in the park," said David. "Weather permitting, we're gonna try to show all of this stuff. Show what happened to the people out there, you know? We're gonna try to make it happen at this music thing that the Yippies are putting together at Lincoln Park."

This was the first inkling I had that David and the Videofreex were not exactly totally working for CBS. I was working for Don at CBS, but the Videofreex had their own political agenda. When people asked, "what's this for?" David would say it was an underground media thing. I realized television could be something that was not even remotely like CBS. This was beyond television as I knew it. And it occurred to me that I might not be there just because I was working for CBS, either. This was new, this was conceptual. It wasn't TV, it was VT. It was dyslexic. We were on the flip side and I liked it there.

WE MADE CONTACT with Abbie Hoffman and the Yippies in their basement coffeehouse headquarters. The defendants had been in jail but were now released on bail, so there was a party atmosphere, laughing and camaraderie. David pointed the microphone at Abbie, his

19

old college pal. Parry was holding the camera in his hand shooting. "You've had TV interviews before and, uh—no? You haven't? This is your first?" asked David, getting a big laugh from the assembled group. "Is there anything you'd like to say?"

"Fuuuuck!" shouted Abbie as the crowd roared with laughter.

"Are you having fun?" Abbie ignored the question, saying, "What's this for? What are you gonna do with this after it's done?"

"Maybe we'll put it on television."

"Network TV?"

"Yeah. What do you think about network TV?"

"My favorite shows are Lawrence Welk, and Land of the Giants. It's the truth. I thought I was just making fun of that because, you know, because they're kinda campy. But then I figured out like they're the only shows I watch so I must like 'em. I don't like baseball. I like the news," Abbie concluded.

Abbie and David went on to discuss the radical Weatherman faction.

"What do you think about the Weatherman action last night when a brick was thrown through a barbershop window?" asked David. Abbie thought it was stupid. "You have to lay an action so that you have some morality on your side, so you can split the ruling class. What they did unites the ruling class," he said. Then David asked him if he thought he was going to get a fair trial.

"I'll get the usual fair trial. Chicago style. They're building gallows on the third floor. Some people say that's a pretty pessimistic sign but I don't know. There's guys practicing a drum roll. Aarrgh!"

"It's a little scary," said David.

"No. No, not scary. Until the last day. Then shocking. But it's never scary. No. It's just the last day, they say, 'Guilty.' You say, 'What? After all this shit? Three fucking months? Guilty?' And the poor jury! They're doing time. They're just locked up. They can't fuck or nothin'. They can't watch TV!"

"That's a good state of mind to put them in, for the judge, isn't it?" asked David.

"Well, there's a thing that happens when they're locked up

20

because all they do is have contact with government people. U.S. marshals are the only ones they see. So eventually they feel like an important part of the government team. This judge, the past four years, he's had twenty-four jury trials and he got guess how many guilties?"

"How many?"

"Twenty-four." Everyone laughed uproariously. What else could they do?

"You know, somebody said you want to be convicted so you can be martyrs," said David.

"Oh, no. We would've put a brick through a barber shop window last night if we wanted to be martyrs. We wanna live to see it. Live to see the overthrow of the government. Be a great fuckin' movie."

ABBIE'S TESTIMONY AT TRIAL began like this:

Mr. Weinglass: Will you please identify yourself for the record?

The Witness: My name is Abbie. I am an orphan of America.

Mr Schultz: Your Honor, may the record show it is the defendant Hoffman who has taken the stand?

The Court: Oh, yes. It may so indicate …

Mr. Weinglass: Where do you reside?

The Witness: I live in Woodstock Nation.

Mr. Weinglass: Will you tell the Court and jury where it is?

The Witness: Yes. It is a nation of alienated young people. We carry it around with us as a state of mind in the same way as the Sioux Indians carried the Sioux nation around with them. It is a nation dedicated to cooperation versus competition, to the idea that people should have better means of exchange than property or money, that there should be some other basis for human interaction. It is a nation dedicated to—

The Court: Just where it is, that is all.

The Witness: It is in my mind and in the minds of my brothers and sisters. It does not consist of property or material but, rather, of ideas and certain values. We believe in a society—

The Court: No, we want the place of residence, if he has one, place of doing business, if you have a business. Nothing about philosophy or India, sir. Just where you live, if you have a place to live. Now you said Woodstock. In what state is Woodstock?

The Witness: It is in the state of mind …

AFTER THE VIDEOFREEX INTERVIEWED ABBIE I called my mom in Detroit from a phone booth and told her starting now not to say anything about my job when she called me because I was pretty sure our phone was gonna be tapped.

The next afternoon we videotaped members of the Chicago chapter of the Black Panther Party. The Black Panther Party was founded in 1966 by Bobby Seale and Huey P. Newton. Electronic surveillance of the Panthers led to the indictment of Bobby Seale as an eighth defendant with the *Chicago 7* for inciting riots at the 1968 convention, but he was ultimately tried separately. Earlier that year, twenty-one members of the Black Panther Party in New York had been indicted on charges of conspiring to blow up five department stores, a police station, railroad tracks and the Bronx Botanical Gardens. The "Panther 21," being held in prison, had student radicals black and white uniting behind them, asserting the Panther trial was part of the federal government's nationwide "extermination campaign" against them.

David had arranged, probably through Abbie, a private interview with the Chicago Panthers at the beautiful Old Town home of Lucy Montgomery, a supporter.

The Black Panthers had a fearsome power and energy and Montgomery's beautifully appointed parlor room was electric with excitement when we arrived. The Panthers were laughing and talking and I heard someone shout out "Off the pigs!" in a jovial manner. "What do you mean?" I asked a Panther named Omar. "The pigs are the police," he explained. "And, 'off'? You don't get that?"

"I'm not from Chicago," I said. I got big laughs.

Fred Hampton stood out among the Panthers as the thoughtful soft-spoken leader. Parry asked the first question. "You and the people around you always seem to be in danger. You could be killed as you walk out of here. If you are killed, will the breakfast program go on, on day-to-day level?"

22

Fred Hampton answered "Last year we started a free breakfast for children program and this year we gave it to the people and they are running that program already. Our whole program is geared toward educating the masses of people—and say, that free health clinic we have, the people in the community are going to run that clinic. And after a while we're going to give them that clinic and we're going to move on to higher levels because we understand the difference between the vanguard and the people.

"We're not worried about them killing anybody. I think that you know, they jailed Huey P. Newton and they ran Eldridge Cleaver out of the country and they jailed Bobby Seale and we've got David Hilliard up there now who's very capable, most capable of running the Black Panther Party. So they can just take all of them they want to, and we'll have someone to fill that position. Because that's the type of organization the Black Panther Party is.

"We don't produce buffoons. We produce leaders and anybody in the Black Panther Party and any type of cadre, is becoming a leader. Our deputy minister of health in the state of Illinois can run the Black Panther Party and so can anybody in this cadre, so all they're involved in is an excursion in futility. Because anybody that tries to deal with wiping out the leadership of the Black Panther Party is dealing with a time waste.

"It's a futile effort to seize some type of power that can never be seized because it's a type of unending flow of this power. Everytime somebody moves, we're just producing more and more people. You know, the story goes, they wiped out Martin Luther King, and they wiped out Malcolm X, you know what I mean, and they wiped out all these people, and these people were produced. So I think that in the near future you'll see programs initiated by the government. They'll probably have the CIA protecting people like us. Because when they wiped out Huey P. Newton, and Eldridge Cleaver popped up, I know very well they be saying, 'I wish the hell we would have kept Huey P. Newton on the scene, because this motherfucker's out of his mind.'"

There was righteous laughter and nods of "Right on! Right on! Right On!"

ABBIE INVITED US to the conspiracy defense office of the *Chicago 8*. Dave Dellinger, renowned pacifist and activist for nonviolent social change, and oldest of the defendants, was there, along with William Kunstler, the fiery defense attorney, Abbie Hoffman of the Yippies, and Tom Hayden of SDS (Students for a Democratic Society).

Tom Hayden, a dedicated civil rights worker, was now an anti-war activist. There was a lot of activity in the office, discussing, planning, and strategizing for the defense. We had been videotaping for over an hour and nobody said anything about the camera and the microphone. It was Tom Hayden who ultimately turned to us and asked "Who are you with?" David said, "Well, it's partly an underground thing, but we're also showing the footage to CBS."

That's all Hayden had to hear and he refused to let us leave the office with the footage. After a long, long debate, David erased major sections of video while Hayden, who didn't trust CBS, looked on. After the meeting, I called Don in New York and told him, "We've run into a little snag here and I was wondering if you can tell me, let's just say that if the FBI calls you and asks to see footage we're shooting, would you show it to them?" Don said, "Yes, I would have to." He said that CBS had a history of cooperating with the government. He assumed everyone knew that CBS Chairman William S. Paley himself had served as deputy chief of the psychological warfare branch of General Dwight Eisenhower's staff during World War II. That was another war and another time, but probably if the intelligence community wanted to look at footage at the network today, probably, quietly, they would look at it. What was going on? If we shot video in the counterculture and gave it to CBS, it was as if we were working for the government.

MEANWHILE, DON, WITH a working title of "The Real World," had gone back to Fort Hill in Roxbury to videotape Mel Lyman's commune with the crew from WGBH. They shot videotape all day. Not the portable half-inch kind the Freex were using, but the old clunky two-inch tape with a TV studio type of system. After the shoot, the crew went back to Boston and Don stayed at the commune to play back the video footage for the commune family. The story goes that the family hated the tapes. They told Don it was "bullshit" and "superficial." There were about thirty commune members there and they really ganged up on Don. Don told us family member David Gude confronted him shouting "You talk about 'The Real World?' This is 'The Real World!'" Then he pulled out a German Lugar and put it in Don's face. "This is *our* real world!"

So, in the power struggle over Don's heart and mind, the Videofreex had surged ahead, through no fault of their own. Actually the commune was pretty much out of the picture after the gun incident, but they still lurked around the project until the very end.

In any event, even with all the special treatment for the Videofreex, there was still only a slim chance any of their footage would ever make it to the small screen. This was largely because of Mike Dann, Vice President in charge of programming at the network. And although Dr. Stanton was ultimate boss at the network, he was not himself in charge of programming. Mike Dann was. Mike Dann was the first and last word in programming at CBS. Notably, he brought them the *Beverly Hillbillies*.

ON DECEMBER 17, 1969, Don West and the Videofreex made their presentation of *Subject to Change* to the CBS executives. It was live from the new Videofreex studio/loft on Prince Street in SoHo. We led Mike Dann and the CBS execs into our neighbor's adjoining loft, across the hall from our studio set, and seated them in front of a specially wired closed-circuit monitor so they could catch a glimpse of the future of television. They were smoking expensive cigars, smelling up our neighbor's loft. They burned a hole in our neighbor's futon.

In the Videofreex studio next door, we opened the show with Buzzy Linhart, our house band, doing a grinding and sizzling rendition of "Reputation." The cameras were switching furiously from Buzzy and his band to the audience shouting and grooving, to the monitors, to the cables running across the floor. Then bam! It was a hard cut from live studio chaos, to the crowds protesting on the streets of Chicago. No introduction. It seemed raw, with no voiceover to explain what we were looking at. We were asking the audience to figure it out for themselves.

The last several days had been tense and crazy, peppered with technical problems and horrendous realizations of what it might really entail to produce a television program. The Videofreex had taken all their videotapes upstate to a rented house near Albany where they toiled around the clock figuring out how to edit the video together using reel-to-reel video decks and a stopwatch. They were trying to integrate the gritty images and shocking events that had been recorded from coast to coast, including our interview with Fred Hampton who had been murdered in his bed by the Chicago Police just weeks after we saw him.

The Videofreex had decided not to let Don see any of their footage until the last minute. They did that for a couple of reasons. First, David was afraid the poor quality of the video image would scare Don off. And also because there was a fear that the government was asking CBS to see the footage and that they might take it and use it against the people on our tapes.

Don finally got to see the edit the Videofreex produced when David brought it to New York on the day before the presentation. It was pretty disjointed, cutting from New York to Chicago to California, with no warning or explanation. Don was livid and he was scared. "What is this? Are you kidding me? It makes no sense!" He paused, then shouted "What have you done? How could you do this to me? I want all the original footage. Now!"

"It's upstate. I don't have it." David said.

Don chartered a plane and flew the tapes back to New York. He spent the night before the presentation re-editing from scratch: forty hours down to thirty minutes. Because Fred Hampton had been murdered just a few days earlier, Don had obtained footage of his funeral with heavy dirge music and wanted to insert it as a lead in to our interview with Hampton. Parry felt it wasn't so much the funeral that didn't work, as much as the nature of the funeral footage. "It was film," Parry said. "Film is the old medium, distant, inflexible, elitist and impure."

The next day, the day of the presentation, Don brought his new edit with him to the Videofreex loft, demanding that his new version should be rolled into the live program. In a tense showdown, Parry refused to put Don's tape on the deck. "Don, if you try to play that stuff

26

about Hampton's funeral, I'll disconnect so many cables you'll never get this show on." Don had lost control of his program and blown his one big chance to become a television producer. It was turning out to be exactly the disaster his comedy writers had predicted when they walked out on the show.

"This is my show and I'm going to put it on!" shouted Don, waving the reel with his version in Parry's face. Our friends, the studio audience, were scrambling for seats on the newly constructed bleachers, thinking that perhaps the show had already begun. "I told you I'll pull all the plugs and there won't be a show," said Parry. Down to the wire and defeated, Don said, "I won't put my tape on because I don't have any choice. But I'll never work with you again. If this is the greatest show in the history of television, it's all yours. And if it's the worst show, it's all yours." There was a stunned silence for a short moment. The Videofreex had won. But what?

OKAY, SO IT WAS TRUE, there was no stage set built yet, or any graphic opening or any good lighting to speak of. But we did have bleachers set up so everyone we knew could be here for the live program, and monitors set up all over the loft showing every camera angle live. We had Buzzy Linhart's band and, most importantly, we had the video and the video had that eerie ring of truth about it.

Once it started, *Subject to Change* came gushing down tumbling over itself, seemingly (and virtually) un-directed. At the conclusion I was squatting under a table piled high with monitors, pressing the palms of my hands into my eye sockets. At the very end of the show the crowd went wild with enthusiasm and there was bedlam in the gallery as David tossed the cards with the credits on them into the bleachers and the Videofreex threw their arms up and walked off the set. I pulled myself together enough to say goodbye to Mike Dann and his cronies. "It's a piece of shit," Dann told me, nodding happily and smiling. And as he was disappearing out the door he added, "It'll be five years before people will be ready for something like this." I didn't have the time or the presence of mind to tell him the new revolutionary video had already been tested and proved to be feasible and profitable only five months earlier on July 20, 1969, when a live transmission of video from the Moon was seen by 720 million people around the world as Neil Armstrong stepped onto the moon's surface. The picture was kind of grey and jerky and one might have argued that it was difficult to understand what was happening. But it was the content. The content, get it?

IT WAS MIDNIGHT. We sat in the smoldering wreckage of *Subject to Change.* Carol, Skip and I were with the Videofreex. There was David, Curtis, Parry, tech master Chuck Kennedy, and Davidson Gigliotti, a carpenter/artist with a video camera whom David had met at the bank a few weeks earlier. One thing was clear. We were fired. What now? We did have the Prince Street loft, if we could pay the rent, and the newer larger apartment uptown, along with tons of cables and electronic circuitry. And, we had Videofreex. Videofreex, the future of television.

Subject to Change had come in at about $80,000. Don had given the Videofreex whatever they needed in terms of hardware and tech support, but the concept was never clear. Don had wanted a revolutionary format, but not a revolution. The Videofreex wanted both. From the beginning the Videofreex had known that their program would be unacceptable. That, apparently, was the point.

We all agreed that we should try to get as many videotapes as possible out of the CBS office. We had to do it fast because we were somewhat certain we wouldn't be getting past the lobby security at Black Rock the next morning. Someone had to go up there immediately, before night security heard about the show.

At last: the reason why I had lugged my guitar around with me since college. The instrument was left at the loft and the empty case was used to go up to Black Rock to load the tapes into. It was a little after one in the morning, but the night guy was used to seeing the Videofreex at odd times. Skip walked through the doors at CBS and into the brightly lit lobby. He sauntered casually up to the security desk. "Hi, Kenny," he said, signed in as usual, and got in the elevator. There wasn't much tape left up there. Don must have already taken everything. It wasn't a very successful mission but still it was wildly heart-pounding.

I felt like an outlaw.

Chapter Two:
Freex in Soho 1970

VIDEOTAPE ROLLED CONTINUOUSLY in Soho. Seemingly insignificant events became important simply by pointing the camera at them. The mundane became art. The person on the street became political. We would shoot all day and have a video show every Friday night at the Prince Street loft. Video was beginning to happen big in Soho and all the video/political factions were elbowing past each other for attention. We had the multi-channel-crowd, and the stark-raw-politicos, the video-as-art-gang, the techies, the video-as-money-crowd, and sure, the video-as-television-art-money-politics-crowd. We were into all of it.

It was good to be conceptual. In New York back then, you could still do just about anything in the streets. Performance artist Tosun Bayrak had no trouble getting a permit to take over all of Prince Street between Greene and Mercer one Saturday afternoon for his perform-ance of *Love America or Live*. Tosun had his players acting out in various ways, most notably a young man and woman naked and fucking on a big sheet of white butcher's paper in the middle of Prince Street while Tosun poured buckets of cows' blood out of a sixth floor window onto them. People were sloshing around naked fucking in cow's blood on Prince Street. Then later, Tosun had a huge feast in his loft where he had beautiful young women squatting on the banquet table, peeing on French bread. Fresh Sweet Girl-Pee on French bread was listed on the menu. The other dishes were pretty much unidentifiable (in the "sweetbreads" category), but opulent. The guests reclined around Tosun's big table, being served by slave boys and eating with gusto. The Tosun tapes were a big hit with our Friday night crowd at the Videofreex loft. But none of this seemed to be paying the rent. That's why I took a job at ASCAP, the songwriters union.

I went to work at 5 p.m. and got off at 11:45 at night, Monday through Friday. With hours like that I was able to spend all day at the

Freex loft doing video, go to my job at ASCAP at five, and the party would just be getting good by the time I got home a little after midnight.

In order to be a signatory of ASCAP, a radio station was required to provide an audio tape of eight consecutive hours of their music programming per month to the union to be monitored. It was my job as a music monitor to listen to the reels of audio tape and note down on a form every song or melody or piece of a song or any bars of music or any interpolation of any melody inside another song. The findings were tabulated and the songwriters would get their royalties based on these figures.

I was the only girl working on the night shift. Music nerds, old jazz guys, and me. It was pretty laid back. We all sat in one big room, each at our own desk with headsets and a tape recorder. You had to know a lot of songs to get the most out of this job. If you monitored more than forty hours of radio tapes a week you started to make bonus money. So the trick was to name that tune and then fast forward the tape to the next music. That worked well for the pop stations but you could miss an interpolation here and there with that method if you were monitoring jazz. If you found a piece of music you couldn't identify, you could give a signal and play a section of the music to the rest of the room through a speaker, and if no one recognized it you could look it up in the do-re-mi-files, called the solfeggio. The solfeggio files contained thousands of index-carded melodies, and their titles. I hardly ever got stumped and always made maximum bonus. Not surprising since I had spent a lifetime learning songs.

My first achievement, at about one year of age, was a popular song of the day called "Breathless." It was a complex little ditty which I picked up in one afternoon. When my dad got home from work, my mom had me sing it for him.

> If I had a dictionary
> I would use the customary
> Compliments and phrases
> How I love to sing your praises,
> But I'm up to here in trouble

My adversity is double
And to make the matters worse
(TAKE A BIG BREATH)
… I'm breathless …

I went on to sing the bridge and another chorus. Just the way my mom sang it to me. Of course my dad was astonished and elated. My mother was delirious. I went on to add "Oh, How I Hate to get Up in the Morning," "The G.I. Jive," and "Open the Door, Richard" in quick succession to my repertoire. I found I could get along okay in the world as long as I sang those songs on request. I had a large collection of record albums which I enjoyed. My favorites included Bing Crosby and the Andrews Sisters' "Don't Fence Me In," the Marine Corps Marching Band playing all the official songs of the different armed forces. ("Up we go, into the wild blue yonder … ." I loved that.) Most of all I liked the life stories of the great composers. Especially I liked Mozart and Schubert because they wrote all these great tunes when they were still little kids.

The Baldwin spinet piano arrived almost right away. I loved to play it. The notes were easy to find and the tones were all in a row so it was pretty simple to poke out the melodies that I heard on records and on the radio. But now Mrs. Fleischer had begun coming over on Wednesday afternoons for what they called lessons. This changed everything. I learned to read the notes she showed me but had a hard time playing them without making mistakes which in turn frustrated me and I was beginning to kick the piano. Not good. My mom said that in order to learn these pieces correctly I would have to practice, which meant playing the same thing over and over. I didn't know how long I was going to be able to do that.

When I was four, Mrs. Fleischer told my mom I should begin a more serious study, since I was talented. She suggested I attend theory class every Saturday morning. Theory class was held in a sunny conservatory room behind the Detroit Art Institute and I went in a carpool with other talented children from my neighborhood. They were all at least four or five years older than I was and I became hysterical (only on the inside) because I had no idea what they were talking about in the car. I decided I'd better be quiet until I figured out what was going on. I was quiet for a long long time—many years, actually. At the theory class they gave us music paper printed with only the lines on it. We were supposed to put the notes in. I was watching the teacher talk but since I was hysterical I didn't understand what she was saying, yet I appeared to be listening. I utilized this virtual silence that I discovered at theory class when I started kindergarten, and on through the fourth and fifth grades. That's when I decided that I wanted to change instruments. My mom was great about it. She didn't bat an eye when I gave her my decision, and was even willing to drive me way out to the east side so I could get lessons from the great Tony Dannon at the Accordion Institute. "Lady of Spain"? Sure, I could play it. Dick Contino? I had all his albums.

Even though it's pretty easy to play the accordion, I was only person at Bagley school who could do it. Once you learn the eight-note scale on the bass side where the buttons are, you can play the scale in any key just by moving up or down. It's all the same configuration. And each note has chords. A chord from just one button. Major, minor, seventh, and diminished. I could play "Tico Tico," "Dizzy Fingers," and pieces too numerous to mention, like "Hungarian Dance Number 5." There was a wide selection of sheet music at the Accordion Institute. So now I knew pretty much every song and they loved me for it at ASCAP.

IN FEBRUARY 1970, while I was still working at ASCAP, Abbie Hoffman and four others of the *Chicago 8* who had been found guilty were sentenced to five years in prison and a $5,000 fine. In his statement to the court, Abbie Hoffman recommended that the judge try LSD. Tom Hayden stated that "... we would hardly have been notorious characters if they'd left us alone on the streets of Chicago, but instead we became the architects, the masterminds, and the geniuses of a conspiracy to overthrow the government. We were invented."

Were they guilty? Abbie Hoffman said, "I don't know whether I'm innocent or I'm guilty." Norman Mailer, novelist, and witness for the defense, pointed out that the alleged conspirators "understood that you

32

didn't have to attack the fortress anymore. All they had to do was surround it, make faces at the people inside and let them have nervous breakdowns and destroy themselves." He added, "Left wingers are incapable of conspiracy because they're all egomaniacs."

"Conspiracy?" said Abbie, "Hell, we couldn't agree on lunch."

It was soon after the conviction, but before its reversal by the Seventh Court of Appeals, that Abbie contacted Parry at the Videofreex loft. He wondered if the Videofreex could give him a set of instructions on how to build a pirate TV station. He was writing *Steal This Book* and thought that would be good information to disseminate for the coming revolution.

Parry didn't know how to build a pirate TV station, so in the spirit of the project, he went to a university library and stole a paperback on the physics of television. Then he and Chuck began working on it. The Videofreex had to invent new tech daily. Chuck would listen to what we said, scratch his head, and dive right in. When it came to electronics, he would try anything. The first thing he would do when we got a new deck or camera was open it up and take a look at the innards. Nothing was impossible for Chuck. As a matter of fact, he was the world's foremost expert. Sony did not know what the Videofreex needed, but Chuck did.

Chuck was born in the Bronx and spent a large part of his youth in a Catholic orphanage. At a certain point, he was given the choice between reform school or the Army, so he joined up. In the Army, Chuck learned electronics and saw the world. When he came out of the service he got a steady job. He was making good money and living in a funky penthouse on Central Park West when one day David Cort came into the video shop. Chuck was in the back at the bench soldering circuitry and David said, "Chuck, come on with us. We've got a great gig with an executive at CBS to shoot portable video and we really need someone who can fix this equipment. And then he added, "We can get you three hundred a week." So Chuck got up from the bench and followed David out the door. Just like that.

Parry and Chuck watched as Abbie wrote a check for $325 for them to purchase the transmitter that would make it possible for him to pirate the airwaves, and Parry and Chuck began to build the system.

A few days later, Abbie came back to the loft for a demonstration of their invention. Parry and Chuck were proud to show Abbie they could actually transmit all the way from Chuck's shop to the control room next to it. No longer did they have to shout through the wall. Parry recalled that Abbie looked annoyed. "He might have settled for broadcasting to Manhattan, but what he really wanted was the five boroughs and the suburbs," said Parry. What Parry and Chuck were showing Abbie was a toy. "C'mon boys, what's it gonna take?"

"We'd need an amplifier ... a radio frequency amplifier." It was falling outside Chuck's immediate experience. He'd have to build one from scratch and he didn't know where to start. Abbie stalked out of the loft, cursing. He left the transmitter behind.

IN THE SPRING OF 1970, David thought Bart Friedman was someone who could do a little business agenting for us because Bart used to work at the Ashley Famous Talent Agency. David talked to him on the phone and Bart came right over.

I was surprised to see Bart at the Videofreex loft. We had met in the days before video, two years earlier at Sire Records. I was in a singing group called *The Bead Game.* We were recording a few songs acoustically for Richard Gotterer and Seymour Stein as a demo. Bart was a friend of theirs and was around the recording studio a lot. Back then he had been planning to leave the Ashley Famous office to become a talent manager. He already had some good acts, including the great singer-songwriter Peter Kelly (if you can ever find his record, grab it— you've got a treasure), and the astonishing magician Ricky Jay. Not only was Ricky's sleight of hand flawless, but Ricky Jay was so incredibly powerful he could flick a playing card from across the room and imbed it in a whole watermelon. Bart produced Ricky Jay over on 8th Avenue at the Elgin Theater after the midnight showing of the (even then) cult film, *El Topo*. Bart heard The Bead Game sing and loved our sound (four voices and a twelve string guitar), and might have liked to manage us. But instead of staying with the group, I gave up show business, married Alan and left town.

34

Now Bart walked into the Videofreex loft, picked up a hammer, and began building the studio with the rest of us. There wasn't much discussion about it. He stayed. And pretty soon he moved in with me, Skip, Carol and Parry, at our larger-than-ever West End Avenue apartment which I had rented in a fit of confidence during the CBS project. David, Curtis, Chuck, and Davidson were living at the Prince Street loft. That's when the Videofreex began to set up a not-for-profit corporation, Media Bus Inc.

We were now going to be fundable. Incorporating our many interests, we began cranking out video shows, gallery and museum installations, exhibitions, and video workshops, traveling all over New York state showing people how to shoot video and use it for themselves. When media arts money became available through the New York State Arts Council, there was a big scramble for the funding. Media Bus and three other video groups emerged as the leading contenders. They were Peoples Video Theater, Global Village, and Raindance Corporation—each wanting the media money.

Raindance proposed the creation of what they were calling the Center for De-Centralized Television. Not an oxymoron to them, it was going to be a video viewing space with production and editing. Global Village wanted the same thing. Peoples Video Theater was shooting video out on the streets doing politics and also wanted the video viewing space and post-production facility. Media Bus wanted all of that and we wanted new vehicles with portable production equipment to drive the video technology all over the state. After a fierce competition, the arts council, instead of granting the total funds to one organization, divided it between the organizations. So, to a certain degree, we were all funded, but barely.

IT WAS 1971, one year after the Kent State University demonstration where four students were shot dead by the Ohio National Guard. To commemorate that event, protestors were going to Washington to close down the government by blocking all major roads into the District of Columbia, and the Videofreex were going to document it. On April 29, David, Davidson, Chuck, Parry and Carol prepared to drive down to

D.C. to meet the May Day Video Collective, media students, and groups from colleges and universities all across the country. David, who had essentially put the video production together, and Davidson, were counting cables and packing the gear while the rest of us loaded the van. David and Davidson had met in a bank on West Broadway one day in 1969 during the CBS project. Davidson had a video Porta-pak on his shoulder and a video camera in his hand, which was extremely rare back then, so David brought him back to the Videofreex loft with him.

I remember meeting Davidson at the CBS office and sending him to D.C. to cover a demonstration that day, but he came back with blank tapes. Nothing got recorded. He watched the whole event through his viewfinder, but forgot to push the RECORD button, it seemed. Of course with video a lot of things can go wrong. You couldn't hold it against someone just because they came back with nothing. It happened every day. Ultimately it turned out that Davidson was a true artist behind the camera. Every picture well considered and beautifully framed (a rare quality in those days).

In D.C., the Videofreex met up with the larger video collective, including a lot of kids from Antioch College in Ohio. The May Day Collective had arranged crash pads for activists.

The Videofreex hit the streets. It was loud and tear-gassy, and hovering helicopters were scattering the protesters. On television President Nixon was addressing the nation: "Some people on television may have gotten the impression when they, uh, saw the demonstrations down at the Senate, and that Barry Goldwater's door had red paint on it, I understand, and his office door was locked, and that Washington is somewhat in a state of siege, but, uh, well, let me just make one thing very clear: The Congress is not intimidated, the President is not intimidated, this government is going to go forward. Uh, it doesn't mean that we're not going to listen to those who come peacefully, but those who come and break the law will be prosecuted to the fullest extent of the law. In the meantime, however, I, as president, have my obligation to consider what they say, and all the other things that I know, and then to make the decision that I think will be in their best interest as well as the best interest of other people in the country."

Police were over loudspeakers. "Attention! Attention! This is the Metropolitan Police Department. Everyone must leave the area immediately. Those who do not leave the area are in violation of the law and will be arrested." Helicopters were now landing and military troops were swarming the streets. The sirens were incessant. A man was dragged into the bushes and clubbed by two DC cops. A young boy was pulled from his bicycle and shoved into a paddy wagon by police who trampled his bike in the process. David got clubbed in the knee by a cop for shooting video. A young woman medic wearing a headband and a white T-shirt with a red cross painted on it spoke to David's video camera while people were being arrested and dragged off all around her. She was a modern-day Clara Barton on the front lines, naive, innocent, brave.

"Why are you staying here?" asked David.

"Well, I'm gonna stay and get busted with my people. You know like, uh, some of the medics are gonna go behind the pig lines and use pig tactics and do what the pigs say. I'm not gonna. I'm gonna stay and get busted with my people and when somebody's getting beat on the ground I'm gonna stop the pig from beating him so I can help him. I'm not gonna say, 'Oh, dear sir with the silver badge, can I help you? Can I treat my people now?' Fuck that shit, I'm not gonna do none of that."

Davidson noted in his journal. "May 1. Today we all got up late and I went the national gallery. I was going to go to the Corcoran also but it was closed on account of the riot. I left the National Gallery at 4:30. I ate something poisonous at their cafeteria. I went to the Museum of Science and Technology next door. Now I'm sitting in the park outside. A cop is coming, his walkie-talkie squawking. He's looking me over.

"May 2 I spent the day in jail and was released at 11 p.m. or so. I made a tape in jail. Now David is determined to be arrested. I was lucky of course to be arrested by a policeman in good humor and was let out after a few hours. David no doubt will be beaten to a pulp and thrown in the can for weeks. I don't much want to go back.

"May 4 Riding around DC in Volkswagen buses. This is my fourth day. Parry has created a real efficient headquarters back at

37

Hillyer Street complete with maps, telephone, and bulletin boards. Sort of like a bunker in wartime Europe."

Hundreds of kids were arrested, tossed into buses, and dumped out on a field with a chain link fence around it, thousands of dancing and hooting protesters inside. The video continued to roll because there were way too many people to process them all at once so everyone got to keep their cameras and belongings. Someone held up a copy of the latest edition of a local newspaper for the detainees to see through the fence. The headline read: "7,000 ARRESTED—RECORD ROUND-UP." Cheers erupted.

THE VIDEOFREEX MADE IT BACK to the Prince Street loft with the footage along with a dozen members of the May Day Collective to do a democratic edit where all the participants were represented, and all events witnessed could be seen. We then planned to distribute the program to students across the country and all around the world, for that matter. Each faction wanted to get the most information about their issue into the program, which could only be an hour long for distribution. In the editing room we had the black faction, the women's faction, the Vietnam Vets Against the War faction, the socialists faction, the Marxists faction, and we even had the cross-dressers faction, which was almost unheard of then. "It's fine if I want to wear a dress!" shouted a bearded hippie in a muumuu.

Finally, excruciatingly, we got an hour put together in the nick of time before the electricity was cut off at the Videofreex loft. Then our phone was shut off too. It wasn't the government, it was the money. We didn't have enough of it to work and live in New York City and we had to move. Leaving the city seemed the only way we could have a home and continue to do video. We were going to have to share. Just before the phone was cut off, CBS called Davidson about his jail tape but he told them to get lost.

Chapter Three:
Probably America's
Smallest TV Station

JULY 1971. WE TOOK the New York State thruway to the Kingston exit, then Route 28 north to Phoenicia. From there it was only three miles up Route 214 to Lanesville, and the new home Carol and Parry had found and rented on a frantic weekend real estate search. Paul McCartney sang "The Long and Winding Road" as we sped off with all our stuff and Mushroom the dog in Parry's van.

Mushroom was a funny, shaggy, black dog who looked old but wasn't. Carol got him from a veterinarian over on the east side. The vet found him on the street and was going to have to you-know-what, but Carol happened to be there getting booster shots for the cats, and she saved him. We had meant to name him "Rushmore" because of his noble profile, but someone misheard it and said "Oh, Mushroom. I love it!" Although he was a good natured dog, Mushroom had a horrible spastic shitting problem and would suddenly poop with no warning, anywhere, anytime. Carol had a high tolerance for Mushroom, so he stayed in Carol and Parry's room. Did I mention that Carol and Parry now stayed in the same room?

I read the final directions to Bart as we came up the road. "When you see the sign Maple Tree Farm on the left, pull in and up the driveway ... ." There it was. Oh, it was beautiful! There, sitting on the graceful rise, was our first view of Maple Tree Farm, the stately three-story white frame house. It had a lovely wide porch with white railings and was surrounded by a broad expanse of green lawn lined on both sides by a stand of mature sugar maples, thus the name. My new home boasted sixteen bedrooms. There were enough bedrooms for each of us to have one, and still have extras for visiting artists.

"Mother Nature's Son" boomed through the big speakers in the

39

large center room as we unpacked. Between the ten of us we now possessed hundreds of record albums, thousands of pounds of hardware, miles of coaxial cable on huge spools, boxes by the dozen filled to the brim with assorted electronic paraphernalia, hundreds of videotapes, and the accumulated stuff of this group of strangers who got together making a TV pilot.

Once more I went over my list of rationalizations for leaving the city. For one thing, sharing seemed the right thing to do politically. And, financially, our forty-thousand-dollar New York State Council on the Arts grant wouldn't have taken ten people very far in the city. We had a mandate to fulfill the terms of our grant by doing mobile video workshops upstate, and Lanesville was convenient to the thruway. We were going to be spending a lot of time on the road.

MY FIRST MORNING at Maple Tree Farm I awoke in a charming bright chintzy bedroom, with a cacophony of the first bird sounds in the morning echoing down the valley. There was an aroma of soft summer and a rustle of the breeze through the maples. The first thing I saw was the wallpaper. I was surrounded by thousands of tiny identical pink and green flower bouquets. And, in relief against the tiny bouquets, was one of those heavy white porcelain pitcher-and-bowl affairs sitting on top of a little oak dresser. I had been in Oz, and now I'd suddenly been blown into Kansas. Then I smelled the coffee. I wasn't a coffee drinker but I wanted some. I tiptoed out of the bedroom onto a long corridor and down the stairs, and followed the chatter to the kitchen, peeking into the various rooms as I went.

In the new control room I saw Parry's feet sticking out from under the console where he was cabling up our video studio. Already set up was a bank of glowing monitors. Next to the studio was an equipment room and behind that a laundry room. Across the hall from the studio was a TV viewing room where Davidson was at work on his specialty built-in, dovetail-jointed wooden tape shelves. Past the viewing room was a huge center room with a soon-to-be-poly-urethaned maple wood floor and no furniture except for Davidson's mother's lovely little spinet piano and an old ornate pedal organ that

Bart bought from my cousin Tommy for fifty dollars. The big room opened onto a beautiful glassed-in sunporch with sofas and a round braided rug. The windows looked out onto a meadow. A comforting hum was emanating, just past the big center room in the very back of the house, the kitchen.

"Hey," Skip smiled, "did you sleep well?" Skip had been in Lanesville for two days already and had apparently become completely assimilated. He was wearing ticked blue and white coveralls hooked up over one shoulder with no shirt underneath, and barefoot. His thick blonde hair flowed down past the middle of his back. The only thing missing was a blade of grass to chew on. "Coffee," he asked?

"Sure," I said. This was going to be my first cup of coffee. I had never tried it. I was raised on Cokes like my mother used to drink. In our house, there was nothing like an ice-cold Coke for breakfast.

ANN WOODWARD POURED the steaming brew into a big white mug and set it in front of me. The Videofreex met Annie soon after the CBS project when we went up to the Rose Art Museum in Waltham, Massachusetts, for the first big Museum and Television exhibit starring Nam June Paik, the father of video art. The Videofreex had set up a live, closed-circuit television system for the museum. Annie was the curator's assistant and a graduating senior at Brandeis University.

A quiet, serious young woman with the whitest peaches-and-cream-complexion, her fine black hair curling all around her face, Annie went to Brandeis University even though she wasn't Jewish. She was a wonderful artist and could draw anything. She had a smooth, sure stroke and was skilled at wildflowers, so this whole media thing with television cable and the mountains of monitors flashing came as a surprise to her. Annie took it all in, and spent a couple of nights with Chuck. They stayed in touch and in the spring, after graduation, Annie arrived at the Videofreex Prince Street loft. She had her bags. Annie stayed. We were glad. It turned out that Annie was a truly accomplished chef, while the rest of us, from what I could gather, were not. I know I wasn't. I knew zero about cooking.

41

IT WAS SLOWLY DAWNING on me that we had all left the city and moved together to Maple Tree Farm. My first day in Lanesville and visitors had begun to arrive. People I had never seen before. We had two guys from Amsterdam, and a beautiful young couple from California. Her name was Vidicon. She had named herself after the small tube inside her video camera. She called her old man Bear. They had arrived in full embroidered and beaded regalia. Vidicon and Bear brought with them video news from a commune out west. They were going to edit their footage at Maple Tree Farm and send copies all around the world.

Video began to arrive from places like England and Poland and France and Prague. Someone brought us a video from Algeria of acid guru Timothy Leary who was on the lam after escaping from prison in California and was now either a guest of, or a prisoner of, Black Panther Eldridge Cleaver in Algeria. Cleaver was also a fugitive. It was hard to tell what was really happening on the video. The picture was gray and the camera was on a tilted tripod, static. Eldridge was speaking and Leary and his wife Rosemary were sitting on the floor leaning against a white wall. Listening? Dazed? There was a lot of rhetoric. A lot of political tapes were coming our way. Conspiracy theorists, revolutionaries, messages from outside the establishment passed from person to person. It was an alternate media system, primitive, like smoke signals.

I looked up at Annie who was placing the coffee in front of me and said, "Thanks. I've never tried coffee before, but the aroma … ."

"Amazing isn't it?" said tech master Chuck, who was darting around the kitchen enthusiastically playing the host. Every morning Chuck would scoop green coffee beans from the hundred pound bag stored in the pantry at Maple Tree Farm. The bag of coffee beans came from a drug rehab program in New York called Phoenix House. We got it in exchange for documenting a fundraiser they held on Hart Island. We also got two dozen pairs of running shoes, and as many pairs of wooden clogs as we wanted, a shelf full of industrial-sized cans of fruits and vegetables, and fifty cartons of Lark cigarettes. These were all items that had been donated to Phoenix House. In fact, Phoenix House had an entire warehouse in Harlem filled with stuff that had been donated to them, like thousands of pounds of spaghetti (we got plenty of that too). Every time the Videofreex did a gig for Phoenix House, we would drive on up to the warehouse and select merchandise from their inventory as payment.

Chuck took the green coffee beans and roasted a couple of handfuls in the oven until that luscious smell happened, then he ground them in the blender and put them in the big old country coffee pot to percolate. Having never been a coffee drinker, only a sip or two of the Videofreex coffee made me feel like, well, God. I rationalized that the coffee would be a small indulgence. Of course, though, there were those Lark cigarettes. I was obviously going to smoke those. We seemed to have an endless supply. And I wasn't the only one smoking the Larks. They were so plentiful that everyone who wanted a cigarette simply opened a fresh pack to get one. Why not? So there were partly-used packs all over the house. Okay, a little coffee and a few cigarettes. And only the pot we grew. Other than that, I was going to eat clean. Maybe even be a vegetarian again.

WHEN I FIRST MOVED TO New York, I often ate at Tad's Steak House on 42nd Street near the subway at Grand Central. At that time Tad's was taking over from where Horn and Hardart's (the Automat) had left off, as the restaurant of choice for indigent oddballs. And there was another Tad's in the Village, right near my apartment. Tad's was cheap and filling and I would sit there chewing on my meat, watching other patrons stuff paper up their noses and babble. After a few weeks of that, I would make a stab at being a vegetarian again.

At dinner in Lanesville, inspired by Annie's scrumptious tofu burgers, people talked about memorable eating experiences. A guy named John had traveled the world and told us about the evening he dined with Salvador Dali. "It was at quite a chic restaurant in Paris," he said.

"What did you eat?" Annie asked.

"Balsa wood" he said. "Balsa wood was all Salvador Dali ate at the time, so we ate it too."

"How was it?"

"It was okay," he said. "Chewy."

Now Annie was pouring a cup of Chuck's coffee for Davidson. I watched him inhale the steam rising off the cup, nostrils flared in the manner of European royalty. A few years ago when I lived on Christopher Street Greenwich Village with Carol and my sister Linda, it turned out that Davidson was living directly across the street from us. On the top floor directly across from our windows were his windows. I was surprised to learn this over Chuck's coffee at the breakfast table in Lanesville. Now I remembered I used to watch him sometimes. He was a carpenter. In Lanesville, Davidson was already busy shooting video for his art installation about dry fly fishing. He had four video cameras set up on tripods in the stream across the road. He planned to play these tapes in a gallery on four monitors making one long picture. You would see the fly-casting pass from monitor to monitor.

Parry and Carol and Chuck and Ann had the two big suites in the front of the house on the second floor. David and his big green parrot Oberon took the side room with the bay windows overlooking the driveway. David had painted the walls of his room white and the wood floor a pale acid green. The only furnishings in the room were David's mattress and a huge dead tree limb where Oberon the parrot stood. No cage. The whole room was Oberon's cage, with David's small mattress on the floor in it.

Just past David's room were the bathrooms. One had two sinks and a tub, and two other cubicles with one toilet each. Past the bathrooms was a door leading to a bridge that spanned the driveway connecting a few more rooms in a back building. The last two rooms on the second floor before the bridge belonged to Bart and me. Did I mention that Bart and I were staying in the same room?

The front room on the third floor was Skip's attic room. Next to Skip was the big sunny room where Curtis lived. She and David had split up and were living on separate floors. Across the hall from Curtis was a guest room. Next to that, the photo darkroom, the bathroom (a large one with an old fashioned tub with feet), and at the end of the hall, the back rooms where Davidson was taking out a wall and making himself a funny angular, modern, sheet-rocked loft space. His room was directly above ours. We could hear Davidson so I'm sure he could hear us too.

Before we came to Maple Tree Farm, a ski club from Brooklyn had been renting the place because of its proximity to Hunter Mountain up the road. They came up weekends and really trashed the house, and painted a lot of stuff black. Sam and Miriam Ginsberg, who owned Maple Tree Farm, were looking for new tenants when we came along. They had run Maple Tree Farm as a summer boarding house for many years. Their guests used to come up to the Catskills from Brooklyn and New Jersey for the summers. Now that they were both well into their seventies, it was getting harder and harder for Miriam to do all that work and cooking and cleaning and washing and linen-changing, so they moved to a small one-bedroom cottage they owned up the road, and rented out Maple Tree Farm, or "The Big House," as Sam called it, to us.

THE FIRST SUMMER in Lanesville I adjusted to life on the farm. Many guests came and went. We planted a garden. We ate together around a big table on the sun porch. The bills got paid. I was never alone. A car trip always included four to six people. We traveled as a group in every instance. We shopped in Kingston at the Shoprite, buying wagon loads of food, all orchestrated by Annie who wanted dinner how she liked it so much that she was willing to cook for everyone to get it that way. As I mentioned, Annie was an inspired chef. She knew at least fifty ways to cook a chicken.

Curtis, now single, wanted, in general, to get married. So one day she met Cy Griffin. A single father of three, Cy was a widower caring for his youngest daughter, Tracy. Cy was on his way to the Rosebud Reservation in South Dakota to fight for Native American rights and other similar adventures that didn't seem right for his nine-year-old-daughter, so when Cy met Curtis in July he was elated. He proposed immediately. She accepted and he left Tracy with Curtis (and the rest of us) at Maple Tree Farm and promised to return in September for the wedding. Tracy was a sweet beautiful child with silky white blond hair that fell past her shoulders. Her seventeen-year-old brother, Jimmy, came and went, and her nineteen-year-old sister, Janet, often visited along with her boyfriend Bob.

Bart went with Cy and several Native Americans from the Rosebud Reservation to Washington D.C. in 1972 when they staged a sit-in at the Bureau of Indian Affairs building. The American Indian Movement (AIM) was founded in 1968 to encourage self-determination among Native Americans and to establish recognition of their treaty rights. During the takeover Bart was there with the video camera, but a lot of the Native Americans who were sitting-in didn't trust him and it was tough for Bart to get any intimate footage. But later, when it was over, the Native Americans had learned to like him and insisted that he at least take one of the IBM typewriters. To refuse would have been an insult. The Native Americans took everything from the offices when they left the building. After all, it was their Bureau, right? Their building. It was pretty easy to see their point. They complained that the government had created the tribal councils on reservations in 1934 as a way of perpetuating paternalistic control over Native American development.

IN ACCORDANCE WITH OUR arts council grant, all through the summer before Curtis and Cy's wedding, we drove up and down the New York State Thruway doing workshops and video shows. We were friendly outside agitators and this video thing that was happening was a media revolution. With this new technology, people could control the information about themselves. Television pictures didn't have to go to some central place in New York or Los Angeles. It was that simple. And, it had become obvious that TV news coverage wasn't fair. Everything was decided by a limited number of people with similar views. So the media revolution was saying that all available channels should be opened up to the people—indigenous video production.

We went to Utica and Schenectady and Syracuse and Rochester and Buffalo. People gathered at the YMCA or the art museum or the library or university and we showed them how to run the cameras and we sent them out on the streets to record events. Then we went over to the cable company with them and their videotapes and explained to the cable executives about the access provision in their license agreement for the cable franchise with the town which mandated a free access channel for the community. Usually the cable companies didn't like the idea and we had to make a big fuss before they handed over the channel to the people.

The way our money worked was that Media Bus paid for all of our expenses. Food, rent, supplies, travel, medical, dental, all of it. And as long as we were within our budget (which wasn't always), we each got paid $35 a month. In cash. I rarely spent mine. There was nothing to buy. It was great.

Curtis' wedding lasted for three days. Tents and tepees were set up in the back meadow and there was drumming day and night. Parry, a mail-order Minister in the Universal Life Church, performed the ceremony. Shirley Clarke, the great madcap filmmaker-turned-video-artist and documentarian, shot a Marx Brothers style movie with the action all set against the background of the wedding party. For this production she had Skip play Harpo, Bart play Chico, and Shirley herself playing Groucho. Finally, Curtis rode off into the sunset with her instant family. We waved goodbye.

WITH THE ARRIVAL OF SARAH, Carol and Parry's baby, Maple Tree was beginning to feel like home. The garden was tilled and planted, and groups of visiting video freaks came and went. One day, Annie was creating a magnificent dinner in the kitchen. She had been simmering her sauce for the spaghetti all day. As always, Annie's dinners were a work of art. And no one was looking forward to this meal more than Annie herself. The aroma of Annie's sauce permeated the editing room where I was putting together Bart's Cowboy Show For Kids of All Ages. Carol was cradling Sarah in her arms. As Annie swirled the big wooden spoon through the steaming sauce there was the sound of an un-muffled engine, and the shift of gears. Something very large had pulled into the driveway. Annie rushed to the window. It was big and blue. It was a school bus. It was the Hog Farm, a merry band of people-loving hippies touring the east as a change from their communal home in Oregon.

The bus roared up to our back door and ground to a stop. At least a dozen hippies scampered out and approached the kitchen door. A rotund clown-like presence in tie-dyed velvets, a fools cap, and a huge wide smile, was in the lead with a thick orange electric cord in his hand. He beckoned to Annie through the screen door to allow him to slip the plug end of his cord through her open window and into an outlet in the wall. Annie smiled politely with visions of her spaghetti dinner. She instinctively stepped in front of the stove, shielding the view of her sauce from the visitors. Carol gazed silently at the scene. Her fantasy of the quiet nursery was slipping away. The Hog Farm had arrived.

Bart greeted the busload with glee, knowing they would help him set up the Blue Calzone, a giant inflatable TV screen and projector that Davidson and the Videofreex had built for the back meadow. He immediately invited them to dinner, slapping an arm around Annie while extolling the delicacy of her special sauce. Little puddles appeared in Annie's eyes. Bart continued, "They'll park the bus in the driveway and run a line into the kitchen for electricity." It's not that Annie wasn't generous. And everyone knew the Hog Farmers themselves were famous for feeding masses of people for free. The Hog Farm had famously fed a hundred thousand people breakfast at the Woodstock Festival.

Still, Annie thought, why now? "What about dinner?" she asked. That's when Bart came up with his great idea for a way to stretch out the spaghetti to feed twelve more people. He was already busy doing a big pot of popcorn which he planned to mix with the spaghetti. Now Annie was mad. She hadn't tended that sauce all day to eat it over popcorn. But that's what happened. And then after dinner, we all danced around the Blue Calzone, our inflatable TV screen in the meadow while live pictures of ourselves in punchy black and white were projected on the screen. Carol rocked her baby Sarah near the upstairs window and watched.

ON A MAP, LANESVILLE can be found exactly in the middle of the Stony Clove Valley which is shaped like a V, with Route 214 running right up

48

through the notch. Lanesville is a tiny dot on a winding road through a narrow valley with high mountains on either side of the road. It was easy to see that there was going to be no television reception in Lanesville. What to do? Parry and Chuck figured that if we took a few hundred yards of coaxial cable we could string it up to the top of the mountain behind our house, attach it to an antenna and see what came in. Yes! Two separate channels of television looking perfectly clear popped on to the screen. They were coming from Wilkes-Barre, Pennsylvania. Even though Wilkes-Barre was many many miles away and none of us had ever been there, we now knew everything about the greater Wilkes-Barre area. We would usually start our viewing day in Lanesville with Hogan's Heroes every evening at 5:30, followed by the local news from Wilkes-Barre.

Our neighbors, the Hells Angels next door; and next to them, a family of sand hogs (tunnel diggers) from the Bronx; and beyond them, our landlords Sam and Miriam Ginsberg, were also happy because we split the cable and ran a line over to their houses too. So now they could all get TV from Wilkes-Barre. And sometimes really late at night in the middle of an old movie, the screen would suddenly turn to snow and we would know that the porcupines were feasting on that sweet foamy insulation inside our coaxial cable and that we'd be climbing the hill to splice it back together in the morning.

LANESVILLE TV, Probably America's Smallest TV Station, was broadcast live on Channel 3 whenever we turned on the transmitter and pointed the camera at something. But we could always be found live on Saturday nights starting at seven o'clock. Since no one in Lanesville got any television reception unless we provided it, Lanesville TV was a popular attraction in a town of fewer than three hundred inhabitants. It was the only station that came in on every set in town.

Lanesville TV pretty much owed its existence to our friend J.P., who was a true radio pirate. He had in fact been busted by the FCC for broadcasting without a license and he wasn't even political. He was messing around with a transmitter in his mom's basement in Yonkers, broadcasting rock and roll, and one night he asked the people in his audience to call if they were receiving the signal. The first call he got was from Grosse Pointe, Michigan. Yes, J.P. had a powerful signal. The FCC came and warned him not to do it, but he couldn't resist, so the Feds came back and took away all his equipment. J.P. was still on probation. He wasn't allowed to leave the state.

With the help of J.P., we built a small transmitting antenna out of a few pieces of copper wire and a little math. It may actually have been dangerous for J.P. to turn on Lanesville TV, but we figured we weren't doing any interstate stuff here, so Lanesville TV went on the air. We used the small transmitter that Abbie Hoffman had given us right before we left the city. We kept the transmitter in a closet on the bridgeway to the back building. It took a couple of minutes to warm up when we turned it on but then up would pop the Lanesville TV logo (hand painted by my dad during a visit), along with our theme song, "A Sunny Disposish" by Manhattan Transfer, and we'd be on the air.

Cut to tape of Bart wheeling a baby carriage up Route 214 with a video recorder instead of a baby nestled on a pillow in it. The road was deserted except for an occasional car whizzing past. Trolling for news, Bart meandered around Lanesville.

"So, Elmer, how are the pigs today?"

"Oh fine, fine."

A little further down the road, Rabbi Kelley flagged Bart down and took the microphone:

"Hello this is Rabbi Joseph K-E-L-L-E-Y, Kelley," he said in his heavily-accented eastern European-style English, "reporting that I have a three-room apartment empty, ninety-five dollars plus utilities." Still holding the mike, Rabbi Kelley continued, "My wife was away for three or four days but she extended it to fourteen or fifteen days and during her being there she wrote to me a letter with ten words. That she is coming back on Friday and that she is well."

"Eay Ayh," the local folks would grunt, speaking from their homes, their barns, town meetings. Speaking from the bar, the beauty shop, the church supper, and the truck stop at the thruway exit. Their conversation ranged from what roads to take to the gravel pit, to the most recent bar brawl, and even to gossip about local cops.

50

We would take turns hosting the broadcasts and taking phone calls from the viewers, which was always a lot of fun. Carol was probably our most popular host. Parry described her perfectly in his book, *Videofreex*. "Carol's sweet face and soft voice in no way prepared you for her unadorned straightforwardness, on the air or off. She spoke her mind in a guileless, conversational tone that disarmed most callers. 'That sounds like fascism to me,' or she'd say, 'Have you lost your mind?' She bypassed stickiness, remained sweet but firm, and viewers seldom raised a sound in protest."

LANESVILLE TV BREATHED LIFE into every community event. Characters came alive for the cameras. Everyone played a part. Lanesville TV would begin to tell a story and the townspeople would take over. Here's one story that grew and grew and grew. The goal? To raise money for the rescue squad up the road in Hunter and Tannersville. The method? A prize fight. Lanesville TV began to get the word out. Everyone played along. And presto! Two new folk heroes emerged. As large as Paul Bunyan, as enduring as Rip Van Winkle.

Frank "The Fist" Farkle and "Rocky" Van, peaceful men from sleepy villages in the Catskill Mountains, stepped forward to help raise money for the Hunter-Tannersville Rescue Squad. Yep, Frankie and Rocky were actually going to climb into the ring and punch each other for charity. Everyone on the mountaintop was talking about the prizefight. First a video survey. We popped into the liquor store in Tannersville. Behind the counter, Doug was thumbing through the newspaper.

"Who do you think is gonna win that fight?" Bart asked him.

"Oh, I don't know, I'd have to give it to Frankie Farkle, Frankie the Fist."

"How come?"

"Well, fact is, I know him a little better. He's been in training for about a week and he's really putting in to it."

"Is he fast?"

"Oh, he's like lightning. He's gonna knock Rocky out in the second round."

51

"You think so?"

"Yeah, I think so."

"How about Rocky?"

"Oh he's a cupcake. A Freihofer's cupcake."

"What do you mean by that?"

"Oh, he's gonna be easy. Frankie's gonna hit him and one-two he's gonna go down."

"What's his weak point?"

"His weak point is he's gonna show up half in the bag."

Over at the luncheonette, the guys behind the counter were bursting with pride about Frankie. They talked into the camera: "Sure! Frankie got his start here in the restaurant as a pearl diver. He was a dish washer. He was a husky lad even then."

"Have you got a prediction?"

"I think Frankie Farkle is gonna knock him out."

Now to Haines Falls where the folks were stringing a banner across the road "Welcome to Haines Falls, Home of Frank "The Fist" Farkle." We knocked on Frankie's mom's kitchen door. Over tea we asked, "How do you feel about Frankie taking up a career as a fighter?"

Frankie's mom answered calmly and slowly in her cigarette-husky twang. "Well, I'd rather he didn't because I don't like to see men hurt or injured. But, as this is for a good cause, I thought that this would be his one and only fight. Because years ago I made sure he had no fights with children, and I'm rather upset about it, but he's promised me he'll be as easy as he can on him." She kept a straight face for a beat before we all started to laugh.

Frankie's training session: There he is running up the road toward Hunter Mountain, his distinctive beer belly in perfect profile against the rugged mountain landscape behind him as our car pulls alongside keeping pace. "This is Frank 'The Fist' Farkle in his training session. He's been running five miles today he's got another eight to go. How do you feel Frank?"

"Great!" [He coughs.]

"What's your prediction for the fight?"

"I say he's gonna hit that canvas floor in four. [He coughs again.]

52

Never felt better!"

The night of the fight the whole town packed the school gymnasium in Tannersville. There was hooting and stomping for each contender. The crowd seemed equally divided. The Hunter Mountain crowd strongly behind Rocky Van, and the Tannersville-Haines Falls crew for Frankie. After three rugged rounds with more than a few well placed punches, the judges declared a tie. Everyone knew it was best that way. The valorous rescue squad was saved. The folk tale was twentieth century media product, and community theater no one on the mountaintop would ever forget.

When we got home from the prizefight, I noticed a big bubbling pot on top of the stove in the kitchen, and the strong smell of what seemed to be turpentine. My god! It was David's white overalls boiling away in a pot of turpentine on the stove! Turpentine! "David! What the fuck are you doing?!" David blinked in the doorway. "Oh, I forgot. I was trying to get the grass stains out of my pants."

AND THEN THERE WERE the road trips. Off to Shirley Clarke's penthouse at the Chelsea Hotel, the camp and seedy stopover for artists and Bohemians in New York City. Shirley was already famous as a filmmaker. She made *The Connection* and then she made *The Cool World* and now she had immersed herself in video. Shirley's place was happening twenty-four hours a day and we often stayed there when we went into the city.

I began to feel the buzz of Shirley's penthouse while we were still in the elevator and I recall feeling an actual blast of energy as I stepped out and into her sea of cables, cameras, glowing monitors, her miniature poodles, Morris and Max, and a half dozen college students. I threaded my way through the front room and found Shirley at her dressing-table mirror with a palate of clown make-up displayed in front of her. "Nancy, sit down. Come on, make yourself up. Let's see what you come up with!" Within a minute of my arrival, I was turning myself into an angry beast as Shirley was turning herself into a sad, baggy-pantsed hobo with a bowler hat and cane. "What's going on?" I asked.

"Oh, the laser is coming so we're going to shoot some scenes with it."

"The laser?"

As twilight fell, more people began arriving. Arthur C. Clarke (no relation to Shirley), the science-fiction writer who lived downstairs, arrived, bringing with him his pal Hugh Downs, the television host. Out on the roof garden the cameras were set up all along the perimeter, focusing down onto the avenue below. The laser looked like a long thin flashlight made out of a black brushed metal of some kind and it sent out a highly intense ruby-colored bead of light that appeared on the first object it touched wherever you pointed it. Even if that object was at a great distance.

The amazing thing about this ruby bead of light was that there was no beam or shaft connecting it to its source. The red bead of light just appeared. So when we aimed the laser downward the ruby bead appeared as a red dot on the sidewalk. People on the street started to notice it and would become fascinated. People were looking all over the place trying to see where it was coming from. And we were up there in the penthouse garden looking down on the scene and manipulating the dot. We videotaped with three cameras. Sometimes we let the ruby dot stay with one person all the way down the block. One guy was convinced he was communicating with the dot and tried to coax it to come around the corner with him. He came back from around the corner a couple of times in order to try again but sadly, the dot couldn't go home with him. It could do a lot of things but it couldn't make the turn.

When Shirley and I finished our clown makeup I asked why we were doing the make-up. "I'm getting in character for my piece with the laser. I don't know why you're doing it." I spent the rest of the night made up like Spider-Man but no one mentioned it.

Charlie Chaplin would have tipped his bowler to Shirley Clarke that night. Her sad little tramp walking down 23rd Street and meeting up with the ruby bead of light was a work of art. It was choreography. Shirley danced with the laser light. She lauded and applauded it, she argued and flattered the ruby bead. She teased, vamped, and vixened it.

She bullied and played and otherwise engaged the ruby bead, and ultimately Shirley charmed the entity. We watched from above in astonishment.

The next day the Videofreex got down to business. Parry and Chuck were designing a little video camera for Shirley that would wrap around her wrist with a miniature viewfinder at the end of a long cable that snaked around so that she wouldn't have to put the camera to her eye. Shirley wanted to use it as part of the art piece she was doing for Yoko Ono's new show, *This Is Not Here,* that was opening at the Everson Museum of Art in Syracuse. We were all going up for the opening, which would be jammed because John Lennon and Ringo Starr were going to be there too.

And it was true, in the crush of people, there went Ringo. He was being swept past us into the main gallery. "There he goes. Hi, Ringo!" He was gone but we could play our video as much as we wanted to. "There he goes. Hi, Ringo!" "There he goes, Hi, Ringo!"

THE ROAD TRIP TO ANN ARBOR: Media Bus was hired to stir up some video at the public access channel there, so David, Carol, Skip, and I went. For relaxation we decided to take the pastoral Canadian route instead of the Pennsylvania Turnpike. We drove up New York State and crossed Ontario to Detroit. We were going to stay with my mom and dad overnight and then drive out to Ann Arbor in the morning.

O Canada! No traffic, country roads all the way. It was an idyllic day, at least for me, riding along as if we were free. Canada had a different vibe and a slower beat. After a while I relaxed and stopped thinking that we were going to get pulled over by the cops at any moment the way I did when we were on the New York Thruway system, for example. It was a sunny, happy day away. That is, until it was time to re-enter the country at U.S. Customs. That was the price we paid for taking the scenic route. We had to pass through U.S. Customs, which is always a complex and dangerous game.

Sometimes it's not paranoia. Sometimes it's intuition. Sometimes you know your number is up. That's the way it was when I saw that the customs inspector walking toward me was a woman. She escorted me alone through a door into a small anteroom. They had already ripped our car apart and taken our video reels out of the boxes and held the tapes up to the light. They had already taken out the back seat, where they said, they, "found a seed." Jesus, a seed. Maybe they did. Shit. But they would have stopped us anyway because we fit a profile. Skip with his thick blond hair flowing way down his back and David with his black beard out to there, and Carol and I were not exactly in business suits either, and well, I guess we did seem a suspicious bunch. The customs inspector was closing the door behind us. She stared at me. Dry mouth and heart palpitations (mine, not hers). The little leather pouch of pot was burning a hole in my shirt pocket. I was a guilty murderer.

"You'd better give it to me, because if I find it, it's gonna be way worse."

Poomb! Poomb! I heard the squishing of my blood pumping past my ear drums. I examined my options and handed over the pot. And I kept my mouth shut. Now she wanted me to strip and squat to make sure I didn't have anything else stashed up inside me. Hey, it's just a little dignity. Go ahead. Take it.

They searched Skip and David and Carol too, but they were clean. Now the four of us were sitting on a hard bench waiting for the Customs Inspectors to come up with the next scenario. Here they came. The deal was that we were guilty of bringing a controlled substance across an international border in a vehicle, and the United States government consequently was going to take ownership of our vehicle.

"Wait a minute. You mean the government now owns our car?" Skip asked incredulously. Yes, it was true. That was the bad news. The good news was that we could buy it back from them for only one hundred dollars. Wow, really? Because this was a brand new 1973 Dodge Dart four-door—the same model and shade of green as the phone company cars, to keep a low profile on the highway. A hundred dollars was a bargain for such a fine vehicle. We bought it (leaving us with about $30 between us), and were kicked unceremoniously out onto Jefferson Avenue, Detroit Michigan, USA. It was nighttime.

We arrived at my mom and dad's late, and we were all excited about our border experience, which we related breathlessly, leaving out the part where they found my pot.

Producing our video-chaos cable television extravaganza in Ann Arbor was as controversial as ever. Live television with open phones in a college town was edgy, but nothing topped U.S. customs for a thrill.

BACK IN LANESVILLE, Harriet called to me from the door of her trailer as I was walking to the post office. "Hey, do you want to see my baby?" Harriet was married to Bobby, one of the Benjamin boys. There were plenty of Benjamins in Lanesville. The Benjamins had been in the Stony Clove Valley for more than two hundred years and the story goes that their ancestors had been awarded the property in a land grant from King George of England. Since then (and this is nothing against the Benjamins) they had stayed in the valley and married their cousins. Maybe some escaped and went away to college and never came back, but a lot stayed. Like Elmer Benjamin up the road in Edgewood, who stayed and had eleven kids of his own.

Willie Benjamin was the patriarch of the Benjamin clan. Willie lived with his grandson David (who was "slow" and in his twenties) in the house right across the road from his son Bobby Benjamin and his wife Harriet Benjamin and their five kids. Willie was completely crippled with arthritis and walked with tremendous difficulty using two canes. But he could still drive the snow plow and the tractor. No problem. A snow storm would make Willie shout with glee. "Pennies from heaven," he would bellow and then laugh, looking up with his very blue twinkling Benjamin eyes. And even though crippled, if Willie ever spotted a bit of metal or copper wire down on the dusty road, he would poke it around with his cane, and Bobby or one of the kids would pick it up for him.

Bobby and Harriet Benjamin lived in the tiny trailer next to the post office. It was one of those scrubby looking plots with a poor, sad, growling dog who never got walked, chained to a stake out front. When Harriet motioned to me from the doorway of her trailer and asked if I wanted to see her baby, I said yes. As I entered, I could hear, through a lot of static, a country western radio station from Albany squeaking out a popular favorite: "... so darlin' dream your dreams, every night and day." Harriet listened, holding her baby Todd on her hip.

"Here he is," she said. "Oh what a dear little man, the hamburger boy." She gave him a small bit of raw chopped meat with her fingers from her kitchen counter. And there was Scotty, the second youngest who was four. Then Johnny, who was six and smart as a whip, then Louise who was ten, and Paul, the oldest, who was twelve. These seven Benjamins lived in this two bedroom trailer.

I began videotaping Harriet at home. "Here comes the school bus" she shouts in the misty dawn, and walks the three older kids up to the road.

Harriet nibbles a piece of toast at the kitchen table. "The only time I can control my eating is when I'm on diet pills. It's the truth," she tells me.

Harriet reads to me from the New York Daily News: "See, here's Mrs. Crimmins: 'I have always said I was innocent and I'll keep fighting to prove my innocence.'" Harriet resonates to the Mrs. Crimmins story. Mrs. Crimmins was in jail for murdering all her children so she could run off with her boyfriend. Now Scotty is up on the kitchen table making animal sounds and squirming all over it. "Oh, he's been a devil all day long."

Then Harriet's husband Bobby comes home with Willie and David at lunchtime and Harriet dishes out the hot dogs and beans. "The woman who lives across the road from Gert Benjamin is dying of cancer," she tells them.

"Who?" says Bobby. Harriet repeats her statement, this time a little louder.

"She's done nothin' but throw up for fourteen days now!"

Paul and Louise begin fighting about who gets to go out that night. "You went to Dot's last night so you can't come!" taunts Paul to Louise.

"Ma, Paul says I can't go," whines Louise.

"Oh shut up, Louise," shouts Harriet.

I videotape Harriet packing her suitcase, grabbing it, bursting out of the trailer, slamming the door behind her, tossing her suitcase into the back seat of the old family station wagon, getting behind the wheel, and speeding off down the road singing "Roll Out the Barrel."

"Goodbye, Lanesville! I've had enough of it! I want to see something different!" She laughs maniacally and drives on for miles with me in the front seat with the video camera. At a certain point I begin to wonder if this is for real. It takes Harriet five miles to stop laughing.

The Benjamins became regular players on Lanesville TV. When we produced *A Saucer Lands in Lanesville*, we interviewed all the Benjamins about what they saw.

"We interrupt this broadcast to bring you a special bulletin. We switch you now to Harriet's trailer in downtown Lanesville."

Willie Benjamin is sitting on his tractor and shaking his head. "Wow! It was traveling! First one I ever seen. Looked like a big flat piece of material."

A gaggle of schoolgirls in front of the general store are excited. "It was a sudden thing. We were just waitin' for the school bus and we looked up and there it was!"

THE UPSTAIRS AT THE DOWNSTAIRS was famous for its musical revues when I first went to New York City in the mid-60s and got a job in the cabaret show there. I was hired to replace the most beloved and adored member of the cast, Miss Genna (Dixie) Carter, who was leaving the show and going to California. Everyone at the Upstairs at the Downstairs was referred to as Miss or Mister on the program—for that air of class or camp I'm not sure which. Anyway, no one could imagine the show without Miss Genna Carter. And, as it turned out, I, Miss Nancy, was no Miss Genna Carter, but I learned the show fast and loved doing it. We played two shows nightly (except Sundays) at 9:30 and midnight. In-between shows we would go down one flight to the Downstairs at the Upstairs to catch Miss Joan Rivers' show. Miss Joan Rivers was a comic who worked hard and would no doubt soon be famous. She wasn't that friendly. Meanwhile, back at the Upstairs at the Downstairs, it seemed that cast member Miss Madeline Kahn may not have liked me much. It may have been that she missed Miss Genna

59

Carter. Or maybe it was because I said one of her lines by mistake on my opening night. Nerves, you know. Fortunately for me, my old pal Miss Lily Tomlin from Detroit was also in the cast and she was always sweet so I didn't feel totally ostracized. Lily was performing a lot of her own material in the show and during the run, she had gained a job on *The Gary Moore Show* replacing Carol Burnett. That was her big break. From there she got *Rowan and Martin's Laugh-In,* so it was not that big a surprise to find Lily Tomlin's face smiling up at me from the cover of the *Time* magazine that was tossed on the kitchen table at Maple Tree Farm in Lanesville. Can you get bigger than that? Lily was on Broadway. She was on the cover of Time.

Lily Tomlin's Broadway debut, a one-person show called *Appearing Nightly,* written and directed by Jane Wagner, had a lot of video in it. She was projecting huge video images on a screen behind her. Always the perfectionist, Lily wanted to re-shoot some video in her felt poodle skirt, playing the part of a teenager at a school dance in the Fifties. Lanesville was only about two-and-a-half hour drive from the city if the roads were clear, but it was February and they weren't. So Lily drove up by herself in a snow storm and ultimately arrived at Maple Tree Farm for a late dinner. Bart had cooked a corned beef that was so tough there was no way it could be chewed. No way to even pretend that it could be chewed, much less swallowed. Bart was mortified because he prided himself on his deli specialties. His family was in the business. His dad and brother owned King Arthur's deli in Canarsie, Brooklyn. Lily never mentioned a thing about the corned beef and did not join in on the shoe leather jokes and complaints.

By the next morning it had snowed a couple of more feet. Bart and Skip and Parry helped me set up for Lily's shoot at the Tannersville high school gym. We made it up the mountain by following the snow plow and got the school principal in Tannersville to okay our use of the gym and then found that Lily's poodle skirt was wrinkled. Okay, there was a dry cleaner over in Hunter, let's go. Lily and I rushed the skirt over and cajoled the woman behind the counter to press it for us right away. She said okay, come back in an hour. In an hour we were setting lights and Carol went back to the dry cleaner for us.

"Who was that who brought in this skirt?" the woman asked Carol. "She looks so familiar."

"That was Lily Tomlin."

"No, not her, the other one."

"Oh, that's Nancy from Lanesville."

"Oh yes, that's right. I saw her on Lanesville TV."

THE LIVE, ONE HUNDRED and seventy-first broadcast of Lanesville TV was also going to be seen in New York City on Channel 13 on Russell Connor's weekly series, *Videotape Review*. Russell came up to Lanesville with his crew for the broadcast. He was going to appear live on the set with Bart who was hosting the show. Russell was wearing his safari jacket and sporting a dashing mustache. He was a cultured and artistic guy. Well mannered. He opened his program about Lanesville TV on June 26, 1975:

"One of the familiar clichés about portable video is that it decentralizes television, allowing for a genuinely local use of the medium. To see how it works, we went to the country, to Lanesville in the Catskill Mountains. There, one of the pioneer groups in video, Media Bus, formerly known as the Videofreex, has been running what may be the smallest television station in the world, reaching, on a big night, as many as three hundred people. Lanesville TV could be one of the signposts toward a future in which we'll all have video cameras. It certainly is the most neighborly television around."

Bart was welcoming the viewers: "... and for those tuning in here in Lanesville, be sure to adjust your Fine Tune to assure the best reception." Bart then turned to Russell and explained, "A lot of people have old TV sets and it takes some time to tune in." Call us at 7084 if you'd like to talk about anything—something to sell, lost dog, new cow? There are some new cows in Lanesville, we noticed."

One of the Benjamins down the road called to say the show was coming in good this week and then Bart announced that Parry's new tape, *The Circus Comes to Lanesville,* a fantasy about a goofy guy (played by Parry) who runs a video camera, but really wants to be a clown in the circus, would be coming on. The one-ring circus came to

Phoenicia (down the road) every summer. When Parry's circus video was over, we cut back to the live scene in the studio where Sam Ginsberg had arrived from his house up the road to put in his two cents' worth. He pulled up a chair on the set. Russell was surprised. He was taken off guard, realizing Lanesville TV was not on guard.

"Oh! We have a surprise guest who just walked in and this demonstrates the neighborliness of TV up in Lanesville," said Russell.

"May I introduce to you, Sam Ginsberg. Our neighbor and best TV fan."

"Well Sam, can you tell the people in New York what it means to have these people (the Videofreex) up here?"

[Speaking in his finest heavy-Russian-accented English.] "These people? I'm glad. See here, four years ago I don't figure what kind people these guys, now after I met them and I know them, I'm very glad to have these people in Lanesville and this is okay."

"Do you watch this program often?"

"Every Saturday night," said Sam, "I like it. I'd like all America to see this picture. See, here in our place it's mostly all reactionaries in Lanesville. Lanesville is not liberal people. Lanesville is all Republicans." Russell laughed nervously. "These are Nixon's people," Sam shouted agitatedly, being the true lefty he was.

Russell laughed again, but faintly. "Yes. Well ..."

Sam turned to look into the camera, speaking directly to the viewers. "Nixon's people!" Sam accused the audience.

"All right, all right," said Russell.

"Yeah," Sam continued, "one day George McGovern was running and this guy is coming up to me. A fellow, a milk driver says so who you gonna vote for? And I say I'm not gonna vote for that bum Nixon. So the milk driver he says he's not going to vote for McGovern the bum. Now I don't see him today but if I do I would say to him I'd say Charlie, how's your bum today?" Russell continued to laugh nervously. (Watergate was still a big story). "That Nixon bum, you're gonna see what's four more years!"

"I think it's great for you to come by," said Russell, turning to Bart. "That's the kind of er, uh, candid television you do here."

62

"Yeah. A lot of it is," said Bart. "When it's strictly a Lanesville TV show, we talk about the lawn."

"The lawn?"

"Yeah, we talk about the rain. We talk about Nixon, we still talk about Nixon. We talk about the anarchists and the CIA ... ."

Robert Sklar in his book *Prime Time America* noted: "... with an effective radius of three miles, Lanesville TV numbers its potential audience at around three hundred. Nothing to make William S. Paley quake in his boots just yet. But wait: Lanesville TV may merely be a little ahead of its time, a straw in the wind, a harbinger of television's future."

Chapter Four:
TVTV

THEY SAY MICHAEL SHAMBERG came up with the name TVTV (Top Value Television), while he was doing Yoga one day, and he knew instantly that's what he would name the company he was creating to cover the political conventions in 1972. Shamberg, who had been a reporter for *Time* magazine, who wrote the book *Guerrilla Television* (which postulates the theory that politics are obsolete and that information tools and tactics are a more powerful means of social change), who founded Raindance Corporation, a media think tank which had published *Radical Software* (a periodical), and who now, as TVTV, intended to conquer television. It was Michael Shamberg, Megan Williams, Allen Rucker, Hudson Marquez and Tom Weinberg, as TVTV, who put the big convention production together. And, one of the first calls they made was to Lanesville.

The Democratic Convention and the Republican Convention were each happening in Miami Beach that summer. Back then the political parties actually chose their candidates and agreed on their agenda during their conventions. That's what conventions were for. The Democrats went first, in July. The Democratic convention was wild and the sessions would go on late into the night sometimes until two or three in the morning. One night I was standing right next to candidate George McGovern in the lobby of the Fontainebleau Hotel so close I could see the thick orange pancake make-up he was wearing for the TV lights.

The Democratic convention was interesting, especially the part about Senator Thomas Eagleton. George McGovern had selected Eagleton to be his VP so then of course the media searched for dirt and revealed that Eagleton had taken shock treatments for depression at one time so McGovern had to take back the offer, eventually going with Sargent Shriver of Maryland. It was a huge fiasco. That, along with

McGovern's anti-war stance, insured that the Democrats were a hundred percent screwed.

Now it was the Republicans' turn. I already knew my way around Miami and where to get the good Cubano coffee and fried bananas. I was a seasoned veteran. TVTV had rented the same house on the canals on Pine Tree Drive that we stayed in the previous month for the Democrats. Now we were back. Like a summer camp reunion. I was feeling good. "Hey, hey, waddaya say? Nixon, Agnew, all the way!" The Republicans were going to have an event that would be more like a coronation for the sitting president than an actual convention. The entire Republican convention was completely pre-planned and timed out with the media given a script of the whole event. It was the first-ever convention produced entirely for television.

At the TVTV headquarters on Pine Tree Drive, Jody Sibert was again at mission control. Jody was the central office coordinator at the TVTV Headquarters. There she was, her golden hair back lit by the afternoon sun flickering through the French doors with the blue pool sparkling at her back. She was unselfconsciously topless, revealing her perfect breasts in the tropical Miami August. She listened with the phone to her ear while simultaneously ripping a page from the AP wire service ticker. Behind Jody, taped on the wall was this reminder from the TVTV management to the video shooters.

> ARE YOU ON TO A BIG STORY?
> Does your big story connect with the others?
> Is your Little story part of the Big picture?
> THE BIG STORIES
> 1. The Underbelly of Broadcast TV
> 2. The Vietnam Vets
> 3. Those zany Republicans, young and old
> 4. The White House family/celebrities.

I gave Jody a hug, feeling happy to be back and eager for a second round of politics-for-the-hell-of-it. There were seventeen of us this time, including the Ant Farm who had arrived that morning from

65

Texas. The Ant Farm, conceptual artist/architects, Chip Lord, Doug Michels, Curtis Schreier and T.L. Morey arrived in Miami Beach in a customized gray van with TVTV written backwards on the front. Like AMBULANCE, you know, so you can read it through your rear view mirror. They brought their own unique vision to the political convention. Chip Lord had an unimpressed, wide-angled point of view while he was shooting video and could often be heard on his tapes humming as he walked along. Chip was the only video shooter who left his camera running as it went through the security X-ray machines, so his camera discovered the inside of the convention floor by itself and waited for Chip to pick it up again.

TVTV HAD A SMALL BOOTH with the rest of the media over at the Jackie Gleason Convention Center. Our booth was four canvas walls held up by large plastic paper clips. We had a bunch of convention floor passes that worked by rotation and in half-hour intervals. Each half hour we had to turn them in and then get back in line for another round. Fortunately we had enough people in rotation for floor passes that we usually had two crews on the convention floor at any given time.

On the first day of the convention, Skip and I found ourselves standing inside the NBC News booth. which seemed to be suspended above the convention floor by wires. We were shooting hand-held black-and-white video of the NBC network announcer with his hand over his ear, speaking into the microphone: "NBC News continues its coverage of the 1972 Republican National Convention brought to you by the Gulf Oil Corporation."

We checked our briefing instructions. They were typed.

"The Media: We need to document the media presence. This can be done partly through visuals which show equipment, crews, and interviews; and partly through sound: either newsmen [sic] talking to each other, or interviews with newsmen. In fact, newsmen are the only people we would consider doing a formal interview with. You should also make friends with newsmen as they'll give you tips about events and processes. Chances are they won't feel threatened by us but will be amused and want to help."

66

On the convention floor, Skip had the mike and I had the camera and we searched out all the network news people to see how they were covering the show. Mike Wallace was vaguely condescending but tolerant of Skip's questions:

"What's going on right now," Skip asked, indicating to the crowd that was cheering and chanting "Four More Years."

"It's a moderately interesting story," said Mike Wallace. "What's going on right now though it seems to me is the first genuinely heart-felt spontaneous thing that has happened on this first night of the convention, wouldn't you agree?"

"Yes."

"It's quite obvious. Particularly those young people over there seem to feel very genuinely an affection for Pat Nixon."

"What do you think about the Republican youth?" Skip asked.

"I don't know enough about them. It's such a general question, isn't it?"

"Well, what kind of stories do you cover here on the floor?"

"Well, tonight I have covered none," said Mike.

"So it's been kind of dull?" asked Skip.

"A little bit, yes," said Mike

"Why haven't you been able to cover any stories?"

"Well, because so much of the action—you see, CBS quadrants the floor and the states that I have, I have about 16 or 17 states, that really, there's not been a great deal of action in. Most of the action has been on that side of the VIP area and Dan Rather has that part."

"Do you cover delegates?"

"Oh yes."

"Do you ever get a chance to get to know the delegates and sort of hang out with them?"

"We do a little by the end of the convention."

Then Skip started to talk about the tight scheduling the Republicans had done and how the networks were sticking with the platform and platform issues.

"If you could loosen up the format a little, sort of get into more advocacy reporting, would you …"

"Advocacy reporting?" Mike Wallace smiled in a world-weary fashion, shaking his head. "No. I don't ..." He stopped again and shook his head and laughed palely. "I'm not a big fan of advocacy reporting. It seems to me that my chore is to tell what happens, analyze a little bit what happens if I can, try to go into the background, try to reveal what goes on underneath the surface. But as for advocacy," he shook his head again, "that's not mine."

"If you had an open rein on what you wanted to cover, how would you go about it?"

"Here? I think I might rather watch it at home. Honest."

"Okay, thanks a lot."

Then we spotted Roger Mudd, the network correspondent on the convention floor. He was sitting on the sidelines taking a break, smoking a cigarette. We approached him with the camera rolling. He was sitting on the edge of a temporary barrier in front of some seats so that we were below him and had to hold the microphone up towards his face. Roger looked down on us, puffing on his cigarette. He was wearing headsets and was nodding with a tight-mouthed smile/smirk. He refused to speak, still staring directly at Skip.

"Just don't have time?" Skip asked him. "You wouldn't talk to me last convention either. You don't speak at all?"

Roger shook his head no. He took a drag of his cigarette while giving Skip the dead eye.

"How come you're so much trouble tonight?" Skip turned to the camera. "I think we have a good interview going so far." We waited for a few seconds. "He won't say anything. I think he's serious about it. He won't even tell me no. He won't tell me why." Skip tried one more time. "I'm serious. Won't you just give me a reason why you won't speak to me?"

Skip looked up at Roger Mudd hopefully once more. Roger exhaled smoke through his nose, shook his head no, his smile growing weaker.

"Just tired?" asked Skip.

Roger smiled silently and stared at Skip.

"Okay, that's fine. That's real good."

Roger raised his eyebrows.

"See ya later." Skip continued speaking as we wandered across the convention floor trolling for news. "Do you believe him? Do you think he's really tired?"

From behind the camera I was thinking, sure, I believe he was tired. And I believed Mike Wallace would rather be at home. That was the difference between TV and TVTV. Skip took out his harmonica and held the mike right up to it like Bob Dylan and played "The Republican Convention Drag" as we walked through the crowded hall. The security cop waited until Skip finished the chorus to stop us and check the press pass hanging around his neck.

"Did you like the way I played?"

"I'm not a music critic," said the cop.

WALTER CRONKITE SAT DOWN for us in his portable office in a trailer outside the convention center. He talked about television news:

"I don't think they ought to believe me. I don't think they ought to believe Brinkley or anybody else on the air. And I don't think they ought to get all their news from one television broadcast, or even all their news from television. I think they ought to read and they ought to go to opinion journals and all the rest of it, and I think it's terribly important that this be taught in the public schools because otherwise we're going to get to a situation because of economic pressures that television is all you've got left and that would be disastrous. We can't cover the news in a half-hour every evening. That's ridiculous."

Cronkite might have said some other stuff at the very end of the interview but I was a little nervous about actually shooting Cronkite and I re-wound a little bit at the end of the tape to make sure I'd recorded it. Of course I had been recording, but I failed to fast forward up to the end after I checked, so I by mistake taped over Walter's ending. Instead of Walter's last words, there is video of the empty hall after the ball kind of scene with melting ice sculptures and garbage on the floor. Shamberg was really really pissed off.

THE REPUBLICAN CONVENTION was to be the last patrol for the ragtag Vietnam Veterans Against the War. Twelve hundred vets led by three men in wheelchairs marching silently down Collins Avenue, the American flag unfurled, flapping upside down above them. In front of the Fontainebleau Hotel, where delegates and VIPS were staying, the vets approached 500 heavily armed police who were guarding the building. The two groups stood facing each other for several tense silent minutes. At last a vet spoke through a bullhorn: "We want to come inside." The vets were denied entrance to the hotel.

Republican Congressman Pete McCloskey tried to appease the vets. Sure he was a Republican, but a liberal one. He was behaving as if he was on their side. He himself was a veteran. McCloskey explained calmly to Ron Kovic, who was leading the procession in his wheelchair, that the vets should understand that "the government fears you." Ultimately the vets didn't get into the hotel but they made several speeches for the media which were mostly drowned out by helicopters and general chaos.

Outside the convention center, I was running with a crowd of just-gassed people and you could hear the canisters popping and see the smoke in the air and people were gagging and tear-stained, and we were all choking—but Bart was still shooting. He saw a network news truck parked at the curb, and all the crew guys were wearing gas masks, standing on top of the vans with big cameras on tripods watching the melee. And he went over to them as if he had found his long lost brothers, and asked if they had an extra gas mask and they told him they did, but they had to save it in case they needed it later. And the gas was so painful and pervasive that even some of the Republicans trying to get into the hall got a whiff. Middle-aged lady delegates who were entirely innocent were gasping and choking. "Is this your first time?" Bart asked them. "Yes, yes," they sobbed. "Oh isn't that wonderful!" Bart said.

Inside the hall, however, everything was orderly. President Nixon was about to be nominated, then Spiro Agnew was going to be nominated, and the platform was going to be adopted. Everything was on schedule for television. Doug Kiker was one of the few network reporters who still had some energy and excitement. When Skip asked what he would do if he could loosen up NBC's format, he said, "I guess

70

I'd like to have more time on the floor because, as Brinkley is fond of pointing out, "The delegates are the convention."' Doug Kiker seemed actually to be prowling the floor looking for stories, which was very non-network.

ON THE LAST NIGHT of the convention there was a buzz on the convention floor because Nixon himself was going to appear. Of course, all the media wanted to be on the floor, and the rotation line for the floor passes was huge but TVTV managed to have two crews out at this time. Chip Lord was out with one camera and Michael Shamberg was out with the other.

Jody Sibert had been running the office for the whole convention and hadn't yet experienced being on the convention floor, so she was going to tag along with Shamberg to see what it was like. The next time I saw Jody was about forty-five minutes later and she was sitting in the TVTV booth, pale and shaken while being debriefed on video about her experience. Jody said she and Michael had come through security and were entering the convention floor where Nixon was already speaking. "He looked very very tiny way up on a platform way way in the distance. Like the size of a Ken doll," she said.

"He spoke into a microphone so you could hear his echoey voice and see his little gesticulations. The place was packed and, through the din, I heard a faint voice shouting in counterpoint to the whole hall chanting "Four More Years! Four More Years! Four More Years!" Jody heard a lone voice crying out, "Stop the bombing!" Stop the bombing!" She said that she decided to follow the sound and check out what was happening. "Stop the Killing! Stop the Killing!" The chant was faint but strong. She threaded her way through the crowd and there they were, three Vietnam vets. One of them, Ron Kovic, was in a wheelchair. Jody gazed at Kovic, who was at his most Christ-like for this event. Eyes upward, medals spangled across his chest. "Stop the bombing," he beseeched the throngs.

The vets were positioned in the visitors section, each with an authentic visitors pass. They were surrounded by enthusiastic Nixon-lovers who gazed steadfastly and zombie-like away from them, refusing

71

to hear or notice them. And the vets were pleading and weeping and shouting "Stop the bombing! Stop the killing!" They were starting to cause a small disturbance which attracted Doug Kiker and his crew from NBC. Kiker was talking frantically into his microphone trying to get the control booth to cut away from Nixon's speech and over to him, where something was actually happening at that very moment. Jody and the vets were suddenly surrounded by a swarm of Secret Service. "Stop killing innocent women and children!" "Stop the bombing!" Ron Kovic's eyes were rolling up in his head. "Stop the bombing! Stop the killing!"

The Secret Service had started to muscle the vets away and that's when Jody made eye contact with a secret service guy. She looked into his flat cold eyes and realized who she was dealing with. At that moment she made her decision. "I stepped over the line," she said. "Not just the hippie-journalist line, but the fearless-hero line. I took hold of Ron's chair and wouldn't let go. We were all grabbed from behind and I held on and held on and the band began to play and the balloons began to fall and they pushed and pulled us and kicked us and I shouted, 'Take your hands off me, I'm with the press,' and then—we were out on our asses through these huge side doors onto the sidewalk."

Shaken, Ron turned to Jody and said, "You were the only one. Sister, sister, you were the only one." And then he asked her plaintively, "Did they hear us?" And Jody, who saw the anguish in Ron's eyes, said, "Yes, I know they did," even though she knew they didn't.

Lucky for TVTV, Chip Lord caught some of that scene on tape until he too was surrounded by secret service and his camera suddenly went dead. So nobody recorded Jody and the vets getting strong-armed out of the building. (Rumor had it that the Secret Service could zap your camera anytime they wanted to.)

When Oliver Stone made Ron Kovic's book, *Born on the Fourth of July*, into a movie in 1989, he used that particular scene on the convention floor, taken directly from the TVTV footage, and he staged it almost exactly the way it happened with Tom Cruise playing Ron Kovic, but Jody's part wasn't in the scene. It wasn't in the movie but Jody probably saved the vets from getting roughed up by Nixon's goons.

OUTSIDE THE CONVENTION, beefy plainclothes cops were hustling frightened Republicans into the hall. "We're in a gas situation out here. Move 'em through. Let's get 'em inside or they're gonna get gassed." The plainclothes cop listened through the plug in his ear as he spoke. "They're using gas over on Washington Avenue. Let's let 'em in now just calm and easy. Slow and easy."

Pop! Pop! There it was and it hurt like hell. Not again! Oh, ugh, aarrgh, my throat was closing and burning and my eyes were on fire. Aarrgh, ugh, there was no way to stop it. I was being gassed. People were rushing past me. I saw them pixilated against the yellow acrid smoke that was hanging in the air. Achhh, I needed to rub my eyes to scratch aarrgh, ucckkkhh, no that was worse! Oh my throat, my throat. Then the soldiers and the cops in black gas masks wielding sticks arrived, oh god, my eyes, aarrgh! What were they doing this for? The cops were so much over-reacting to the demonstrators. It was stupid. The demonstrators wanted non-violence. The cops wanted violence.

I caught up with Doug Kiker later on the convention floor and I was all tear-streaked and smelly. He told me, "Never wash your face with soap in a gas situation like this. Use apple vinegar." He indicated how you should pour the vinegar into a hanky and hold it over your nose. He said he learned that in Northern Ireland.

All in all, the Republican Convention was a grand rip-roaring week of politics. Polaroid flashes of the swimming pool, tanks of nitrous oxide, balloons, and whipped cream, filled TVTV's scrapbook along with memos and memorabilia from the conventions including lots of hand-held video shooting advice such as "KEEP BOTH EYES OPEN." And, jotted on the margin of the photo album was this metaphysics advice based on Carlos Castaneda: "Find a spot for shooting (see Don Juan), then move the spot with you."

A COUPLE OF YEARS LATER I had another adventure with TVTV, video-taping Republicans. We had geared up to cover the impeachment trial of Richard Nixon as a four-part series for public television which would have obviously been a great video, but Nixon resigned and left us with *Gerald Ford's America*. TVTV had rented a townhouse headquarters in

73

Washington and Michael Shamberg was again at the helm. This time our angle wasn't quite as well defined as it had been in the past. Gerald Ford was no Nixon. Skip and I were covering Congress. We got permission through Representative John Brademus, whom we were profiling, to videotape a few minutes of congressional banter before a meeting of the House leadership who were planning to discuss the CIA involvement in the Middle East. The TVTV crew was supposed to leave as soon as serious discussion began, but right away, over their sweet rolls and coffee, they started talking about the situation with Turkey and Greece, about Cyprus, and the conversation started heating up and the congressmen were really going at it. We kept shooting, thinking that any moment they were going kick us out. But since we didn't look like a network crew with big obtrusive equipment, we got away with videotaping the entire meeting which ended when the doors were flung open to let in the reporters for their briefing. And the first visual the reporters saw was Skip in the midst of the congressmen pointing his camera at them. In the front of the pack of reporters was Roger Mudd, who so laconically refused to speak to us at the Republican Convention two years earlier. Hi, Roger.

Shooting video around Washington with TVTV made it glaringly obvious that we would never really fit the mold of the press corps. For example, we used to actually pass the camera around among us. That was the Videofreex method. The news media would never do that. Plus, we would shoot way, way too much tape. Because we were looking for some authentic moments and we wanted a scene to unfold naturally. We weren't going out for 30 second bites to roll into a newscast. Another difference was that in the press corps there was a clear division between the reporters and the technical guys, to the extent that they sat in separate areas of the press room. Upon entering the White House pressroom, you go to one side or the other. Techies liked us even though (or maybe because) they didn't take us seriously.

IT WAS ELECTION NIGHT IN 1974, a mid-term election during the early days of *Gerald Ford's America*. We were at the Republican National Committee's opulent townhouse headquarters in Washington, DC to shoot some video of their election night victory party. Only it wasn't a victory party. The Republicans had, at long last, lost that year. Nevertheless, we loaded up our rented station wagon with gear and headed off to the event.

There was a subdued tone as we entered. On the dark wood paneled walls of the large anteroom hung the official party portraits of each Republican president throughout history. The other news crews were setting up for their evening sound bites. As we loaded in our equipment from the car, we stacked it all up against the wall beneath the Republican Party's official portrait of the Nixon family. As we were piling up our boxes, unloading our equipment, one of us slipped the portrait of the Nixons off the wall and onto the floor, leaning it behind our light kit box for the duration of the party. A lounge band was playing "Happy Days are Here Again." I taped the entire number. I thought it was funny being that they lost the election big time and also because "Happy Days Are Here Again" was the traditional song for the Democrats! Nobody noticed.

We shot video of the Republicans for hours, long after the other media had packed it in. We interviewed anyone and everyone. We snooped around and listened in, waiting around for a great moment. Then at the end of the evening, we simply loaded out the portrait of the Nixons with the rest of our stuff. I'll admit that this caper wasn't my idea, but I felt good being a part of it. From that day on, the Nixons' official portrait would hang proudly in the small office of a rural grassroots media center somewhere in America.

AT SUPERBOWL X, the Woodstock of corporate America, it was the Dallas Cowboys against the Pittsburgh Steelers. As an extra added attraction for this production, TVTV had recruited Harold Ramis and Bill Murray (before *Ghostbusters*) to add another layer to our coverage. TVTV was evolving. Some characters now were fictional, and others were not. You had to have been watching Lanesville TV to come up with such a novel idea. It was also a good idea for TVTV to give a portapak video rig to the football players to take home and tape themselves when we weren't around.

75

Lynn Swann of the Steelers showed all his body scars. Ernie Holmes of the Steelers explained, "I'll tell you why I enjoy playing football. I enjoy kicking ass. I'm an ass-kicker."

The National Football League, or the NFL was very intimidating and everyone did what they said. No joking around with the NFL. Yes sir, they were the final word. The perimeter of the football field was ringed with Doberman Pinschers. So even if you got past the NFL, nobody got past the NFL's dogs. But somehow I had a field pass, and a camera crew, and I was standing on the field during the game—an otherworldly feeling, bizarre and surreal. The din was shattering. And then it was over. There was a rush of silence. After two weeks of living and breathing Super Bowl, it was over and the fans were gone. Miami was quiet. The stadium was dark, the tension was gone.

The TVTV crew was clearing out of the old mansion on Palm Island that had been our headquarters, but Bill Murray wanted to do one more scene. He wanted to go back over to the stadium and do a little monologue as "The Last Fan." Everyone just stared at him. Nobody wanted to put the gear together again and go back out to shoot. Billy tried his pleading yet endearing look and I said okay, I'll go back with him but only with the black and white camera. Not the color equipment or lights.

Back we went to the Orange Bowl looming gray and silent. Only a couple of hours ago it was filled with camper trucks and hooting fans. Bill Murray was the last fan. He was a poignant guy, a little dim-witted maybe, with a slight speech impediment who couldn't bring himself to leave. And I, who had zero interest in football and never believed actors, was actually moved by the lost soul I saw in Billy's eyes. Here I was, believing him for a hot second.

Nice little piece. It didn't make the cut.

Chapter Five:
Perhaps it was the Fermi
Fast Breeder Reactor

GODDARD COLLEGE in Plainfield Vermont is a small progressive school where you can get a degree in Social Ecology and other esoteric sciences. During the summer of 1976, Media Bus taught a course on how to build a community television station and how to broadcast video all over the campus. The new campus-wide TV channel had been dubbed "Piña Colada TV" by the students.

The program was working out well, but I was having a hard time concentrating because there was something very wrong inside my body. Whatever it was, I could feel it growing inside me like a string of pearls along the inside slope of my right hip. It had begun to hurt me after I took a tumble sledding down the back trail in Lanesville the previous winter. Now it was summer and I could no longer deny it. One day in the staff dorm, I showed Bart. "Look, feel this." I guided his fingers with my own. "What do you think it is?" He jumped back when he felt it and said I should go right over to the campus clinic, so I did. I showed it to the junior doctor and he was stumped. He said I should watch it and if it continued to grow I should have it checked again. "Maybe it's a knot in your muscle," he speculated.

In August, we brought all our students from Goddard down to New York City with us to cover the Democratic National Convention. We were doing five nights live coverage on Manhattan Cable. Three hours each night. We called the show *The Five Day Bicycle Race,* because we were bicycling our tapes from the convention floor over to the studio where our live show was being cablecast. It was by no means a done deal in terms of who the candidate would be that year. Of all the candidates at the Democratic convention, Jimmy Carter's folks were the friendliest. They had brought the whole family up from Georgia including aunts and uncles, a dozen cousins, all working the press, glad-handing us at the buffet tables. Even the Carter kids were willing to be interviewed and were actually taking a moderate position on pot.

Among the video shooters, things were getting competitive. Who could get the biggest candidate? Skip got Mondale, who would ultimately become vice president. I had to get on the ball. I needed a candidate. I waited around Jerry Brown's hotel lobby for three hours just to track him from the elevator to his car at the curb. Lucky for me his car wouldn't start and Jerry improvised some jokes about the car being a kind of metaphor for his whole campaign. "It just ran out of gas at the last minute." The driver was grinding the ignition. The motor tried and tried and finally turned over, and they pulled away. I got my shot. As they drove off, I felt the pain bloom in my side.

As soon as I got home to Lanesville, I asked a local doctor what was this hard thing and I pointed to the place on my side and he said, "That's your hip bone," and he touched it and, startled, he jumped back slightly the same way the previous doctor had. He said, "Wait, no, it's not your hip bone. I don't know what it is. Don't move. Just stay there." So I was lying on his table and he ran out of the room and came back in with the surgeon from down the hall and they both agreed that I had a big hard tumor and I'd better check into the hospital right away. I was in Rhinebeck, New York, so I went straight to the hospital there. After two days of tests at the Rhinebeck Hospital, the surgeon came in "I'm sorry but this is beyond my medical knowledge." It was a very trippy, other worldly feeling to be told something like that. "I'd suggest you try Sloan Kettering," the doctor was saying. From the way he said it, I understood that I was going to die. I hadn't planned on dealing with that inevitability so soon but now I had no choice. "Can I have your guitar?" said Bart.

"Not Sloan Kettering," I told the doctor. He had nothing else to suggest, but fortunately, an associate of his said he knew the chief-of-surgery at the Albany Medical College, Dr. Powers, and he got him to take a look at me. Dr. Powers was fascinated. This was a very rare tumor and was bound to be a complicated and exciting procedure. At first he thought he wanted to do the surgery himself, but ultimately decided to put his best young surgeon, Dr. Carl Wirth, on the case. Dr. Wirth, a man about my own age, loved the tumor and called it a chondrosarcoma. He liked the way it snaked around between my organs, attaching itself onto my hip bone then winding around behind my kidney. He looked forward to cutting me open and carefully extricating it. He didn't realize at first that he would have to also resect (or saw off) the iliac crest of my right hip to which it was attached. Then of course he had to re-wire all the connections that went from my leg to my hip, and hook them onto my abductor instead. This entailed several drill holes.

On 11-8-76 Doctor Wirth noted: "The patient tolerated the procedure well." And I noted: "I am a long way from my body. I know that I'm dying but it's okay. I feel calm and I have no fear. I try to tell the woman who is shouting at me in the recovery room that she can relax. Dying is so easy."

I'm in the first grade, walking to Bagley school with Eileen E. who lives on my block. Eileen E. is somewhat overwhelming as a companion, but I have no choice. Fate has brought both of us to this block at this time in space. I'm pondering my predicament as we walk down Thatcher, and I'm glancing occasionally at this pudgy little blonde girl with the cold pale blue eyes who has been known to pinch and shove and to point and laugh. What am I doing here? Where would I rather be? From where I stand I'm realizing that the ideal situation for me would be to be able to control what is happening around me, if I only could. But this is my reality. It's a sort of out-of-the blue situation that I apparently will have to make the best of.

I have always sensed that Eileen E. is capable of cruelty. I know that instinctively and until now have taken care to keep a certain distance. But something happens on this day while we're walking to Bagley School. Unexplainably, I experience a warm feeling. It's an oddly hopeful sort of feeling about Eileen E. I glance over at her again. The first inkling of the concept of friendship comes over me. Naively I embrace the idea that Eileen E. feels the same way too. She must. Isn't it all around us? Surely we are both awash with emotion. I'm bursting to communicate. The anticipation of this potential intimacy is visceral. She is my first friend.

"It makes me sad," I say to her, looking down as we walk, "that sometimes the little ants get stepped on by mistake when we're walking to school." Eileen E. stops walking and looks at me, expressionless. Her mouth is open and her nostrils are flared. And yet I continue, "It's weird how the ants are at our mercy." This was something that I had felt, but had never spoken about. The moment the words leave my mouth I feel instant dread for having revealed my thoughts to Eileen E. She looks down at the cement at the long columns of little red ants crossing the cracks, going about their business. She picks up her fat little leg and brings the sole of her brown oxford down, wickedly grinding it into the trail of insects. I watch in horror as she lustily crushes them, one at a time if she can. Eileen E. laughs. She especially likes killing them while she looks at my face. The little ants were dead, senselessly eradicated. If I hadn't pointed them out, they would have still been alive. Everything would have been okay. But alas, it was too late.

Ten days later they wheeled me screaming in pain to rehab and propped me up on the parallel walking bars where I stood motionless with the amputees. I tried to take a step. I concentrated on moving my right leg. It would not move. Tears of frustration and agonizing high-pitched shooting stabbing pain like you get when they saw your bones off. I was doomed. I would never walk again. The slightest movement or twitch in my body triggered involuntary uncontrollable howls. I couldn't move my right leg at all. Bart would sit at my bedside reading to me from the newspaper. In my Darvon haze I was on the lam with Patty Hearst.

One evening, my surgeon asked me if I wanted to go home.

"Very funny" I answered. "I can't walk. How am I supposed to go home to Lanesville if I can't walk?"

"Well", he said, "if you can get to the phone in the hall to call Bart, you can ask him to come and get you."

"How do you expect me to get to the phone?"

"Let me help you stand up. Good. Now hold on to this walker.

Leave the weight on your right leg since you can't move it and step forward with your left." It took me a minute or so to get the message even to my good left leg but I was able finally to step forward with it. "Okay, now drag that right leg up to meet it."

I could walk! But my hip, where was it? Bart had told me I was not going to be happy when they took off the bandages.

Bart and Chuck brought a bed downstairs for me to sleep in because I was unable to climb the stairs. Maple Tree Farm was grey and silent. Only the three of us left. Chuck told me that Skip and his girlfriend Jane Aaron had moved to San Francisco. I didn't hear from them. Carol and Parry bought a house in Phoenicia for their growing family. I rarely saw them.

I was, alone, crying and sniffing because I couldn't even bend my body enough to take off my own shoes. Some nights if didn't remember to ask Bart or Chuck to help me before they went to bed, I'd have to sleep with them on.

I read the papers voraciously. Jimmy Carter was president now. And, as spaced as I was, a story began emerging from the news. It seemed that the nuclear power plants across the country had been emitting plutonium fallout for many years. It wasn't healthy. It caused cancer. It was industrial pollution. How far had I been from the Fermi fast breeder while I was growing up in Detroit? Not very far. Then I noticed a story about Dr. Helen Caldicott, the brilliant pediatrician and anti-nuclear activist, and phoned her at her home in Boston. I asked her if I could interview her on videotape about the cancer-nuclear connection and send the videotape around for showings. She said yes. In an epic snowstorm Bart drove me to Boston so that I could videotape her.

Dr. Caldicott explained it all to me and it wasn't pretty. She said, "The elements that come out of the nuclear reactor are Iodine-131, Strontium-90, Cesium-137 and Plutonium. The first three are beta emitters. Plutonium is an alpha emitter. Alpha emitters (Plutonium in particular) are the most carcinogenic or cancer-producing substances we have ever known. And, Plutonium is man-made! Plutonium didn't exist before we fissioned uranium.

It is appropriately named after Pluto. the God of Hell, because it is incredibly carcinogenic."

As she was talking I was thinking that no one was concerned about my tumor back in the fifties, and no one was thinking about it now, even though the truth was out. "In every cell in the body there is a regulatory gene which controls the rate at which that cell divides," Dr. Caldicott continued. "And if you have an atom of plutonium sitting next to a cell, giving off its alpha particle, and the particle hits the regulatory gene, it will damage it. But the cell will survive. The cell will sit dormant for about fifteen years. And then one day, instead of dividing normally, it goes berserk and produces millions and billions of cells. That's cancer." Then she made the leap by adding, "And, if we proceed with nuclear power and nuclear weapons, we're going to wipe out humanity from the face of the earth. The ultimate in preventive medicine is to eliminate nuclear power and nuclear weapons." I asked Helen if she would come to New York and do some kind of public event to make people aware of this issue. She said yes.

We decided to do a balloon release up at Columbia University, where they were messing with nuclear materials in their labs. A couple of weeks before the event, Parry went in and interviewed the professors and scientists about their experiments and they showed him their little nuclear reactor, so we knew it was really in there.

Dr. Caldicott did a rabble-rousing rant on the sidewalk outside the lab building. Speaking to the shockingly sparse crowd, she talked about what it's like to see children die from cancer. "It's no use treating cancer once it occurs. It's too late! Have you ever seen a child come into a hospital with some bruises, have a blood picture done, got leukemia, put in a little room all by himself, treated with nasty drugs, make him feel sick? His parents can't see him unless they wear a mask and a gown. He lies in a state of abject terror while everyone smiles at him and two weeks later in the middle of the night, he dies, bleeding from his mouth, nose and rectum." Then she said, "Einstein predicted this would happen. He said, 'I wish I had been a locksmith' when he saw the atomic bomb. We are the curators of life on earth and we hold it in the palm of our hand," concluded Dr. Caldicott.

Then poet Louise Bernikow stepped to the microphone: "... People dying of cancer are not writing letters to congressmen or to you, not marching, not shouting, not bombing, not rebelling, not shaking their fists in the pestilent air. Heartless, inviolate, the pestilent air, disguised as a lover, plants its insidious caress on grandmothers, lovers, California, Oklahoma, is really a rapist, the air invades lung, liver, cervix, breast, bladder, while the muse recoils in dizzy horror, and hearty dark-eyed poets tear their own hair."

Then, one hundred black balloons were released with a message attached to each one. "If this had been a nuclear accident, the wind would have blown the fallout to where you found this balloon." We asked anyone who found a balloon to please mail the card back to us so we could track where the contamination would have gone. We received two cards back, both mailed from Connecticut.

MY NEW CLIENT was dying fast. He was 40, handsome, and rich. He lived in Chicago with his wife and kids. Life was good. Suddenly he gets a pain. He drops in at his doctor's office after lunch. It must be a pulled muscle from his tennis game. But, no. His entire insides are riddled with cancer. He has very little time. He starts treatment. He keeps his positive attitude. "Go for it," he says when the doctors explain his chances. "Do everything you can think of." Sure, he would have said that. And somewhere in his secret heart he must have thought he hoped that somehow the impossible would be true for him and he would be back on the tennis court and people would be marveling at modern medicine.

What he wanted from me was to help him make an inspirational television show featuring interviews with well known people who had survived cancer. All my friends had turned him down and told him to try me, since I already had survived cancer (so far). I flew all over the country with him and his wife and a video crew. We went to Kansas City and interviewed one of the Block brothers (of H&R). He had survived cancer. We interviewed Butch Waltz, a pro tennis player. He had survived cancer. And of course we went to Florida where pretty much everyone had cancer. I sat next to the camera and asked the questions:

When did you get cancer? How did you treat your cancer? What are your feelings about cancer? How do you cope with cancer? What is it like? How are you now? What can you tell us?

In the end my client became too ill to travel, so I went to Rancho Mirage, California to interview Betty Ford without him. She had survived cancer, too. "What about a cure for cancer?" I asked Mrs. Ford hopefully, as if she'd know. She replied "I leave that to the scientists. They're making wonderful strides. Why, every day ... ." No mention of the power plants.

Before we left, as we were packing up our gear, I asked Betty Ford about her life after the White House. "When there's nothing on the calendar," she joked, "we develop a seminar."

My client died one day after I got the Betty Ford videotapes to his bedside.

What is luxury? The Yacht Club in Boca, Townhouse Number Seven, with three bedrooms? Is luxury a condo at Turnberry in Hallandale? Swat team at the gate with riot guns and 45's? What is luxury? Is it a one hundred and twenty eight pound marlin? A triple bypass? Philanthropy? The best treatment? The top doctors? The perfect chemo cocktail?"

Albany Medical College
Division of Orthopedic Surgery
Cain, Nancy

Nancy Cain appears at this time. She is now three months post-radical resection of an extra osseous chondrosarcoma of the right lower quadrant of the abdomen. She has had whole body computed tomography at Syracuse University, which has been read as unremarkable and will be used as a baseline for follow-up of such tomography next summer. Chest X-ray today is normal and physical examination reveals a well-healed wound at this time. This young woman is doing extremely well at this point. She will be seen in approximately three months for a new chest x-ray. Carl R. Wirth, M.D.

Chapter Six:
Something Entirely Different

BART AND I WENT to Spain. Emotionally spent, Bart's mood was still somewhat tense and grim from my surgery and slow recovery which he had been enduring, but we planned to have a wonderful trip, regardless. We flew to Madrid and took the train to Sevilla where my Aunt Lois and Uncle Richard had rented a house for a year. Richard, an artist, was painting bulls and Lois was taking care of everything else, including their social life. She encouraged me to speak in Spanish instead of English. We gave it a try with a Japanese gentleman at the jai alai matches. Lois asked him in Spanish what he liked best about Spain and he answered, "Aceitunas rellenas." Of everything in Spain, this guy liked the stuffed olives best. The olives were that good in Spain. Sevilla featured stone streets and siestas. It was warm in Sevilla and still light at ten o'clock at night when we would have dinner. We haunted the little automatic photo booths, taking pictures of ourselves, then cutting out and pasting our own heads onto postcards of the saints.

"It's all about healing, right?" I said to Bart. "About my physical self healing."

"Of course that's what it's about," said Bart.

"I don't want to be a victim. My leg is hurting."

In Madrid the unregulated motor emissions and air pollution were so intense that it was impossible for Bart to breathe and he was feeling anxious so we headed over to the Costa Brava, then decided to leave Spain altogether and go to Morocco. We spent our last night in Spain in a dreary high rise Miami Beach style hotel where a double room cost $12. A tourist in the lobby told us it was so cheap because the Brits who vacationed there refused to pay any more than that. We had arrived at the hotel on "Travesty Night" and the hotel guests were abuzz. All the men were dressed up in ladies' clothes. That's what a travesty is. It was all in good fun. From the Costa Brava we took the night ferry across the Straits of Gibraltar to Tangier. We arrived at midnight after a smooth boat ride and candlelight dinner with a view of the Rock of Gibraltar floating by.

It was midnight in Tangier at the boat dock. We chose a Mercedes taxi because the driver said he knew a room to rent for the night even though it was very late. He left us off on a narrow dark street and pointed to an unlit doorway. Luckily it really was a room to rent. We fell asleep without a sense of where we were.

We were awakened in the morning by the Muslim call to prayer from a loudspeaker. We were in a small tiled room with a window opening onto a view of minarets and blue sky. We stepped out onto the narrow street which was now bustling with activity. We were immediately accosted by several young boys, each wanting to be our guide. They hovered around us, sticking close as we tried to hurry past them, but they tailed us trying several languages while we were shaking our heads no and shooing them away, until finally I turned and shouted at them in English that I was an insane person and they had better back off. Bart was furious with me for making a scene but, thanks to my outburst, we had an uninterrupted Moroccan coffee and a big bun for breakfast at the café on the corner. We decided to get away from Tangier, which seemed like a border town, and taxied to the train station where we decided to go to Fez.

In Fez I rode on the back of Mohammed's motor scooter. It was excellent physical therapy for my leg because you hold on with your thighs on the back of a scooter. You hold on tight. Bart rode with Mohammed's brother, Abdul. We all smoked fresh hashish rolled into Camel cigarettes and scooted through the Medina (the old city) day and night. Mohammed and Abdul even took us home with them where all the men danced and sang for us. I was the only female at the table. The women were covered and looked at us through the slats in the kitchen door. I had no opportunity to communicate with them even though I wanted to.

One day I was strolling along the outer wall of the Medina in Fez where a few scruffy merchants squatted next to their wares. I noticed a man seated beside a large bowl of teeth. The man next to him was selling plastic kitchenware. Why was this man selling teeth? I squatted down and looked into the bowl. He had all kinds of teeth in it. I looked up at him quizzically as he tried to explain to me about the teeth. He stirred his finger around in them and nodded happily up at me. "But what do people use them for? Why would they want to buy them?" I asked in English. He laughed.

"You are English?"

"No. American." He laughed again and nodded, and I did the same, and finally I strolled on. It was only later at the hotel that our waiter explained that I had been speaking to the dentist and that the bowl of teeth was his advertisement. It showed he was experienced.

We were really hungry as the train pulled out of Fez to take us back to Tangier. And just as the train was pulling out, a man appeared selling chicken sandwiches through the open train windows. "Over here," we were shouting. "Over here!" Oh good, he saw us. The sandwiches were huge with bread on both sides and even a piece of succulent chicken sticking tantalizingly out of one edge. We grabbed the sandwich and stuffed a pocketful of dinars into his hand as the train pulled out of the station. The sandwich man waved cheerfully. What luck. This should be plenty for both of us. We opened the sandwich and guess what? There was nothing between the pieces of bread but that tiny succulent bit that was showing at the edge. One tiny bite of meat and two big pieces of bread. I thought that was so clever. Who could ever complain?

When we got to Tangier we still had a little chunk of hash left. So rather than pass through customs with the chunk, or worse yet, throw it away, we cut it in half and swallowed it with our last cup of Moroccan coffee and boarded the plane for Madrid.

Sparkling Madrid with a chunk of hash in my tummy and the streets were paved with gold and silver. Madrid aglow. Drenched in sunlight. So different from the dreary Madrid we had left only last week when it was totally polluted and Bart became ill from the car fumes. Now our taxi floated above the glittering pavement and whisked us to our hotel. And the Prado! In one flash we absorbed every brush stroke. Goya, Van Gogh, the Guernica by Picasso, Las Meninas by Velázquez.

We had an anxious moment or two as we left the museum, trying to remember the name of our hotel or where it was. The streets seemed to have toned down some by then. It was all fading to gray.

TIME-TRAVEL WITH ME to a place where only royalty, the great Hawaiian chieftains, the kings and princes have climbed. Up the great mountain as the days become weeks along the wet jungled way. Waterfalls cascade hundreds of feet over the lava-formed landscape, and we're only half way there. Weeks dissolve into months as we climb to the cloud covered top of the sacred mountain where the secrets of the universe shall be revealed, and we pray we will not die from the knowledge. Or, we could take a helicopter.

On Kauai, we browsed at the Rain Shop in Hanalai, watched the sunset at the end of the road at Ke'e Beach, and took the helicopter ride to the mountain peak from Princeville. Then we hiked the trail up the Na Pali coast. I was getting stronger. I was healing, naked on the soft sand. Bart ran his finger down the length of the jagged scar on my hip. I surrendered myself to the sun. We floated in the warm ocean.

On Kauai the mushrooms grew right out of the fresh cow-pies deposited nightly behind our rented house. And every day at dawn we arose at first light and plucked them from the dung before the sun dried them out. Then we shook a few bananas out of the tree and tossed them into the blender along with the mushrooms. We always had a delicious breakfast and a fine perspective on the day.

The pot was so strong on Kauai that only a couple of tokes and we locked our keys in the trunk of the car. We had to hike down to the road into town to get a new key from the rental company. But we didn't mind. Soon enough we were driving up the winding road again, nodding and waving to the smiling workers walking barefoot in the sugar fields, each equipped with a backpack loaded with two tanks of pesticide, misting the crops. And a few minutes later, there they were, a small group of protesters holding signs up, apparently for a political candidate. We pulled the car over and turned on the camera. I asked them what was the story with the sugar cane being sprayed. A man holding a baby in his arms answered, "A lot of pesticides and herbicides that are being used in Hawaii are no longer allowed on the mainland. Like Paraquat. They tested Agent Orange on this island years ago for Viet Nam and nobody here even knew about it until last year."

His wife added, "And they're still using 245T. They're still using DBCP on this island. Those are the deadly chemicals that they've already banned. The Pentagon banned them in 1971, and we're still using them on this island now. At this very moment, people are walking around spraying. We've had a lot of dead animals. They say it's a dog poisoner, but we feel it's the wide use of pesticides. We've had a lot of miscarriages when they spray the fields." I nodded. I knew that I had to go home and face the politics of the planet.

Chapter Seven:
Free Speech and
Dangerous Television

CHUCK, BART, AND I tapped the maple trees in Lanesville that spring of 1978. Then, in the summer Chuck moved to New Paltz with his girlfriend Marji Yablon and they had a baby, Rhea. Parry and Carol had already moved down the road to Phoenicia, and now had three daughters, Sarah, Emilia, and Chloe. Parry would soon become the editor of the weekly *Woodstock Times*. Davidson had long ago gone back to New York and so had Annie, who had soon become an editor for Barbara Walters' television specials. David had moved to Boston, married and had twin daughters. Skip and Jane had gone to San Francisco. Bart and I decided to give up Maple Tree Farm and move the office and editing studio to Woodstock, about ten miles down the road.

We rented our friend Douglas Schmidt's beautifully designed barn home in Saugerties. We were secluded, yet only a couple of miles from our Tinker Street video studio. Maybe Media Bus could make something happen in Woodstock, which was loaded with artists. The first thing we did was get the cable access channel turned on. Channel 6, Woodstock Access TV.

We kept Channel 6 on the air twenty-four hours a day. When there were no programs playing, the automated message wheel did the work. A stationary camera would be pointed at a small mechanical wheel with 30 slots for index cards. Every ten seconds, the little motor would flop a card over and the next index card would appear with a public service announcement or a community calendar event:

June 21, See Barry Commoner,
presidential candidate for the Citizens Party
at the home of Howard and Ann Koch in Woodstock.

As the wheel turned, we played audio from the national weather service, which, we were told, got a lot of people to tune in.

In the little shed/studio behind the community hall, video producer and station manager Tobe Carey was setting up for his show *This is Not the News.* He was going to play my coverage of the Woodstock Town Picnic. Tobe turned on the camera and pointed it at the title card then switched to the live picture.

THIS IS NOT THE NEWS
CHANNEL 6 WOODSTOCK
WEDNESDAY NIGHTS 9PM.
Tonight: Woodstock Town Picnic.

AT THE WOODSTOCK TOWN PICNIC, I tucked my camera under my arm and piled my plate high, then found a place to sit on the grass next to a beautiful, rosy-cheeked woman. I introduced myself. She said, "Hi, I'm Molly Rush and I'm one of the "Plowshares 8."

I turned on the camera. Molly Rush looked into the camera and told me that four of her fellow activists were still in jail after their sentencing for entering the King of Prussia plant at a re-entry division of General Electric in which first-strike nuclear warheads were produced. "And what we did," she said, "was simply take little household hammers and baby bottles full of blood, and we walked past the security guard, got inside the plant and we took out our hammers and we took two of the nuclear warheads, which were not attached to bombs at the time, but would be, when attached, the equivalent of twenty-five to thirty Hiroshimas, and we hammered those warheads so that they were unusable and we committed what has been described as the first act of nuclear disarmament in thirty-six years."

Molly had been sentenced to 2 to 5 years but was currently on appeal awaiting the judgment of the Superior Court of Pennsylvania, and that's why she could come to the Woodstock Town Picnic.

Later I took the video over to see the African musicians and storytellers at the Creative Music Studio workshop. We all gathered in a circle and the storyteller began, "Can anyone tell me what is the most

91

dangerous thing in the jungle?" The group was silent. I hesitated but since no one else answered, I guessed "A man?"

"Ha Ha" laughed the storyteller. "A fruit! A fruit is the most dangerous thing in the jungle. Something very beautiful and sweet tasting—it may be poison."

"Oh," I said. "Sure, it's a fruit. Okay."

ONE DAY WHILE TROLLING for news stories on the village green, I ran into local Woodstock personality, philosopher, and letter-to-the-editor-writer Farmer Frank. He lived out in Willow, was retired but worked on the town crew part time. He also delivered the prepared food for *Meals on Wheels* and he cared a lot for old folks. Of course the folks were essentially trapped when Farmer Frank came over with lunch and would have to sit and listen to him go on and on before he would give them their food and leave. There was no way to say "Can it, Frank," or "See ya later."

Sometimes I tagged along with Frank on his rounds, shooting video to play on Channel 6 and helping him get people to volunteer for *Meals on Wheels*. When I turned on my camera that day, he immediately began preaching the Gospel to me. He said he was going to quote a great Jew to me and then he said it was (surprise) Jesus! He stood real close to me, and then he moved even closer. "It all depends on what you give to others," he confided to me. And then he said he was involved with a group called "Jews for Jesus." He said that he was a Christian who was helping them out and that there were fifty chapters. "It's such a great thing to see the Christians and the Jews get together for Jesus." Then he asked, "Do you know anybody who would like to get into it?" He was waiting for me to say I would. So I told him, "You wish!" We both laughed. I said, "But I'll keep it in mind in case I ever run into anyone who is interested. And thanks for the info."

Frank threw in a Bible quotation and was off, stepping gingerly over a bearded man, whom we had been ignoring, who was rolling in the grass mumbling curses and shouting out intermittently, next to us. We knew the cursing shouting man as "The Runner." Folks called him that because he would run as fast as he could to get from one place to another. He never walked or strolled or even jogged. He just flat out ran as fast as he could. He bathed winter and summer in the Sawkill River that runs through town. He looked young, barely twenty. He was in a very angry mood most of the time, but I was told by those who had spoken to him that he was a bit of an intellectual. "Hey, how ya doin?" I said, as I stepped over him.

HERE'S A MAJOR THING I learned while I was programming director at Channel 6 cable access TV in Woodstock. It's not enough to know the days of the week and the dates. You have to know the meaning of each day and date and be sensitive to what holidays are observed on which days and how people feel emotionally about them.

Channel 6 had been humming along nicely with our policy of allowing all producers to play or say whatever they wanted to on Channel 6 with absolutely no pre-screening or censorship of any kind. Each producer would choose a time slot on a first-come-first-served basis, which I still think is the best way to do it since producers know when their audience can watch. And everything was fine until this new show called *Men in Film* was scheduled by a newcomer named Lou Maletta, who had a vacation home up in Woodstock but lived in the city. So I talked to Lou on the phone and he said his show was about men in films and that he reviewed these films and showed clips. He said he'd like a late-night slot. I said that he could have Thursday nights at midnight.

Lou had only been playing his show for a couple of weeks when, what do you know, it turned out to be Christmas Eve on this particular Thursday and all the kids were out of school and staying up late and families were gathered around the TV hearth and suddenly *Men in Film* comes on and it turns out to be clips from gay porn movies on video that Lou Maletta is reviewing, and selling. ("And for those who like your boys hairless ... .") The police department in Woodstock was flooded with calls. So now the cops and the town board and the district attorney were involved and it was my fault for letting such junk on our town cable.

What was the offensive image that the unsuspecting townsfolk

93

saw with their families on Christmas Eve? Well, there was a banana in it. When I finally, after the fact, viewed the program in question, I thought it was hilarious. A naked guy was eating a banana. They cut from his face with the banana in his mouth, to a close-up of his ass and the banana coming out of his butt. Then they reversed the film and the banana goes back the other way This was causing such a furor that the entire town became polarized and now the town board was ordering us to pre-screen all programs, and when we refused they begged us. "Please, please," begged Mescal Hornbeck of the Woodstock Town Board, "just take that one show off and nothing else. Please, please." We had to say that we couldn't do that. So now they were starting something called the Community Decency Board. This couldn't be good. So much for Woodstock Nation.

Now the town meetings began in earnest. And I mean the steamy meeting hall filled with shouting people. A member of the Community Decency Board was shouting above the din, "I don't want it coming into my house if this is going to happen!" Someone else yelled, "What about the evening news, you want that censored too?" The decency board member shouted back, "We've been through all that. I don't want to pull the plug on Channel 6 per se, I want to pull the plug on homosexual love, or whatever that was." This statement brought the house down, pro and con.

Finally Liza Cowan took the floor. "I'm a lesbian," she shouted. A hush fell over the crowd. "And I'm really really upset about you! What's your name?" She brazenly pointed to the man from the Decency Board. He answered somewhat sheepishly, "Carl." He even said his last name, like a schoolboy. "Carl," repeated Liza. "Carl, unfortunately I can easily believe you said that. But I'm really appalled to live in a town so rabid with homophobia."

Carl got back a bit of his bluster. "I don't mind your homosexuality," he said to the lesbian, "I just don't want it at my house."

"Well, hey, don't invite me over." The crowd laughed.

"I don't want it on my TV either, is what I'm saying ... ."

This sort of dialogue went on for weeks. But at least they weren't bothering us about the other shows on Channel 6.

ASSASSINATIONOLOGIST Rush Harp's *Conspiracy Update* came on as scheduled 8 p.m. on Wednesdays. No problem. Rush laid it all out. Just like it said on the billboard he had put up out on Route 28. "WHO KILLED JFK, RFK, MLK, & MJK?" The sign attracted a lot of attention. Most people who saw it for the first time asked, "Who is MJK?" And we would say, "Mary Jo Kopechne," who died in Teddy Kennedy's car at Chappaquiddick Bridge. Rush Harp said that's how the CIA in effect assassinated Teddy.

Rush had a conspiracy for every death, and each seemed reasonable the way he told it. Rush customarily ended his show by saying, "... so this is what we're supporting. Our money is going to the CIA and causing the death, destruction and torture of people all over the world and I think it's time we stopped them. My motto is, 'Do away with the CIA, and do it today.' That's the way I feel."

At the time of Rush Harp's death, he had been waiting to meet a certain Colonel from the United States Army who was going to show him the documentation concerning the government's role in the Jonestown murders. The last story Rush told me before he died was about the death of Harry Chapin, the songwriter and singer. Rush said, "The Long Island Expressway is a good place to kill people. They can put on the steering wheel a chemical that will absorb into your hands as you drive the car, and you have what appears to be a heart attack and you black out. And of course when you're driving a car on the Long Island Expressway, and you black out, chances are you're going to die. The truck driver, I'm quite certain, was not in on the murder. It was just very nicely planned and nicely executed at 11:10:46 a.m."

Rush told me he always received his information secondhand, but in the next two months he expected to be directly interviewing someone who was at Jonestown. "I'm gonna get firsthand information about that little fiasco. Jonestown was definitely put on by our military government, and they don't think anything about killing us for a military coup. They love it." Unfortunately this was not resolved because Rush died suddenly and mysteriously in his home, slumped over his telephone.

And, amazingly, the Community Decency Board wasn't bothering

Ruth Simpson over at *Minority Report,* 10 p.m. Fridays. Ruth, a warm, grandmotherly woman with a sweet lilting voice, spoke softly and directly into the camera, "You know, one of the first questions that I get asked is, 'When did you decide to be gay?' Like I woke up one morning and it was a nice sunny morning and I looked out the window and said, 'I think I'm going to be a lesbian.'" Ruth always made the crew laugh.

And nobody was bothering *Woodstock's Talking Youth,* 4 p.m. Tuesdays. Kids out interviewing each other live from the Pin Ball Parlor.

"Do you think police in the area give kids a hard time?"

"No, I think that they do their job."

"Well, I think the police force is really lame. I think that they're really misers in the cold. They're not nice. The cops just aren't nice."

"Not nice to everybody or just the kids?"

"I think they're not nice to people that they think are not perfect citizens."

CHANNEL 6 WAS REALLY GOING STRONG. I hated to see Lou Maletta's *Men in Film* take the whole channel down. If this continued, pretty soon someone was going to start to complain about *Men Who Love Trucks.* "I've always loved her," said Robert Monroe, kissing his Chevy Blazer on the lips.

Our usual late night entry, *Intellectual Free For All* which played Friday nights after the *Night Owl Show,* was under the radar now that the gay guys were taking the flack. The program featured our funniest guys, Robert Monroe and Lester Nafzger.

Lester: It's interesting, the derivation of the word "disrupt."
Robert: Rupt?
Lester: Disrupt.
Robert: Disrupt. Dis, meaning dis. Dis, it's an article.
Lester: And rupt?
Robert: Rupt?
Lester: Clearly a derivation of rump. Dis-rump, dis-ass …
Robert: Dis-ass …"
Lester: Based upon an Italian insult."

Robert: Oh! Oh yes! Ass-sumay, dis-ass, dis-assumay . . .
Lester: That's right. To make an ass of you and me.
Robert: At a distance.

And thanks to *Men in Film,* no one was bothering anyone over at *The Velvet Trigger* where Linda Jovin Halback was asking poet Teresa Marta Costa to read her latest gem. She obliged:
"He entered my box of Ivory Snow
sucked off my Panasonic ovaries
and electrocuted himself."

OUT BEHIND OUR HOUSE in Saugerties, the green lichen glinted off of the bluestone wall as the sun moved slowly across it. Two wasps tussled on the flat gray stone slab. Giant woodpeckers drilled low on the fir tree, then flew to the willow. Robins pecked worms out of the freshly turned soil in the garden. Two tiny birds sang "Jeepers Creepers" across the meadow to each other. And down in the bottom of Paciti's pond were two big old catfish. Every year when the ice melted, I peered into that pond to find them still there. They lived in a rusty old frying pan at the bottom.

I put the flame of my red Bic to a fat joint, the herb in it grown in this very garden only last summer. And now again it was spring and I lived and breathed. A long black snake slipped slowly out of his skin beside me. I wished I could do the same. I watched a thousand sparrows test the wind and I wanted to fly with them, but instead, I videotaped Bruce Bart, the tattoo artist as he buzz buzz buzzed away on his girlfriend's tummy up in Tannersville. And as he worked he told us a story about a tall, lanky young boy who wanted the word "Shorty" tattooed on his arm. His mother was with the kid and she said it was okay. "But why?" asked the tattoo artist. The mother said, "He's the shortest of my triplets and the tattoo will identify him." And she chuckled. Since the kid's mom thought it was funny, Bruce went ahead and did it. Then he told his story about a pale young girl who wanted a swastika tattooed on the fleshy part of her arm. Bruce agreed to make the tattoo but refused to accept any payment. No payment? The girl

97

seemed confused, and no longer certain. "Only for free" said Bruce with inked needles poised. "But why?" asked the girl with the ivory skin. And Bruce thought about Shorty and said, "To identify you. So we'll know who you are," he said.

I BEGAN SPENDING LESS TIME at Channel 6. My last live coverage was going to be election night in Woodstock. As the on-camera host that night, I sat silently and read comic books (to myself) while waiting for the returns to begin coming in. Later, things got going and tons of call-ins came in from the precincts, and the videotapes were rushed in from the festivities at various parties with the candidates, and we got the results from our exit polls, and people called with news and predictions. And then everyone poured into the studio and congratulated each other on the great coverage, even though no individual could take the credit or the blame. Anyone who looked at Channel 6 could see the simple truth. It worked by itself.

Spaghetti City Video Manual. Text by Parry Teasdale and art work by Ann Woodward.

Top: Freex in Soho, 1970, in our Prince Street loft. Standing from left, Skip Blumberg, Chuck Kennedy, Davidson Gigliotti, Parry Teasdale, Curtis Ratcliff and David Cort. Seated, Bart Friedman, Carol Vontobel, Nancy Cain, and Ann Woodward *(Bill Cox). Above Left:* Don West. Producer of "Subject to Change" for CBS. *Above Right:* Freex Tongue Group.

Top: Abbie Hoffman, Chicago 8 co-conspirator taped by the Videofreex for "Subject to Change" 1969 (*Michael Curran*). *Above:* Fred Hampton of the Black Panther Party interviewed by Videofreex for "Subject to Change" 1969 (*Michael Curran*).

Community Contact. A flier by Davidson Gigliotti announcing the services of Videofreex and Media Bus, showing how all roads lead to Maple Tree Farm (*Media Bus archives*).

Top: Videofreex library and viewing room. Ann Woodward and David Cort looking through the tapes. On the monitor, Carol Vontobel interviews Elmer Benjamin who tries to remember the names of his twelve children (*Media Bus archives*). *Above:* In the kitchen in Lanesville. Playing around with the video. From left, David Cort, Scotty Benjamin (clown), Bart Friedman (with camera), Parry Teasdale, and Sarah Teasdale (*Media Bus archives*).

Top: The Blue Calzone, our inflatable TV set, set up at the Alternative Media Conference at Goddard College in Vermont. The video projector was housed inside, with the image presented to people outside on the rear projection screen mounted at the front. It also served as as tent for some Freex during the conference (from *Videofreex* by Parry Teasdale). *Bottom:* On the Set of Lanesville TV. I take a call from Willie Benjamin, while Harriet Benjamin reacts and Russell Connor, who headed the video program from the New York State Council on the Arts and co-hosted "Video and Television Review" looks on.

Top: Academy Award winner director Shirley Clarke produces her video version of a Marx Brothers movie within the wedding of Curtis Ratcliff and Cy Griffin at Maple Tree Farm. Skip Blumberg is Harpo, Alan Sholom is Groucho and Bart Friedman is Chico (*Larry Gale, Media Bus archives*). *Bottom:* Tech master Chuck Kennedy at his workbench in Lanesville.

Top: Parry Teasdale and Carol Vontobel with baby Sarah. June 1972 (*Collection of Parry Teasdale*). *Above left:* Harriet Benjamin, Willie Benjamin and Little Toddy Benjamin. *Above right:* Chuck Kennedy and I are at the controls for a Lanesville TV broadcast.

Top: TVTV in Miami during the 1972 political conventions. From left: Colonel Sanders, Allen Rucker, Anda Korsts, Tom Weinberg, Skip Blumberg, Michael Couzins (behind Blumberg), Judy Newman, Steve Christiansen, Chuck Kennedy, Ira Schneider (kneeling), Martha Miller, Michaell Shamberg, Chip Lord (kneeling), Andy Mann, Nancy Cain, Hudson Marquez, Jody Sibert (seated), Curtis Schreier, Joan Logue, and Jim Newman(*TVTV*). Bottom: On the convention floor. Skip Blumberg interviews Douglas Kiker and I record. For "Four More Years." Republican National Convention, Miami, 1972 (*TVTV*).

Upper left: Nancy Cain of TVTV videotaping the Republican National Convention in Miami, 1972 (*TVTV*). *Upper right:* Tom Weinberg of TVTV and All Things Chicago, 1973 (*Jac Stafford.*) Above: Superbowl X Bart Friedman, Nancy Cain Tom Weinberg, and Elon Soltes of TVTV tape the Super Bowl (*TVTV*).

108

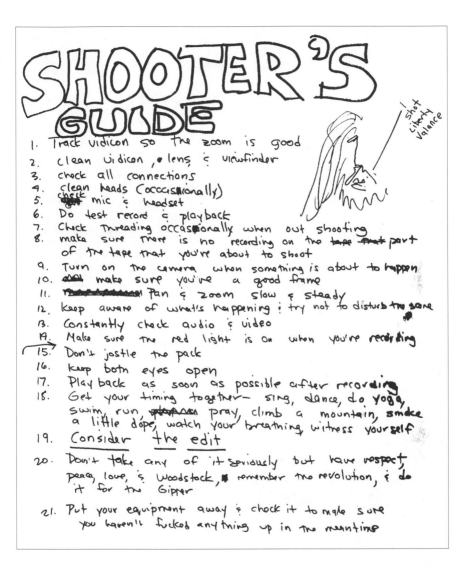

SHOOTER'S GUIDE

I shot Liberty Valance

1. Track vidicon so the zoom is good
2. Clean vidicon, lens & viewfinder
3. Check all connections
4. Clean heads (occasionally)
5. check mic & headset
6. Do test record & playback
7. Check threading occasionally when out shooting
8. make sure there is no recording on the ~~tape part~~ part of the tape that you're about to shoot
9. Turn on the camera when something is about to happen
10. ~~and~~ make sure you've a good frame
11. ~~Keep aware of~~ Pan & zoom slow & steady
12. keep aware of what's happening ; try not to disturb ~~the scene~~
13. Constantly check audio & video
14. Make sure the red light is on when you're recording
15. Don't jostle the pack
16. keep both eyes open
17. Play back as soon as possible after recording
18. Get your timing together— sing, dance, do yoga, swim, run, ~~practice~~ pray, climb a mountain, smoke a little dope, watch your breathing witness yourself
19. Consider the edit
20. Don't ~~take~~ any of it seriously but have respect, peace, love, & woodstock, remember the revolution, & do it for the Gipper
21. Put your equipment away & check it to make sure you haven't fucked anything up in the meantime

A page from TVTV's scrap book of the 1972 political conventions (*Skip Blumberg*).

The 5 Day Bicycle Race. Five nights' coverage of the 1976 Democratic National Convention in New York. Tapes were shot on the convention floor and bicycled over to the live studio at Manhattan Cable where they were played and talked about. *Top:* On the set from left (on couch) Bart Friedman, Nancy Cain, Joel Gold (with phone) Maxi Cohen and Bill Marpet. Back row from left, John Trayna, Joanna Milton Tom Weinberg (standing) Andy Aaron, Shalom Gorewitz and Elon Soltes. Bottom: Image Union Press Card, PBS Press Card, TVTV News Press Card, Lanesville TV Logo (*Leon Wayburn*).

Upper left: Who Killed JFK? Here I am as the producer of Assasinationologist Rush Harp's "Conspiracy Update." Channel 6, Woodstock (*photo booth at the dime store*). *Upper right:* Bart Friedman at the Media Bus Studio in Woodstock. *Above:* The Velvet Trigger. Linda Halback is host of the popular poetry show on Channel 6, Woodstock, 1982 (*Sandi Young*).

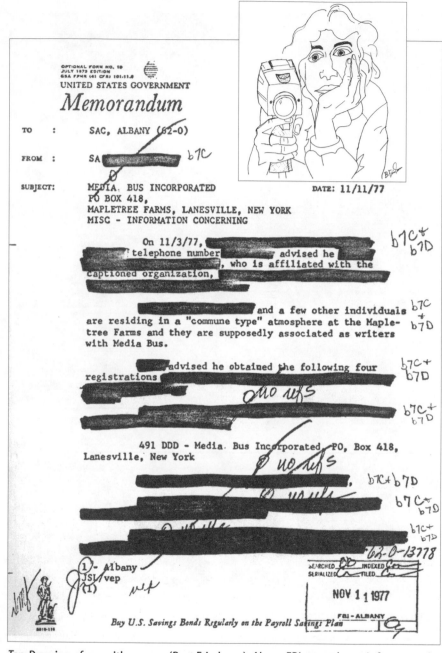

OPTIONAL FORM NO. 10
JULY 1973 EDITION
GSA FPMR (41 CFR) 101-11.6

UNITED STATES GOVERNMENT

Memorandum

TO : SAC, ALBANY (62-0)

FROM : SA ▓▓▓▓▓▓▓ *b7C*

SUBJECT: MEDIA BUS INCORPORATED
PO BOX 418,
MAPLETREE FARMS, LANESVILLE, NEW YORK
MISC - INFORMATION CONCERNING

DATE: 11/11/77

On 11/3/77, ▓▓▓▓▓▓▓ *b7C+ b7D*
▓▓▓ telephone number ▓▓▓▓ advised he ▓▓▓▓▓▓
▓▓▓▓▓▓▓▓, who is affiliated with the ▓▓▓▓
captioned organization,

▓▓▓▓▓▓▓▓ and a few other individuals *b7C + b7D*
are residing in a "commune type" atmosphere at the Mapletree Farms and they are supposedly associated as writers
with Media Bus.

▓▓▓▓▓ advised he obtained the following four *b7C+ b7D*
registrations ▓▓▓▓▓▓▓▓▓▓▓

▓▓▓▓▓▓▓▓▓▓▓▓ *b7C+ b7D*

491 DDD - Media Bus Incorporated, PO, Box 418,
Lanesville, New York

▓▓▓▓▓▓▓▓▓▓▓▓▓▓▓ *b7C+b7D*

▓▓▓▓▓▓▓▓▓▓▓▓ *b7C+ b7D*

▓▓▓▓▓▓▓▓ *b7C+ b7D*

62-0-13778

1 - Albany
JSL/vep
(1)

SEARCHED ___ INDEXED ___
SERIALIZED ___ FILED ___

NOV 1 1 1977

FBI - ALBANY

Buy U.S. Savings Bonds Regularly on the Payroll Savings Plan

5010-110

Top: Drawing of me with camera (Bart Friedman). *Above:* FBI report by an informant who
visited Maple Tree Farm. (*Collection of Parry Teasdale, from Videofreex, by Parry Teasdale*).

Top left: Here I am recently born with my parents Leon and Mil Wayburn. *Top right:* Who doesn't have a picture of their dad (or mom for that matter) as Groucho? Leon Wayburn, 1942 (*Ruth West*). *Above:* "Milky's Movie Party" premiered on December 16, 1950. The two-hour show featured cartoons, Westerns and Milky's magic tricks and the weekly winner of the "Sunshine Smile" photo contest. Produced by Leon Wayburn (*Luckoff and Wayburn Advertising, Detroit*).

Top: Cowgirls. Here I am with my sister Linda in 1949. *Bottom:* Here I am with my sister Linda Grossman in Lanesville in 1974.

114

Top and above right: Two pictures of my dad, Leon Wayburn, as Nathan Detroit (black suit, center), 1959 in Detroit (*Wayburn archives*). *Above left:* Phil Gaberman, musical director of Guys and Dolls, at rehearsal where I met him.

115

Top: My Dad and Mom, Leon and Mil Wayburn. Mid-century moderns in their home on Canterbury Road, 1954 (*Warren Coville*). *Above:* The Wayburn family, dining at the Northwood Inn. Here I am at the left, a strange boy from another table, Mil and Leon Wayburn, and Linda Wayburn.

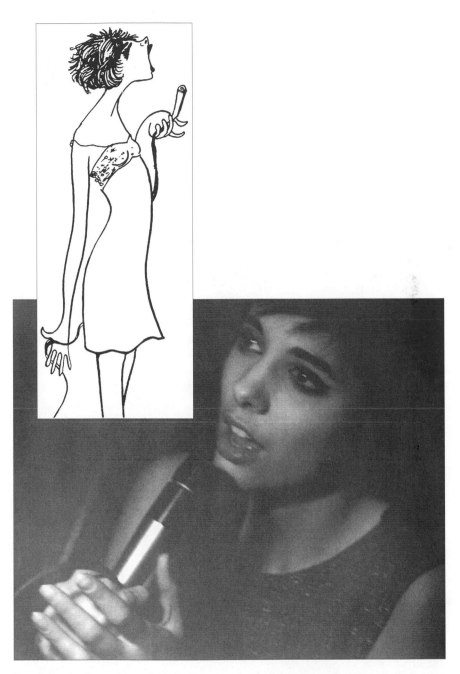

Here I am singing at Momo's Cocktail Lounge with the Phil Gaberman Trio, Detroit 1963 (*Dwight Hooker*). Drawing of me singing at Momo's Detroit 1963 (*Win Wells*).

117

This is Yogi Ramaiah who was living as a guest in our apartment in return for teaching us his brand of yoga. A lot of discipline was required. We had to wake up at 5 a.m. for certain asanas, and learn breathing techniques. We chanted "Om Kria Babaji Om."

My alter ego, Roxy Banner, in Hollywood, 1984 (*Jody Sibert*).

Top: Portrait of Mary Feldstein, the first Film/Video Historian of the New York Public Library, pictured as the Mona Lisa with Sony videocassette box (*Ger Van Dykk*). *Above:* Here I am with Mary Feldstein trying out the Anonymous scene in Los Angeles (*anonymous photo*).

Top: Ian Stafford, Freddie Stafford and Rita Xanthoudakis at city hall wedding. *Above:* At Eric and Mary Wright's in Malibu for the Easter Sunday Grand Trample, Egg Hunt, One Mile Hike and Potluck Supper, 1985. Front row (from left) Tara Sibert-Procter, Jody Sibert (seated), Paul Krassner, Jody Procter, Kit Sibert. Standing (from left) Freddie Stafford, Ginny Newsom, Tom Morey, and I (*Rita Xanthoudakis*).

Top: Rita Xanthoudakis and Freddie Stafford's wedding ceremony at City Hall. From left, Jody Sibert, Barbara Bottner, Rita Xanthoudakis, Stanley Young, me, and Paul Krassner. *Above:* With Jody Sibert in Hollywood.

122

Top: CamNet founders Judith Binder and Nancy Cain near their studio at Venice Beach, 1994(*Wired Magazine*). *Above:* CamNet's Ace reporter, the great video journalist and ecological warrior, Jay April (*Jay April's archives*).

123

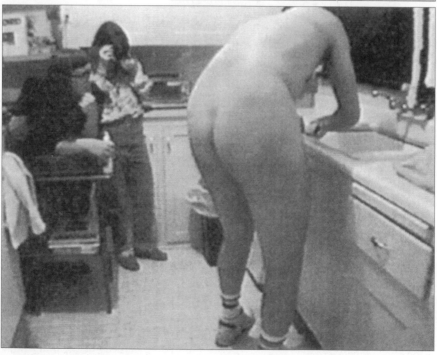

Top: Judith Binder, co-founder of CamNet. *Above:* Nude Handyman on CamNet (*Judith Binder*).

Beth Lapides covers the 1992 Democratic national convention in New York for CamNet (*Dona Ann McAdams*).

Top: Paul and Nancy in Malibu (*Rita Xanthoudakis*). *Above:* In the rose garden (*Jody Sibert*).

Chapter Eight:
Art and Life

HOT WOODSTOCK July twilight. The aroma of chicken barbecue wafting, mingling with the olfactory prick of rich dark pine forest, the sweetness of the lush deep blood red summer blossoms, as I sped up the mountain to the Zen Center in Mt. Tremper. There were already fifty or sixty cars parked along the roadside for Linda Montano's art event. I found a spot and walked up the steep winding trail, huffing-puffing even before I got to the meadow. Suddenly a group of nuns appeared. They were walking in the waist high grass, each wearing a Walkman headset. Then several twirling brides emerged and a Transvestite-Madonna and Child were wading slowly through the grass and wild flowers. The ceremony had already begun.

I watched from the perimeter. There she was! Linda Montano! She was surrounded by a priest and several peasant-skirted women with castanets, performing a Spanish dance around and around her.

Linda Montano was playing the part of her own alter-ego, Rosita, and Rosita was playing the part of Saint Teresa of Avila. As Saint Teresa, Rosita reclined on her bed in the clearing. The nuns circled around her. (The original Saint Teresa had an experience with Christ early in her life and ran away to Morocco with her brother to die, but joined the Carmelites instead and had many religious experiences and was often misunderstood. Something happened to Saint Teresa when she was forty and she died, giving off the scent of violets. Even months later when her tomb was opened, her flesh had not disintegrated even though her habit had.)

Linda Montano had herself been a Maryknoll nun. And, about suffering, she had already endured the death, at a very young age, of her own husband, Mitchell. When Mitchell died, Linda Montano hung her entire face in acupuncture needles, her face dripping with needles, as she chanted for him.

Now in the meadow, over and over again the litany was intoned, bouncing off the mountains, as the nuns circled Linda Montano as Rosita, as Saint Teresa, and it was all building to ecstasy as the nuns took off Saint Teresa's gown and dressed her in a priest's black suit with a turned-around collar. Then they attached a mustache to her lip. Saint Teresa, as the priest in the black suit with the turned around collar and mustache, got up from the bed with everyone in the meadow forming a circle around her. She sat down quietly on a stool. Then Paulene Oliveros, accordion player, poet, conceptual artist and the lover of Linda Montano's alter-ego Rosita, wearing a top hat and Hawaiian shirt, approached Linda Montano/Rosita/Saint Teresa/priest in black suit. She held a huge orange scissors in her hand. She took Rosita's hair roughly in her fist and ruthlessly began shearing it off, tossing hunks of hair to the crowd of 200 or so friends in attendance.

I moved forward, shocked, assaulted. I stepped closer. Linda Montano/Rosita/Saint Teresa was in a trance. And now her hair was clipped to a fraction of an inch and you could see little patches of her scalp. Paulene turned and motioned to a man waiting at the end of a thick yellow extension cord. He stepped forward with the electric barber's sheers, looking very sinister as he approached Linda Montano/Rosita/Saint Teresa/priest in a black suit.

I now realized her head was going to be shaved in front of all of us. The sound of the appliance was as shattering as a lawn mower. Her head was so tiny. She was so tiny. Her neck inside the white turned around collar was so tiny. Bzzzzzzzzz, and it was done. I was horrified and a little nauseated as Linda Montano/Rosita/Saint Teresa/priest in black suit lead the procession of nuns and brides back behind her A-frame house in the meadow.

Everything was quiet as we waited for the next scene. Suddenly we heard a blood-curdling scream. She screamed and screamed again and then there was silence. We all waited in the meadow quietly until Linda Montano appeared before us once more. She had no mustache, and she was bald. The performance had ended. I went to her. "Rosita, what have you done?" I cupped her head in my hand. I gazed into her blue eyes. "Look at you," I said. We embraced and the reception began.

Now Rosita was Linda Montano, and she would be leaving Woodstock for New York City that very evening where she planned to be tied by an 8 foot rope to a beautiful young Asian performance artist, a young man several years her junior, for an entire year. She handed me her statement:

"We, Linda Montano and Tehching Hsieh, plan to do a one year performance. We will stay together for one year and never be alone. We will be in the same room at the same time, when we are inside. We will be tied together at the waist with an 8 foot rope. We will never touch each other during the year. The performance will begin on July 4, 1983 at 6 p.m., and continue until July 4, 1984 at 6 p.m."

They would remain tied together with the rope for one year, living life without touching. I got an eerie feeling that what Linda Montano had decided to perform as art, Bart and I had been doing as life, and for a lot longer than a year. "Have a wonderful art life," I told her. "And thank you."

THE VERY NEXT WEEK I was on location at Hampton Beach, in the shadow of the Seabrook Nuclear Power Station, shooting video with producer Susan Milano. Susan Milano was the originator and producer of the *Women's Video Festival*. She and Bart and I had recently mounted a gallery video installation called *Taxi*. We interviewed a lot of taxi drivers in New York City, shooting video of the back of their heads while they told wonderful taxi stories. The audience sat in the backseat of course, and we played back the video on a monitor placed where the driver's head would be. Another channel of video showed the city streets through the windshield. The cab was a Checker so we could fit in four or five people per show. Occasionally, during the taxi stories, we would sit on the bumper and bounce the vehicle a little bit for a more exciting ride. We mounted the taxi show at museums in New York, Syracuse, and Hartford.

Now, in Hampton Beach, Susan, her production partner Marilyn, and I were videotaping the story of Ted and Ruth and their children Barbara and Charlie. Ted had worked at Los Alamos in 1944, carrying long uranium rods in his bare hands while employed by the govern-

129

ment who told him only that the work he was doing would end the war.

Ted said it was all science-fiction to him and he didn't realize (and why should he?) that someday the palms of his hands and the soles of his feet would bleed spontaneously, and the skin on his hands would peel off in strips and his son would be deaf and retarded and his daughter would have neuro-muscular problems and have to be in a wheelchair because her legs stopped working and the government would brand him a radical because he put two and two together and the courts would throw his case out. We videotaped him in color on three-quarter-inch cassettes.

After the shoot we all went to Markey's Seafood Restaurant for dinner where I, an animal with my shell on the inside, ate a lobster, with its shell on the outside, on a porch, under an awning silhouetted with seagulls' feet. And I could see from where I sat the Seabrook station nearing completion in the mist perched on the wetlands, and it was raining hard. Then in the arcade we ate fried dough. Big bubbly chewy cakes hot with cinnamon and sugar, at Hampton Beach in the shadow of the cooling towers. *And then I dreamed the new city. I was rising up a steep incline in an elevator, to a new city built on the rubble of an old city. A bright new boulevard lined with gleaming tightly packed buildings. A sparkling Harlem, like 125th Street— with red, white, and blue banners unfurled, marking the Grand Opening of Chinese restaurants and Laundromats. Coils and towers nestled below the electric power plant, which stood at the top of the hill, looming gray against the yellow sky. From the new city I took an elevator up to my home high above the metropolis. The elevator doors opened onto my room. A sterile cubicle. I gazed out. I prided myself on my vantage. I had arrived at the top. The end of the world.*

AS SOON AS I GOT BACK from Hampton Beach, I moved out of the house in Saugerties where I had been living with Bart, and into a one-room cabin in Woodstock. This was the first time in many years that I could recall being absolutely alone. I would listen to the silence for hours and then watch television furtively on a nine-inch screen with rabbit ears.

130

Dave Letterman was talking about a new movie called *The Big Chill*. Michael Shamberg's movie. Remember Shamberg from TVTV? *The Big Chill*—about a group of people who lived together and then separated, but now they were back together, because one of them had died, so they were spending the funeral weekend together. Was that us? TVTV and the Videofreex? Which one of us would die?

THE VILLAGE SHRINK, Joe Trusso, was an extremely intense man, and I'll bet a lot of people were unable to look him in his eyes because they were so black and deep and penetrating. Like a hypnotist. Joe would never lose a staring contest, but it was my game to give it a try for an hour each week. I would face him each week with a new set of excuses for why I seemed unable to escape the endless loop of my life. Joe listened to my dead-end dreams.

"... and I was being helped aboard a high-speed elevator when I realized that the young man assisting me intended to push me into the open shaft. I was saved from the fall by quickly embedding my teeth into his thumb. And there I dangled, pondering my alternatives. In order to express my anger I could bite down hard, thereby severing his thumb from his hand and causing him great pain, while simultaneously causing me to fall to my death down the elevator shaft. Or, I could hold on, causing him mild pain and saving my own life even though I would remain dangling forever."

Joe suggested physical exercise.

THE RADIO BLARED "You'll Never Change the World" as I drove to my workout at the muscle gym in Kingston, New York, while Bart flew to the Kingston in Jamaica. It was Bart's Jamaican holiday. It wasn't that I missed Bart (hip and back, leg extension, leg curl), it was that I dreaded a confrontation on his return (abduction in, abduction out), or perhaps he would never return and I would live happily unresolved forever (calf, back, pull over, keep breathing). I imagined Bart in Jamaica, dancing to de reggae beat with many sweaty people and de beautiful German girls dey stay his place some hot ganja nights. Bart is thin and tan and he knows how to change his money. Miss Elaine brings

131

him juice and breakfast, dinner too, and he goes to de disco in de night and de ladies rub him, and de men dey strut, and he is stoned in de hot dark disco night.

ONE DAY JOE TRUSSO told me he was going to set his bonsai trees free. Come fall, he said, he was going to take them out to the meadow and plant them in the ground. Until that time, he wasn't going to cut them anymore.

"What made you decide to do that?" I asked.

"You did," he said. Strange, because I didn't remember ever mentioning to him how I felt for the little trees, bent to the will of another's vision of beauty, tortured prisoners of the horticulturist.

AFTER ONLY A FEW MONTHS of therapy with Joe Trusso, I was able to give up my complaints and take action. I was free and I got up the gumption to leave.

It was 1984. In the news there were live bombs in Manhattan and bomb trucks and bomb squad detectives and the United Freedom Front, a terrorist organization which had recently caused damage at the South African Consulate on Park Avenue, and the city was beefing up security, putting up big cement slabs in front of all entrances to buildings like the Post Office. People quickly accepted the reality of terrorist acts in New York City.

I began to make plans. I sat down with a notebook and a pen to figure out my assets. Let's see, I had worked on this Media Bus video project for about 14 years now. What did I have? Uh-oh, Media Bus was a not-for-profit corporation. It had no assets. So I owned, let's see, I owned—er, uh—nothing. I had no money. I owned no equipment, I had no equity. Okay, I thought to myself, looking down at my notebook with pen poised. I'll have to be a writer.

INT. LATE MODEL SAAB—NIGHT
MOVING
A freezing, grimy sleet pecks against the windshield.
The wiper blades click furiously, clearing a smaller and

132

smaller path for vision. The windows begin to steam up.
BART is tense, and his driving shows it.
Bart's soon-to-be ex-partner NANCY
sits just as tensely next to him.

                         BART
Goddammit, I thought you said it was over by *People's
Express.* That doesn't seem to be the case, does it?"

Through the fogged up window we see
a maze of highway signs, arrows,
EAST TERMINAL, ARRIVALS, DEPARTURES.

                         NANCY
Sorry. Those were the directions I got.

BART wheels around crazily.

                         BART
Shit. It's going to take us another half-hour to get to
the gate now.

                         NANCY
Calm down, it's almost over.

                         BART
Just shut up, okay?
                       CUT TO:
INT. NEWARK AIRPORT, SECURITY CHECK-NIGHT
BART and NANCY are locked in an embrace as crowds
pass through the gates behind them.

                         BART
I'm sorry.

                         NANCY
Yeah, I know. Me too.

                         BART
I just want you to be happy.

NANCY

I know. I want you to be happy too.

She pauses.

NANCY

So long.

She turns and boards the plane, picturing Bart, driving back along the Jersey Turnpike in the misty rain that had been falling for days, disappearing in the distance up the thruway.

The attendant in the ladies room asks in a Slavic accent if she's all right.

Pale and red-eyed in the COLD BATHROOM LIGHT.

NANCY

Yes, thank you.

Life grinds to a halt as she contemplates her decision.

Chapter Nine:
L.A. 1984

THE HAND-WRITTEN NOTE on a Post-it was stuck to Jody Sibert's bathroom mirror. "I have walked on fire. I can do anything." Jody had arranged a temporary place for me to live and was helping me get accustomed to my new life in California. Her friend Rita Xanthoudakis had a grant to complete her screenplay at a retreat in New Hampshire, and was looking for someone to mind her cottage in Venice for eight weeks.

"It's not a cult," Jody told me, concerning the note on her mirror. "It's a group of people who have found a method, a way, a Technology of Change. Jody had come to California in the late seventies with TVTV and by now she and her boyfriend Elon Soltes had become entrenched in the culture. Elon had joined with TVTV back in the seventies to work on *The Lord of the Universe,* a documentary about a spoiled brat of a fourteen-year-old Indian guru named Maharaj-ji who claimed to be God and was planning to levitate the Astrodome in Houston while it was filled with his devotees.

That was then. Now it was a decade later, and here I was driving with Elon and Jody to their favorite new-age/neo-pagan/voodoo store in Hollywood. "We're burning candles to attract money," Elon explained to me. For an extra ten bucks the salesperson would put a blessing on your candles for you, kind of like a jump start. Elon always bought the blessing. This day they spent fifty dollars on money candles. Candles that attract money are green.

On our way to Venice, Elon said, "You'll need an agent."
"For what?"
"For whatever you get going. And a therapist."
"Why?"
"And an astrological chart, and a car with air conditioning."

THE THICK VINE outside the breakfast room had wormed its way through the crack between the window and the ledge, and was growing gracefully up the wall and across the ceiling inside the little stucco house in Venice. It was going to be two months before Jody's friend Rita, whom I hadn't yet met but whose house I was renting, would return. I embraced my luxurious solitude. I relaxed into a new feeling of unconnectedness and anonymity. Outside, a lone mournful clarinet was playing a big band favorite almost right. The tune wafted lazily on the breeze. It was an idyllic lovely neighborhood afternoon, and young mothers were sunning themselves across the walkway. There were no cars on Clubhouse Avenue because this was a walk street. Instead of traffic we had birds, and pinks and taupes.

Although I hadn't met Rita, I was getting to know her big gray cat, Jamal, and the family of spiders in residence. Customarily spiders are gentle creatures but sometimes they have spats. They bickered about who would get the web over by the gas heater. They ran all over the place. I watched their patterns, their rhythms, their comings and goings. I thought we co-existed, but couldn't be sure.

After a few days at Venice Beach I faced the fact that I had to get some money. What was it that people were looking for in California? What did they want? Maybe I could become a channeler. Channeling was big. Maybe I could memorize some things from thousands of years ago, or I could write messages from the future. I'd have great wisdom flow through me and I'd sell it to people more desperate than I. Maybe I could do it over the phone.

I dreamed I was awake all night and decided to jog around the lake at dawn. As I rounded the turn I realized the Buddhists were setting up to do their morning devotionals around the corner. As I passed them, one priest gave me a push in my ass and I suddenly had more power and was able to move more quickly and propel myself with my hands, while my feet lifted off the ground. I looked around with surprise and smiled at him in thanks.

When I awoke, I rented a car and drove out to Encino, where a few people who had been my students at Goddard College were playing musical jobs at the cable companies in the Valley. Working in cinderblock luxury and rocking in big swivel chairs, they said, "Who cares any more about video and politics? We've got to make a living."

I called Wendy Apple, who had come to LA with TVTV in the seventies. Wendy had gone to NYU film school and had been shooting video right from the beginning. Lunching in the sun in Santa Monica, Wendy told me about her latest exploit into the world of television and production meetings, with men who wore double knits and white patent-leather belts with shoes to match and who, by the way, hated Jews. She put up with them because she was determined to make a journalistic video documentary about porn movies. She was also making a video called *Why Live?* She got varying responses, like from a woman named Sandy, who lived for her shoes.

Lynn Phillips, the great wit and philosopher, once said L.A. is like Siberia. "You're here because you've done something wrong." Lynn now lives in New York. She also said, "Never get into the left lane on Melrose." I made good use of this advice as I tested the terrain in my rented Mercury Lynx. I drove to Hollywood and back. No false moves. I stayed on the surface streets. Venice Boulevard to Fairfax. I could do this. I tried out the Food Barn and the Sav-On. I bought supermarket wine and avocados. I kept my answering machine on. I felt tremors.

At the water's edge one morning I sat cross-legged in the sand. The February beach was overcast and deserted except for the two men making love furtively on a towel a few feet away. I stretched out on my belly and watched them through a small crack between my fingers as they massaged and humped. The muscular dark-haired man was releasing himself from his thin trunks and pushing his dark smooth penis into the slim blonde man beneath him while simultaneously keeping an urgent, watchful eye out for helicopters. Styrofoam containers fought their way through the surf to the open sea. White cups in the white-caps. The sound of a steady stream of traffic played counterpoint to the moving tide. With the hiss of the foam, the roar of the diesel, and the prick of the salt in my nostrils, I dozed.

Suddenly I was about to give birth. Feeling labor pains. So was another woman. I really didn't know what to do. I went outside and waved down a station wagon filled with women holding

137

babies, and I told them, "We are giving birth and could use some help." They obliged, calmly following me into the room. I awakened with a start. It wasn't good to doze off at the beach. I blinked. "Valley Go Home" was scrawled with chalk on the lifeguard station, a kid in a "Nuke 'Em T-shirt" lifted his beer to me.

I stared at my empty calendar of events. I contemplated buying a pack of cigarettes if only to heighten my awareness of inhaling and exhaling. In the coffee shop I marveled at how it was possible for eggs to have absolutely no taste whatsoever. And what about this white toast? And what about those guys in the next booth? What was with them? How was it possible for them to be so happy and optimistic? Perhaps I could drive back to Michigan and disappear into the lake or bury myself in the sand among the hollow reeds. Instead, I put on Rita's hat, a lovely pith helmet made of straw with a dried flower wired to it. It fit. I tried her shoes. Perfect. And her beige linen sun dress? Yes. I thought I'd be Rita for a while and see how it worked.

That night I saw a comet. It was a big ball of a comet with a long blue tail. It streaked across the sky in a small arc and disintegrated somewhere between the Salton Sea and Indio. It happened so fast I almost thought it hadn't. In L.A. people attach special meaning to things like that. A sign, you know. Yes, it could be a sign. It could mean a significant event in another part of the world or maybe a message from my dead father.

MARY FELDSTEIN was the first Film and Video Historian of the New York Public library, and ran an annual buying budget of $50,000, which in the late seventies was a lot of money. She had purchased several of my videotapes for the library's permanent collection. Now, Mary was inviting me to her new home, a one-bedroom apartment in Santa Monica on Pico Boulevard at Ocean. We were happy to see each other again.

Mary played me a rather extensive audiotape from her answering machine of messages that her new boyfriend Tom had left for her. "Hello, Mary? Where are you, Mary?" Like that. Then she showed me where the shopping mall was. Strange that someone with a degree and a good career in New York would dump it all and move to Santa Monica to work in a boiler-room telemarketing office.

"Why?" I asked.

"Well, Plato's Retreat closed," Mary said, making a pale joke about how sex clubs in New York were a thing of the past now that AIDS was here.

The political primaries filled the news, which I watched with Jamal the cat each evening. I commented "Look, there's Hart and Mondale. There's Jesse Jackson." Jamal the cat looked up. "Mondale seems better than Hart as far as the direct confident stuff goes," I continued, "but he keeps saying that 'hamburger' thing, *Where's the beef?*" Jamal looked away. "And when Mondale smiles he looks silly, don't you think? But Hart? I don't think so."

"Reagan will win in '84, most certainly," the cat replied.

I watched NBC coverage of the primaries, sponsored by Advanced Formula Stress Tabs. It was Hart in Oklahoma, Hart in Florida, Hart in Massachusetts, Hart in Rhode Island. It was Mondale in Georgia and Alabama. Jesse Jackson got 20% in Alabama. "Oh, look, Jamal, there's Alexander Haig on the Merv Griffin Show." Jamal yawned. "Jamal, I really really really have to get a job."

"I THINK THIS WILL HELP your outlook," Jody said as we drove up Topanga Canyon to join the goddesses for their spring ritual. Queen Goddess Hugette Lorenz was an ex-Las Vegas showgirl and the now-wife of renowned (at least in Malibu) Robert Lorenz who was running a sort of spin-off of Scientology which he called "The Technology of Change." Jody and Elon had walked on fire with the members of "The Technology" and were volunteering their time to Robert Lorenz, working at his weekend "intensives" helping rich Hollywooders to shout and pound pillows in an effort to free themselves of their horrible parents and other nightmares.

Now Hugette Lorenz and the goddesses had gathered around a rectangular backyard swimming pool with flower petals floating in it. In a scene lifted from a Grecian urn, Hugette raised the chalice and brought it to her lips. She sipped. "Thou art goddess" she whispered to the woman beside her. I followed the cup with my eyes around the circle. And then it came around to Jody. She sipped and turned to me. "Thou art Goddess" Jody whispered, and her lips touched my cheek. I drank of the nectar. Thus the circle was cast and we goddesses took spring into us and loved her, welcomed her, ingested her power. Later, Mary and I went to Burbank and stood in line for seats at *The Tonight Show with Johnny Carson*.

EVERY MORNING I would go to the YMCA in Santa Monica and ride the stationary bicycle for twenty minutes. Then I would work all the Nautilus machines and take a sauna. And I was still a nervous wreck. I curled in the corner, unequipped. I felt skeletal, growing gaunt beneath suntan and ever-circling helicopter surveillance. I decided I had been thinking too much about money and it was beginning to make me sick. I decided to think about art. I picked up the pace on my LifeCycle. The paste-white man with the tiger climbing up his leg, and other tattoos, stole a look at me. I stole a look at him. No one socialized in the basement of the YMCA.

The weeks passed and now Rita had returned from her writers retreat and we were instantly officially roommates and friends, she being so warm and friendly and beautiful. She showed me her screenplay and cooked a chicken dinner. Both were really good.

I worked crew for *Valley Cablevision Arts Magazine*. We set up the video at a little house in Santa Monica where Morton Subotnik and Joan La Barbara were composing and playing music on computers. Their new piece was being written for the upcoming Olympic Arts Festival. I watched the levels on the deck, wound up the cables and set up the lights.

Rita, who had been a member of "The Technology of Change" with Jody, was now well and happy with her new practice as a chanting Buddhist. This was the kind of Buddhism where you could chant for real things. Like cars and houses if you wanted that.

Now Rita's chants vibrated through the courtyard. Nam yo ho— Freddie Stafford was staying the weekend again. Renge kyo—Rita and Freddie were in love. Rita knew Freddie when he was a teenaged

Communist back in Washington Heights where they both grew up. She had a huge crush on him when she was sixteen. So, Nam yo yo, she was sitting in the Rose Cafe in Venice with her editor from *LA Weekly,* and this really handsome guy walked over to her table and said, "Rita?" Rita looked up and she just gazed at him because he was so gorgeous and suddenly, Renge kyo, she realized this was Freddie. "Freddie?"

RITA'S NEW PRACTICE was my second encounter with Buddhists. The first encounter happened on the very day that I quit show business at the soap commercial audition in 1968. After floating home in my altered state, I found another huge surprise waiting in my living room. His name was Yogi Ramaiah and he was seated in a lotus position on the floor in the corner. Alan Cain was beaming at me as I entered the apartment. The Yogi was a twinkling little Indian man who spoke in that sing-songy way you'd think he might. He was wearing only a white sheet.

Yogi Ramaiah, it turned out, wore only a white sheet winter and summer, with rubber thong shoes and nothing else. An extreme vegan, he carried all of his belongings in a straw basket and slept on a narrow grass mat wherever he happened to be. Even in the winter, Yogi Ramaiah wore no coat. He never got cold. Or hot, for that matter. He looked like the Maharishi, whom I had seen at Madison Square Garden a few weeks previously. Or, rather, he looked like the Maharishi's country cousin. Alan said, "Nancy, this is Yogi Ramaiah. I met him on the subway and brought him home."

"Hi."

Yogi Ramaiah was attending classes at New York University and was depending on faith or something like it for all his needs, like for his food and shelter, for example. So Alan with his new consciousness had invited the Yogi to stay with us. In return, Yogi Ramaiah was going to teach us his brand of Kria yoga. Now we were in Yogi Ramaiah's class which was held in our living room and attended by a handful of other people the Yogi had gathered. A lot of discipline was required. We had to wake up at 5 a.m. for certain asanas and to learn breathing techniques. We chanted "Om Kria Babaji Om" and we weren't supposed to turn on the radio, play records, or watch television that might distract us from our practice. This was a sacrifice for me because I had just bought Simon and Garfunkle's new album with "Mrs. Robinson" on it and I wanted to listen to it over and over.

In addition to all this, we were keeping Yogi Ramaiah's dietary rules. It was mung beans mostly. Mung beans for everything. The Yogi said that in a perfect world mung beans would be used to satisfy every need. Hungry? Eat mung beans. Dirty? Wash with mung bean powder. Teeth? Brush with mung bean paste. Mung beans were enough for Yogi Ramaiah but not for me, so the Yogi said it was okay to eat other things. Vegetables were okay and so was fruit as long as you did not ingest the seeds. Anything that could possibly be re-planted and grow should not be eaten. I was given a special dispensation for bananas whose seeds were too difficult to separate from the fruit. There could be nothing with animal anything in it. Like no cheese. There was only one thing that Yogi Ramaiah would kill, a mosquito. "It only wants to suck your blood," he told me.

So okay, I was giving it a try. Alan had found his path. The company that Alan was a sales rep for couldn't relate to him anymore so he was unemployed, and I didn't have a job either. Might as well pack up, buy a van, and drive to California. It was 1968, so on some level we had fewer illusions. Because now, not only had President Kennedy been killed, but so had Martin Luther King, and Bobby Kennedy. It was pretty disheartening. I didn't know much about politics but I thought this could be termed dropping out. If it was, it felt good. The thing was not to worry. I had always wanted not to worry.

IT WAS SIX WEEKS to the day after the soap commercial audition that we pulled out of town in a 1963 Volkswagen van with hand-made chintz curtains on the windows, which we bought from two hippies who had driven it in from Oregon. There was a plywood platform with a foam mattress in the back. Underneath it, we stored a Bunsen burner, a lantern, and a couple dozen reading selections that Alan picked up at the Aquarian and Conspiracy Book Store. I wondered if we'd be compatible on the road.

The people who sublet our apartment waved us off enthusiastically, assuring me that the cats, who stayed with the apartment, would be just fine. In New York City, sub-letters didn't really believe they'd gotten the apartment until the tenant actually left town, so these particular sub-letters could hardly contain their glee as Alan and I pulled away from the curb headed toward the Westside Highway. Through the rearview mirror I saw Yogi Ramaiah waving good-bye alongside them.

I met my first L.A. Buddhist while working at the May Company in Los Angeles 1968, towards the end of that same hippie road trip in search of the miraculous. His name was Seth. He was working at the tie counter on the main floor. I met him in the employees cafeteria. He chanted "Nam yo ho renge kyo," and got whatever he wanted. They chanted for Cadillacs and washing machines. Practical things. He wanted me to do it too. "Like give me an example of how it works," I said.

"Well," said Seth from the tie department, "let's say I don't feel like waiting on customers? I just start to chant "Nam yo ho renge kyo" right there at my counter when I see them coming, and they walk right past."

"Oh, I see."

NOW IN VENICE, leaving Rita and Freddie alone together was always a good plan so I grabbed the video camera I'd borrowed from the cable gig and stepped out onto the boardwalk. Another sect heard from. It was the Hare Krishnas, who had invaded the beach and there was a free feast of mushy sweets with elephant dust for everyone. I walked up to the corner just as the parade was passing. There was a sudden spectacle of ribboned chariots and twirling pubescent goddesses with perfume in the air and rose petals fluttering from the sky, and chants and bells echoed. And then I heard it. I heard it before I could see it. It was a gruff voice through a bull horn.

"Repent Krishna! Repent Krishna! Worship the God of Heaven. Details in the Bible!" I turned to see these biker dudes all tattooed, beer-bellied and snarling. One of them was screaming at the procession through a bullhorn, with the word God printed on it. His voice blasted through the chants and tinkling bells.

"Get to know the God of the Bible! Don't be a Hare Krishna! Children in India are dying each year because these foolish Krishnas refuse to eat the cow! Eat the cow and believe in Jesus Christ! Repent Krishna! Repent Krishna!" Yellow-robed priests bedecked in garlands of flowers moved past the red-faced bullies, lilting blissful Krishnas dancing down the boardwalk. "Believe in Jesus Christ, Krishna! Don't get so caught up in your idolatry! Those false gods cannot save you!" Elbowing me aside he bellowed, "Get out of the way." His "Jesus Saves T-shirt" filled the screen in my viewfinder.

At home, the spaghetti sauce was simmering. It was nice when Rita cooked.

I NEVER TOOK THE VIDEO CAMERA to a pitch meeting, although the thought of recording these encounters was exciting to me. But people in Hollywood didn't like some stranger's camcorder in their faces. So I didn't do it. Was I going to be able to use what I had learned from the video days and turn it into some kind of life in California? Was there any way to do a television show shot on video? I made up a story and a cast of characters, wrote a treatment, and showed it to Louie Rapage, a music video producer, who read it and laughed out loud (which was good). Fifty phone calls later we took the script up to Paramount.

"Well, it's about a dream therapist who has a call-in radio show, and her husband, a dentist, their daughter who goes to USC film school and shoots video, and there's this homeless guy the daughter finds living in a box on the street near school and brings home to Brentwood," I said to the executive. "And it turns out her mom knows the guy from many years ago. I'd like to shoot it all on video from the daughter's point of view. The program would be the video she shoots."

"We like Cyndi Lauper as the daughter," Louie added.

"Have you got anything else?" asked the executive.

So Louie made an appointment for us to meet with Michelle Phillips. Louie thought she would be good in the part of the dream therapist with her daughter Chyna as the video shooting student. We met with Michelle at Junior's Delicatessen in Westwood and gave her the script to read. At Junior's we sat in a padded booth in the back room by the window. Michelle wore a Seiko watch exactly like mine. She said she would read the script. Michelle was okay. She ate a pickle from the tub on the table and showed us a picture of her with her daughter and her son along with the dummy jacket for her new book about the Mamas and the Papas. For Michelle, Louie and I pitched the story as a feature video for the home market, with music. I thought she might like it because of its good politics and how it focused on a homeless situation which not a lot of people were talking about. But, no.

Next we went to Warner Brothers in Burbank. Louie explained that we were "going in on the soft end."

"What does that mean?"

"It means that this guy is the story editor, not an executive."

The story editor couldn't really get into the idea of shooting it on hand-held video. He passed on it but said "I like the story" No doubt the story was pretty good because a couple of years later Paul Mazursky made a movie with a similar plot and called it *Down and Out in Beverly Hills,* with Nick Nolte as the bum. They even had video in it. Things like that happen every day in Hollywood.

Chapter Ten:
Love

JON LAWRENCE PICKED ME as his partner every time we did square dancing in gym class at Pasteur School. Jon was the cutest boy in seventh grade. He had almost platinum blond hair in a silky soft brush cut, and sweet, dark brown eyes. We danced to "San Antonio Rose." Jon put his arm around my waist. I was happy.

On the first day that Jon was absent I was disappointed. I went to school only to see him. On the second day he was absent I was upset. On the third day our teacher announced to the class that Jon would be absent for a long time because he had to have his leg amputated and was in the hospital. Why? I was fearful and nauseated. Our teacher said Jon had cancer. Bone cancer. She suggested that we buy him a get-well card so we could all sign it. One of the boys was assigned to buy the card and he came back with an awful drugstore card that said, "Hope you're back on your feet again soon!" I actually had to point this out to the teacher who had passed it around for our signatures.

When I visited Jon at his house he took a cane and stuck it through the empty leg of his pants and danced around for me. I felt Jon's heart. I loved him. When Jon died, the funeral took place out at the Cranbrook Episcopal Church in Bloomfield Hills and I went with my girlfriends, including Eileen E. We sat in the grey cathedral behind a smattering of mourners in the dank and cold. The men were in suits and the ladies were in hats and gloves. I had an urge to laugh hysterically. I tried to breathe through it, but it burst out and I was unable to control myself from laughing and laughing, and I had to leave the sanctuary. I felt I would not love again.

In high school not every boy liked me, even though my mother explained about hormones, saying that hormones made it so every boy would want to like me and would try to get me to like him too, and that had nothing to do with me personally. It was because boys were compelled by their hormones. I imagined myself kissing the most popular boy. I wrote my name and his name a thousand times on a page in my notebook. As for my sex education, the breeding of Taffy, our Brittany Spaniel, served as a primer. Aunt Ruth fashioned a copper wedding ring in her crafts class for Taffy's collar, and Linda and I were told that Taffy was getting married. While she was pregnant, my mom put her in a little home-sewn smock so she could be modest. The birth was very messy and produced eight puppies, which we kept in the kitchen until we sold them.

After two years at the University of Arizona as a theater major, I was back living with my mom and dad again on Canterbury Road, working part-time for a home decorator on Seven Mile Road, taking a couple of classes at Wayne State University, and hanging out at night at rehearsals with the Temple Players where my mom was the stage manager. A stage manager has to be very organized, which she was. My mom and dad had always had a flair for the theatrical. They were famous for having great parties and costume balls and they and their friends would gather around the piano singing Rogers and Hart songs and later Tom Lehrer. And they would write their own songs and parodies and record them on my dad's reel-to-reel Webcor. One of my dad's greatest compositions was titled "You Can't Buy Bagels in Huntington Woods," a satirical comment on how Jewish people were leaving Detroit and moving to the suburbs.

The Temple Players had mounted several plays like *Ten Little Indians* and *Separate Tables* and *My Sister Eileen*, but never a musical. At Temple Beth El, the house was always sold out whenever the Temple Players did a show. And now, *Guys and Dolls*. I loved the show and of course I knew the entire score. Walt, a TV director at WWJ-TV was staging the show, but it couldn't be cast until they got a musical director. Phil Gaberman came down to the Players meeting to offer his services. There he was. He was at the piano playing softly as people were arriving. He was mysterious and sensual. I watched him lean into the piano with his ear close to the keyboard. His fingers were slender. He tickled the ivories.

Once I had a secret love
that lived within the heart of me.
All too soon my secret love
became impatient to be free …

For a moment he looked up at me. His eyes were dark pools. His lips were ripe and full. His nostrils flared slightly. My mouth was dry, my breathing was shallow. Phil was so incredibly totally cool. He had his own jazz trio, too. He played at Momo's Cocktail Lounge. I was nineteen. I needed ID to get in. I got some. My dad got cast as "Nathan Detroit," and since my mom was the stage manager I hung around rehearsals helping out. I watched Phil Gaberman. He was thirty. How could he ever be interested in me?

The Phil Gaberman Trio played at Momo's Cocktail Lounge on Friday and Saturday nights. Piano, bass, and drums, and sometimes after hours, Jack Brokenshaw from the Australian Jazz Quintet would sit in on vibraphone if he was in town. They played "Satin Doll." Momo's was dark and smoky and seated about fifty. It was the kind of room you would never want to see in the daylight, but at night the mustiness and the music were good together.

Entering Momo's, there was the bar along the right wall with Harold Brown, the owner, sitting behind it near the cash register. Harold's bulldog Spike sat on a big pillow on a stool next to him. Momo's had its regulars. Old neighborhood guys who were there night and day. To the left of the bar and through the archway was "the room." That's where Phil played jazz and people knew to be quiet. The Phil Gaberman Trio played in "the room" at a little piano bar. Think "Green Dolphin Street." Think young sophisticates, lounging on couches and stuffed chairs, drinking scotch and soda. Momo's was midtown. Just a block or two north of the Fisher Building and the General Motors Building. Saks 5th Avenue was practically next door.

One night after Momo's, Phil took me to his apartment. He sat at his piano. Pressing his fingers to the keys, he created a diminished chord of exquisite vibration. He looked up at me. His eyes were half

148

closed. His lips were parted. He modulated his chord. When I sang for him he kissed me softly.

We married. Phil and his friends were all musicians or in the theater, and immediately I was cast in a satirical review opening at the Kenwood Restaurant and Lounge out on Telegraph and Five Mile road. The show was called *Slings and Arrows* and it was getting a lot of press. We did two shows nightly Monday through Thursday and three shows on Fridays and Saturdays. It was my first real paid job in show business and my photo was in the After Dark column in the *Detroit News*. "Here's what's happening around town this week." Lenny Bruce was at the Club Alamo, Paul Mendoza and his Musical Toppers at the Covered Wagon Inn, and I was at the Kenwood.

In the ballroom at the Kenwood Lounge, the audience ate fried shrimp dinners and drank pink wine at ringside tables while we performed. Every night at the dinner show, I became intensely nauseated and had a hard time smiling. Incredibly, it took me until the end of the month to realize it and even then I couldn't believe it was true. After all I had only been married for three weeks. So much for this newfangled contraceptive foam.

So, on this particular hot day, with the sun glinting viciously off the windshield, we headed west out Seven Mile Road to a post-war neighborhood of small lookalike houses, each with a cement walkway and two steps up to the door. The blocks and blocks of little boxes on square lots with driveways and garages and a cement sidewalk rolling by was a knock-out visual which would always stay with me. Phil came around the car and held my door open for me. He took my elbow as we walked toward the front door that matched the address we had memorized.

The first thing I smelled was her perfume. I was sensitive to odors. Then nausea. I focused on her head. She was maybe sixty. Her hair was dyed bright red. Her eyes were black mascaraed and a little smeared from the intense heat. She had a Maybelline red mouth. Was I imagining the cigarette dangling from it? She smiled broadly and welcomed us in an overly friendly manner, as if we were visiting Grandma. Phil was very nice to her. As if he appreciated her or

149

something. We gave her 800 dollars in cash. She told Phil to come back in a half hour and he actually left. She led me into the kitchen where her husband was waiting at the table which was draped in bed sheets. They had me take off my underpants and get on the table. It was stiflingly still and hot. The windows were wide open but there was not a trace of a breeze. The woman's grey haired husband was fingering a metal instrument. Panic rose as I understood that this metal instrument was going to be used to stretch me open. I began to whimper. "Is it going to hurt?" I asked pathetically.

"Just a little."

"Can you put me to sleep?"

"That's not a good idea. You'll want to be leaving here right away afterward. You don't want to be sleepy."

"Oh."

"Open your legs, honey."

I began to cry. "Shut up," she barked hoarsely. "Do you want me to have to shut the windows? Be quiet or the neighbors will hear."

Phil, who had gone away and come back for me, kissed the redhaired woman on the cheek and thanked her sincerely for her help. I guess there weren't that many choices when it came to getting an abortion in Detroit, even though I had heard a rumor that a lot of movie stars came to Detroit to get them. I heard that Martha Raye came once, but not probably to this place.

NOW, IN VENICE, Rita showed me the flyer she had pulled off of the power pole on the corner. Paul Krassner, the political satirist, was coming to town. He was going to be performing a one-person show for a six week run at the Wallenboyd Theater in downtown L.A.

"And he's staying in Scott Kelman's attic apartment" she told me, pointing over to the building across the walkway. "Let's go to his show." Paul—writer, comedian, beloved counterculture hero and publisher of his notorious magazine *The Realist*—was graciously welcomed as a fine addition to the walkway. For example, Rita always invited Paul, who didn't drive, to come with us whenever we went out to eat or to the movies or wherever we happened to be going. We were all instant friends. I could see Paul's apartment window from our house. At least I could see it if I went upstairs to Rita's bedroom and peeked out the tiny window in the corner of her closet. I enjoyed looking out to see his light burning. It felt like love.

One night after Paul's show a whole bunch of us went out to eat. We were waiting outside the restaurant in Japantown. Paul was sitting on a bench. I went over to where he was sitting and kicked the toe of his shoe with my foot to let him know I liked him.

It was Rosh Hashanah, and in celebration I had planned to try the new designer drug called Empathy (which would soon be known as Ecstasy). I had two tabs which I had been holding onto for a couple of months. I asked Paul if he would like to try it with me and he accepted my invitation happily. We swallowed the tabs along with some Vitamin C which he recommended to go along with it. We walked down to the beach and sat in the sand. It wasn't like acid which, for me, erases humanness and replaces it with an eerie feeling of decomposition and impersonality. Empathy was an apt description for this new feeling. We lay in the sand and watched an exquisite bare breasted woman with skin smooth and dark as chocolate pudding and body as lanky as a young stallion, as she bucked her head back under the shower spray. I was comfortable with Paul. We were both comfortable with silence, and I was in love.

Amazingly, the next day I opened the *Los Angeles Times* to find an interview with Paul Krassner. When asked about relationships, Paul, the public figure, was quoted as saying that he had "temporary intimate relationships with women." That was his pattern, he said in the newspaper. He went on to say that it was "hard" to sustain a "long-time" relationship. He said he "got restless."

"I'm not the reassuring type," Paul volunteered that night, hoping to be reassured that I wouldn't depend on him for reassurance. "Okay," I said. "Not a problem."

It was Paul's right leg. His toe would drag when he walked, and there was an obvious spasticity in his gait, as if his electrical system was shorting out. He said it always surprised him when he caught a reflection of himself walking on the street and he would think, "Who's

151

that gimpy guy following me?" It had been that way since he got caught in the after-trial riot in the high-profile Dan White case in San Francisco in 1979. Dan White killed Mayor Moscone and supervisor Harvey Milk and got sentenced to seven years. The ensuing riot in the streets was in reaction to the grave injustice of his short sentence. And so it happened that Paul, who was covering the trial for a local newspaper, received a nightstick in the ribs, and one in the leg, and he never walked right again. Paul's condition was extreme, but he had been successfully ignoring it and pressing on until now.

In January of 1987, an MRI showed that in addition to his previous injuries, there was evidence of "acquired cervical spinal stenosis." Paul's doctor told him that he was a "walking time bomb" and that at any moment the little spurs that were growing on his spine way up by his neck—could suddenly prick through to sever his spinal cord. Like maybe if he sneezed, or ...

I asked him, "What are you going to do?" He said he'd learn to poke out my phone number with his nose. Oh, this was terrible, plus, there was no health insurance. Then I remembered a charitable organization in New York which paid medical expenses for poor or indigent artists and I pitched Paul's case to them and they bought it. They told us to come to the Hospital for Joint Diseases on East 17th street in New York, and Harvey Machaver, the Executive Director, would trade Paul's operation for four paintings or works of art of a certain value. He was mainly interested in oil, watercolor, and unique pieces. So we called a few artists and they said sure, come and get the art.

Paul and I went to New York, and he checked into the hospital and I lugged the canvases through the snow, onto the subway, then dragged them up to Harvey's office, and he called Dr. O'Leary, the finest Park Avenue neurosurgeon and art connoisseur, who would be sawing through Paul's spine and removing the offending sections.

The morning of the operation, in the cafeteria on the 13th floor, I watched two pigeons walking along the ledge of the window while a couple of employees bantered about cross-dressing.

"Ain't no way I let my husband wear lipstick and high-heel shoes in my house."

152

"Baby, this is 1987. You do what you want to do! Have you ever heard of unisex?" I imagined Paul being positioned on the operating table, Dr. O'Leary standing above him. The pigeons on the ledge were lovers, I could see that. They walked side by side, cooing. They flew away and coasted together on the breeze. I waited. They landed on the hands of the tower clock on the church across the park. The hands inched slowly toward 9 a.m. The hospital employees ate home fries and eggs. Dr. O'Leary marked the place on Paul's neck and poised his scalpel.

While Paul was in the hospital in New York I got to know his mom, Ida, who was well into her eighties and rode the train from Astoria, Queens, every day and walked across town to the hospital to see him. She was strong and spry and loved to play Scrabble. I also met Paul's younger sister Marge, a music teacher at Boys and Girls High School in Brooklyn. She directed a huge singing choir and could play anything on the piano. I never thought of Paul as having a family but here they were. He also has an older brother, named George, an engineer. Paul and George were child prodigy violin players and Paul still holds the record for being the youngest person ever to play at Carnegie Hall. He was six when he did it. I kept in close touch with Paul's daughter Holly in San Francisco and Jeanne Johnson, Holly's mother.

Perhaps this terrifying operation had been necessary surgery and maybe it was true that Paul was saved! I liked the way it worked. The doctors were getting valuable collections of artwork while doing good deeds, all in the finest spirit of barter.

Chapter Eleven:
Jobs and Money

THE BANK HAD OFFERED to give me some extra cash over the holiday season by deferring my December car payment to the end of the loan. To do this little favor, they charged $58. That was the deal. Fifty-eight bucks for the privilege of deferring a $140 payment. It was really expensive to be poor. It was time to add another job to my strange list.

When I was engaged to Phil Gaberman in Detroit, his roommate was Dwight Hooker. Photographer and proprietor of the Holland Stevens Portrait studio on Griswald Avenue downtown, Dwight was one of my first employers. Dwight could get any girl to take off her shirt and pose with just a velvet drape, leaning against the fur rug in his photo portrait studio. And sometimes he got them to take the drape off too. If he wanted to. "Wet your lips" he would say, and lick his own lips to show her how. Dwight had black curls and twinkling eyes and you knew right away that he loved women. It was 1960, and my job was in the darkroom. In the darkroom, Dwight stood behind me, pressing himself warmly against the curve in my back, an arm linked through each of mine, and breathing in my ear as he showed me how to take the 4 x 5 negative and put it in the enlarger and frame it just right on the paper, then expose it, develop it, hypo it, sepiatone it, and dry it. I was able to print hundreds of portraits a day in the darkroom where no one was allowed to come in unless I turned off the red light. In this privacy, I listened to the cast album of Camelot continuously and printed portraits all day.

Dwight was entrepreneurial and was building his photo portrait business. He was using a certain sales method. How it worked was that he had people on the street handing out coupons to shoppers and passersby. The coupons were good for one hand-tinted 8 x 10 portrait for the bargain price of one dollar. The men who handed out the coupons were called bums or winos. They were on the streets anyway,

Dwight reasoned, so why not have them pass out the coupons. And if a coupon got redeemed, the wino got 50 cents, so everyone was happy. When the customers with the coupons came into the reception area they were shown to a private dressing room to get themselves ready for their portraits. When they were ready, they were escorted into Dwight's studio where he would take a set of six shots, and of course his photos were fantastic. Every woman looked sexy and beautiful, every man thoughtful and strong.

So then, after the photo sitting, the customer came back the next day and saw the photo proofs. One of the girls at the counter would take the customer into a little booth to display their pictures to them. Seeing the proofs was a private affair. Once the proofs were displayed, it was usually not difficult to help the customer choose a couple of the shots and get a few prints. "Now, how about some wallet-size? And, instead of just a tint, how about a full oil-painting, and what about a frame for it? And, maybe a frame for grandma's print too!"

But sometimes you got a customer who refused to take anything extra. They would only buy the bargain offer. One tinted 8x10 photo for a dollar. And if none of the girls in the front could sell a person more pictures, they would bring in Dwight himself, and he could get an order. No woman could resist him because Dwight gave each customer his total attention. He was interested in everything about her. A woman felt special when Dwight was there looking at her pictures with her. A woman would up her order absolutely for Dwight. The rare individual who got away with one tinted photo for a dollar was called an "Ace." I was glad I didn't have to work the counter very often. I got too many Aces, and I preferred to be in the darkroom.

Dwight took beautiful sexy pictures of me too but I never took my shirt off on his fur rug. Instead, he took grainy black and white photos with his Nikon while I sang at Momo's Cocktail Lounge.

It was at about that time I started to wonder just what I was going to do about my future. I was only making sixty dollars a week at Dwight's photo studio. I wasn't a teacher. What was I? My cousin Tommy, who is a little older than I, said that in the future no one would have to work at a job unless they wanted to. Everyone would do what they want to, and the people who didn't want to work at a job could be taken care of with technology. Like, you know, nobody had to be the garbage man. Technology would be able to take care of that. Tommy was an engineer and he knew a lot about new inventions and outer space. "How soon is this happening?" I asked him. I needed to know. I was semi-desperate for a way to strike out on my own. And then, my big break.

No more dinner theater. Now it was summer stock. I was working the entire season up north in Manistee with the Vanguard Playhouse theater company. Dr. William Gregory, the director, had cast me in a good part for the first production. I was playing "Dulcie" in *The Boy Friend.* I had a feature number. Phil was the musical director and we rented a little attic apartment across from the theater for the season. Manistee was a picturesque if working-class town on Lake Michigan with an equal number of bars and churches, like dozens of them. The playhouse was an ornate remnant of when the opera used to come to Manistee to entertain the logger barons.

In summer stock we would be running one show while rehearsing the next. I loved the pace. I loved the thrill of actually almost dying from heart palpitations waiting in place on stage for the overture to end and the curtain to rise on opening night. All I really wanted to do was to stay with this company when they returned for their winter season at the Vanguard Playhouse in Detroit, and it happened. I got hired.

I was in the resident company of the Vanguard Playhouse in Detroit. Dr. William A. Gregory was the big boss. Now that I was in the company, I called him Bill. Bill cast me as Dolly, a whore in *The Threepenny Opera.* It was going to run for eight weeks. I was earning Actors' Equity scale, $68.50 a week plus I got $5 a night for singing late night at Momo's on weekends.

Later in my first season at the Vanguard, the Detroit police gave us tremendous publicity by deciding that they wanted to close down our production of e.e. cummings' outrageous play, *him*. They said the play was obscene. It was in all the papers. Mainly, they said, it was obscene because of my scene in the barroom (which we portrayed

156

exactly as mr. cummings had it in the script). Apparently the cops were serious. It was the vice squad vs. e.e. cummings.

Even though *him* was written in 1927, our 1963 production was only the second ever mounted. Not because of the striptease but more likely because it was so complex and obscure. It was about a love affair between "him" and his wife, "me." David Atkinson played "him" to Bev Pemberthy's "me." The first act was ordinary enough and seemingly straightforward. Then, suddenly, act two burst into endless abstract ranting and raving about commercials and censorship and fascism and Freud. It might have been a little confusing.

The Detroit police came to the Thursday night show. Everyone knew the cops were coming and might shut us down. The audience knew and the cast knew and everyone was excitedly waiting for my scene, including me. My striptease was performed to the tune of "Frankie and Johnnie." I descended part way down the staircase center stage taking off floaty scarves and a sheer blouse and at that point was wearing only a tiny string bra covering my nipples, a bikini bottom, and high heels. I was usually self-conscious about my skinny bony body but not that night. That night I felt the power. The way the scene was written, actors playing the parts of cops shout "Halt!" from the back of the house. When that happened, the audience thought it might be the real cops because the rumor was out that we might get raided. The real cops in the audience didn't know what to think.

"Frankie and Johnnie were sweethearts, Lordy how they could love," I belted out.

"Halt!" the actor-cops shouted from the back of the theater. I stopped singing and the music petered out behind me. There was silence for a moment as I turned and looked the actor-cops dead in the eye. Slowly, slowly I continued descending the stairway toward them. A chiffon scarf fluttered to the floor behind me. I walked down to the lip of the stage to confront them. They gaped up at me with their sticks and whistles. I never took my eyes off them as I reached into my skimpy bikini bottom and pulled out a bloody banana (as called for in the script), and pushed it toward them menacingly. They were horror-struck. The audience was in amazement. I faced them down in the long silence, savoring the moment. Another gesture with the banana sent them screaming up the aisle and out of the theater and the play continued. While I was doing all this, I was wondering how the real cops who wanted to shut us down were feeling, or where they were sitting for that matter so that I could shoot them a look before I made my exit.

We had the freedom of speech at the Vanguard Playhouse and it felt so good. Happily, the police did not shut us down after all. I thought the whole performance was pretty smart and that Dr. Bill Gregory was brilliant. He got people all fired up about art.

WHEN PAUL AND I RETURNED from New York, I began training immediately for my new job selling the *Encyclopedia Britannica* in the shopping malls. Mary Feldstein, my friend the ex-librarian, was doing it too. The hours were my own and I would get three hundred bucks for every set I sold. How hard could it be?

"The sell is like sex," my instructor Bobby Rolano said, pacing the floor of his sunny office in Century City. "It's about building tension, then releasing it, again and again until the big release—the buy." He explained that the object of the sell is to exchange something of value for something of value. First, you establish the feeling of ownership in the mind of the buyer, and then, you help the buyer decide which set of books to buy. Bobby Rolano was fantastic at this technique. I loved the way he showed the books, pointing out the cross-referencing, revealing the anatomy overlays in the full-color display. He snapped the pages between his fingers.

"Do you know what this paper is made of?" he asked.

"No."

"Silk!"

Bobby's eyes were gleaming. He was combination of Charlie Chan's number one son and a *GQ* model. "The price depends on the binding," he said.

It was four o'clock, and after a long day of training, filling out contracts, figuring monthly payments, and writing up pretend orders, now I was going to spend the evening with Bobby Rolano so that I could observe him work the mall from his little stand at the entrance to Walden's bookstore. The Beverly Center was one of the most massive and monstrous malls in the world. It was like the Fifties on acid and stuffed into a gigantic box. The Beverly Center, with red, red lips, was pony-tail grotesque that night. I glanced at the newspaper headlines on the rack near our encyclopedia stand. There had been a hideous hijacking with killings and grenades on an Egyptian airliner, and the tense standoff was still happening while I was sitting in the mall trying to sell encyclopedias. Suddenly there was a commotion in the building. I heard shrieking female voices and the thunder of running shoppers. I look up to see, not the bomb squad, but a flash of British rockers rushing past me with a ring of security guards circling them, and maybe a hundred teenage girls in pursuit.

"What was that?" I asked Bobby Rolano.

"WHAM!" he said, meaning the band.

The next day I was on my own. Okay. I had to sell one of these people an encyclopedia. I watched the parade of shoppers walk past the entrance to the bookstore where I had my little stand set up. They streamed past me. Suddenly, miraculously, in front of me I saw a family of four, each one holding a hot dog on a stick. They were looking at the books! There they were! Mom, Dad, Sis and Bud. Every element needed to make the sale. I turned the pages of the encyclopedia for them the way Bobby Rolano showed me.

"Do you know what these pages are made of?"

"What?"

"Silk!"

"No one will come to our house, will they?"

"Not unless you beg me."

As my perfect family walked away, a bank of television sets in the next shop blared the nightly news all across the mall. General Electric had just bought NBC. Hey, wait a minute, if General Electric owns NBC now, the encyclopedia folks were going to have to update their edition. The books I was selling were outdated before they were even published. At every moment the *Britannica* must be updated. That was clear. I told Bobby Rolano about how the *Britannica,* as it now existed, was obsolete, and gave up sales. What now?

THAT NIGHT, SITTING ON THE COUCH in the living room with Rita, I must have been looking worried because Rita, said, "The main thing is not to worry." And then she told me that she would be moving out in seven weeks and getting a place with Freddie when he got back from his location shoot in South Africa. So now I had to find somewhere else to live, or get a roommate or a real job.

"Shit, what will I do?"

"I bet you'll think of something," Rita said. I had seven weeks to figure it out. I consulted the television set for a random message that would take on some mystical meaning. "You'll find the answer. Just listen to your heart," said Blake Carrington on *Dynasty.*

The next day I had an interview at KSCI-TV for the position of producer/consultant for a new *TV Horoscope Show.* The boss, Mr. Headly, was a pleasant man, in his sixties. Everyone at KSCI was pleasant. The station was owned by the Maharishi, an Indian spiritual leader, and everyone who worked there was practicing his special brand of Transcendental Meditation. Remember the Maharishi from the Sixties? He was the sweet little bearded guy with the flower. The Beatles did his thing in India. Even I went to see him when he played Madison Square Garden. The Maharishi had invested heavily in media (and real estate) over the years. In the reception area of KSCI-TV there were two big portraits side-by-side on the wall. One was of current President Reagan and the other of the Maharishi.

I told Mr. Headly about my concept for their *TV Horoscope Show* "I see the set as looking like Lucy Ricardo's kitchen except, of course, it's in living color. Nice and bright and cheery. Maybe like *Mister Rogers' Neighborhood.* Guests will be coming in through the kitchen door and chatting with the hosts at the breakfast table. And, friends, and neighbors. will drop in, and each visitor will have a different astrological sign. Then call-ins." Mr. Headly backed away, smiling pleasantly.

It was on my way home from the interview that I heard about The

160

Great Peace March on the car radio. The Great Peace March. It had an edge to it, you know? The Great Peace March. There was a dark, medieval quality to it. Maybe I could get a grant to go with a video camera and cover it. It would be the story of a ploddingly slow foot march inching its way to the Capitol. Thousands of people making the three-thousand mile trek in the name of Peace, marching out of Los Angeles, across the Mojave Desert to Las Vegas, through Utah and Colorado, over Loveland Pass to Denver, past the missile silos of Nebraska to Omaha, through Iowa to Chicago, then, trudging on, through the industrial heartland, with flags unfurled, crossing the George Washington Bridge, and walking down Broadway, past Independence Hall in Philadelphia, and through Baltimore to Washington D.C. Nine months. I figured out that marching would cost less than paying rent in Venice for nine months. I thought probably a lot of homeless people would be going. Maybe I could get a company or some person to sponsor me. I raised my camera to my mind's eye. A moving city of five thousand. The Great Peace March. Would I? In the morning I went down to the ocean to meditate on it. A one-armed man wearing a camouflage jacket approached me on the empty beach.

"You got a cigarette?" he asked aggressively. I shook my head slowly no.

"Got any pot?"

"What?"

"Got any pot?" I shook my head. He walked away, unconvinced, slightly sinister, beaten. As I watched him walk away, I decided to take the mandatory physical exam in case I ended up joining in The Great Peace March.

Young Dr. Mitchell shook my hand in the reception area of the Pro-Peace offices and lead me up the back stairs to an empty room on the third floor where he would be examining me to see if I was fit enough to march. He would do it gratis. He was a member of Physicians for Social Responsibility. He liked my watch ("A Rolex?" "No, a Seiko"), he liked my sweater ("Angora?" "No, cashmere"), he liked my shoes (they were pink). I passed the exam. Then, I was interviewed by Rob, a nice college lefty type.

161

"Why do you want to go on the Great Peace March?"

"For the experience," I said.

"What would you do if a person approached you with intent to be violent?"

"Well, I wouldn't call the cops, I know that much."

"What are you giving up to go on this march?"

"Dunno. My life is a process. I do what I do."

"Don't think this is going to be fun", he warned. "It's going to be long, uncomfortable, miserable."

"Don't forget slow," I said.

"Then why are you going?" he asked.

"Because I'm crazy."

"I think you'll make a great marcher," he said.

Rita didn't seem that enthusiastic when I told her about the Great Peace March. She had recently taken a job as an assistant to a lawyer in Century City. "Please, Nancy, talk to my boss. I'm sure there's a job for you at his office."

"Are you sure you want the job?" said Rita's boss.

"Yes," I said enthusiastically. "I've always wanted to be a file clerk." He took me to the file room and showed it to me. It was an interior room that had never seen the light of day. A room where the aroma of every last cigarette ever smoked in it clung to the stacks of folders (all numerical). It was musty in the file room. The must hung heavy there. The job paid $1400 a month. Eight-thirty to five, and you had to take over for the receptionist when she went to lunch. Maybe they wouldn't hire me. They didn't hire me! I was free!

RITA CAME HOME DISTRESSED. Her boss told her he didn't feel I would be happy in the job.

"How are you doing?" she asked, sympathetically.

"Okay."

"But how are you really doing?"

"Well, er——." Then she sat down. "I've been thinking about this all the way home from the office. I'm concerned about you." She was searching for the right words.

162

"What is it?" I asked.

"I think you should chant." I stared at her. "You could have everything," she told me. "Nam yo ho renge kyo," she said. I told her there was no way I was going to chant for money. "Look Nancy, face it. You lack confidence! You wait for others to do things for you. You wait for other people to tell you what's okay. But it could all be fixed if you started chanting."

Each morning I was awakened at the crack of six by the now familiar drone from Rita's altar upstairs. A tinge of incense hung over the house in Venice which would soon be mine alone for only $800 a month when Rita and Freddie would be moving to their own house. I resisted a ritual of gibberish even though it worked for Rita. For Rita, her true love Freddie had come home from his movie shoot location in Africa, laid his skins and tusks out on the carpet and placed a gold and emerald ring on Rita's finger.

"Does this mean you're engaged?" I asked him.

"I was thinking maybe it does," he said.

I TOOK IN A LOW DEEP BREATH, then exhaled slowly. I was in a room. A meeting room with a certain "church basement" smell. The woman sitting next to me was speaking, and I realized I would be next. This was going to involve public speaking. I hadn't counted on that. Slow motion, I turned my head and scanned the circle of fifty strangers sitting on folding chairs in the community room of the Western Federal Savings Bank in Beverly Hills. It was Sunday. Everyone turned to me and smiled expectantly "I'm Nancy." I stopped and swallowed. They leaned forward. "I'm a compulsive—a compulsive, uh, debtor," I concluded.

Bob Hope smiled broadly from the poster behind me, flashing his credit card. "Hi, Nancy," the group responded loudly in cheerful unison, clearly pleased with my first halting steps down the road to self-discovery at Debtors Anonymous. But even as I said it, I was telling myself it wasn't true. I nodded and smiled but said nothing else. My old friend Mary, the ex-librarian who got me into the *Encyclopedia Britannica* fiasco, was going to speak next. "Hi Mary," they said. I looked at her closely. Okay, maybe Mary was a debtor. Come to think of

163

it, she always had been a little screwy with money. And she must have a dozen pair of Ferragamo shoes.

I wanted to whisper to Mary that I felt strange at the meeting, but there was no cross-talk allowed at Debtors Anonymous. On the ride over she had said, "It works even if you think you don't need it. It's about complete support and unconditional love and you can say anything." This evening Mary began: "All my life I've been screwed up about money." (See? I knew it.) "I always thought that money could fix anything. My earliest memory is when I was three years old. I remember being in a restaurant with my mother and father and saying 'I want that'—you know, pointing at something and getting it. That desire has never left me. It started out in that restaurant, and it ended up in a department store in Chicago six months ago. I was there on a business trip. I was feeling tired and lonely. I walked into the store, opened an instant credit account and consciously bought eight pair of Ferragamo shoes." (Aha!) "They were on sale, down from $110 to $85. I knew I was stealing them. In those days, I would walk into any store and pick up whatever I wanted. They don't call it shoplifting, they call it paying by credit."

There was a low, knowing murmur among us. "When I saw myself buying those shoes," Mary continued, "I guess I really knew that I was in trouble. It didn't feel good. Then, when the bills would come, I'd put them in the cupboard and wouldn't look at them. That didn't work, so I paid a professional bookkeeper $30 an hour to straighten things out. I was going broke and paying someone to tell me so. I was disturbed and unhappy. I bought a 25-inch TV and VCR for $50 down. I felt worse. Then I had a car accident and lost my job. Suddenly my income was one-third what it had been. I still wanted to buy. I started depending on credit cards to eat at restaurants because I had no money to buy groceries. And then I found D.A."

"HI, RANDY," WE SAID. And Randy said "I don't mind if God helps me through my problems. I just don't want my parents to do it. My dad gave me money for tuition and I applied for a student loan so I could use the money he gave me for a slush fund. Is it right to take a car from my folks? I want to be grown-up." I glanced down at the questionnaire I had been clutching in my hand. I uncrumpled the paper. It said if you answered eight of fifteen questions with a yes, you were a compulsive debtor. Let's see:

1. Are your debts making your home life unhappy?

2. Does the pressure of your debts distract from daily work?

3. Are your debts affecting your reputation?

4. Do your debts cause you to think less of yourself?

5. Have you ever given false information in order to obtain credit?

6. Have you ever made unrealistic promises to your creditors?

7. Does the pressure of your debts make you careless of the welfare of your family?

8. Do you ever fear that your employer, family or friends will learn the extent of your total indebtedness?

9. When faced with a difficult financial situation, does the prospect of borrowing give you an inordinate feeling of relief?

10. Does the pressure of your debts cause you to have difficulty sleeping?

11. Has the pressure of your debts ever caused you to consider getting drunk?

12. Have you ever borrowed money without giving adequate consideration to the rate of interest you are required to pay?

13. Do you usually expect a negative response when you are subject to a credit investigation?

14. Have you ever developed a strict regimen for paying off your debts, only to break it under pressure?

15. Do you justify your debts by telling yourself that you are superior to the "other" people, and when you get a break, you'll be out of debt overnight?

I lost. I came in just over the wire with 10 yeses. I went back over the questions searching for two answers to change.

"HI, KEN."

"The first time I came to a meeting, I got physically ill. I became dizzy and nauseated, because I realized I am a compulsive pauper and a debtor …"

"Hi, Sharon."

"I can't believe I've found you! I thought I was the only one. Today, I went out and bought a new front door. I have a front door, but when I saw this one at the hardware store …"

"Hi, Sid."

"My debt is not going to be taken care of by organizing $20 payments. I'm three quarter of a million dollars in. I'm in hiding …"

"Hi, Ronnie."

"Well, I've always just felt justified in having the credit. After all, I'm an American. I have the right to credit."

"Hi, Jack."

"I want to talk about TRW. About panic …"

A montage of never-enough, fear-of-success, adrenaline rushes, spending, borrowing, charging, rose-colored glasses, parking in the red zone, unrealistic expectations, laundry pile-ups, debting, debting-in-relationships, wrong companions, fear, discouragement, car repos, phone shut-offs, bottomless pits, jail, powerlessness.

I imagined the world as anonymous. *Everything Anonymous*. What with Alcoholics, Overeaters, Debtors, Gamblers, Narcotics, Sexaholics, Alanon, Gamanon and even Fundamentalists Anonymous, we could have the great new grass roots populist movement of the decade. No dues, no fees, no memberships, no advice. Not affiliated with any sect, denomination, politic, organization, or institution, engaging in no controversy, endorsing or opposing no cause. *EA* would be autonomous, placing principles above personalities, and offering only total support and unconditional love.

THE MEETING WAS OVER on the dot. We recited the Lord's Prayer together. The circle was unbroken. "Keep coming back, it works!" we chanted and squeezed each other's hands. Some of us hugged and went off to Zucky's Deli on Wilshire for fellowship.

"I found relief to my anxiety at my very first meeting," said Mary on our way to the delicatessen. "I read two books, followed the twelve

166

steps to recovery, and I come back! I keep coming back and it works. I write down all the money I spend and I share out loud for three minutes with my peers when I'm troubled. No one tells me to do anything. I hear what the others are doing. I focus on the solution instead of the problem. It's about truth and trust."

Over soup du jour Mary continued: "It was hard to write my money down, because I'm not an exact person. But I did it. I wrote down everything for six weeks and then I got a 'pressure group' to help me. I picked the people myself. A man and a woman. And then, I opened my accounts to them. I was nervous. It's a very intimate thing to show someone your books. I was afraid that they would judge me, but they didn't. They observed that I was bringing in less money than I needed to live on, so we devised a financial action plan for me. I was to declare a 90-day moratorium with all my creditors. We worked out a letter to that effect. There were some helpful suggestions for things like my car insurance. It was too high. I began comparison shopping. We talked about some financial goals for me. I was able to verbalize what I expected to get out of the group and what needed to be resolved or clarified. We designed re-payment plans. It's been six months and I'm feeling much more confident. I haven't used my credit cards at all. I don't crave going to the mall any more either, because I think about my higher power instead of new shoes. And I feel connected to the greatest force. I have conscious contact with it on a daily basis. And if I have a craving I call someone. Sometimes I call ten people in a row. And now people call me, too."

"You want dessert?" I asked.

"Uh-uh," Mary said. "I'm 19 days sugar free. O.A." (Overeaters Anonymous).

"How many meetings are you going to these days?" I asked.

"Two OAs, three DAs, and an Alanon for my obsession with people. Are you going to come back? It works."

I scanned the twelve steps once more as Mary signaled for the check. Even the twelve steps were only suggested. "Come to the Santa Monica meeting Tuesday night," Mary said, leaving a dollar bill under her plate, and noting it on a small pad.

Stanley, my friend and Yoga instructor, told me he had serious reservations about the twelve-step program. Over beers, he said he thought it was self-limiting. That it wasn't healthy to label yourself as a compulsive debtor or alcoholic, or to believe that you will always be one, and that if you don't keep coming back you are doomed.

The Santa Monica meeting was good. I went twice. I heard the Malibu Alanon was fantastic. I was thinking about it. It was the salted-peanut effect, I thought, as I drove to the 7:30 sunrise Prosperity meeting on Thursday morning. While there, I was moved to tears by a real estate salesman from Orange County who was five payments behind on his car, and who, last night, compulsively spent $165 on Amway products. Well, maybe one more meeting. It's free.

I sold my article about Debtors Anonymous to the *LA Weekly*. I was on a roll at 18 cents a word and had a no-worries holiday with Eric and Mary Wright up on their magical land in Malibu, for the Easter Sunday Grand Trample, Egg Hunt, One Mile Hike, and Potluck Supper.

A profusion of wildflowers choked the hillside, with deep gashes of color pushing through the noir-charred ashes left by the Great Fire of Malibu '85. The mustard fields were shoulder-high. And the purples, the oranges, the blues—each ridge a new vista. A turquoise egg nestled in the fossil bed. Then back to reality the very next day.

Dateline Beverly Hills: The families of the hostages waited outside Gucci's as a gunman held five people in Van Cleef & Arpels. Losses were running $100,000 an hour while Rodeo Drive was blocked off. Kirk Douglas walked by. So did Robert Wagner. Everyone was concerned about the situation.

Chapter Twelve:
I am the Nielsens

UNAWARE OF MY BACKGROUND in television media, there was a note of surprise in the voice of the telemarketing interviewer when I agreed to participate in the Nielsen survey, but she quickly regained her flat tone, telling me she believed I would enjoy the survey week. She told me a letter to confirm my participation would arrive in a few days. When the letter arrived, it seemed urgent. It said the TV industry needed my help. Of course, I agreed. My eye skipped to the bottom of the page. It was signed Art Nielsen, Jr.

And so it was that I, "S., F., 35-44," a clearly eccentric, erratic, indiscriminate viewer, self-diagnosed TV news addict, and known video freak, had become one of the many households across the country whose viewing habits would be used to produce the Nielsen TV ratings. And so it was, too, that I was able to cut down my TV viewing by almost 60% in one short week with the help of my Nielsen TV Viewing Diary.

The diary arrived in a green and white envelope marked First Class. It was addressed to me personally. A crisp dollar bill fluttered out of the booklet as I flipped through the pages. Okay, let's see. "Please list all the members of your household": Just me. "Print first name": Nancy. "Hours worked per week": Not Applicable. Because ... because ... I'm an artist (scratched that out) ... unemployed.

The next question had to do with my TV set, 12 inch RCA portable that Rita left for me. No, it wasn't hooked up to cable. Yes, I used its little whip antenna only. I was to note down each program viewed.

Day One, I circled the set cautiously and at 3:30 in the afternoon I gave in and turned on *Donahue*. I began to become self-conscious sitting on the sofa, stilted, unnatural. I turned the set off at 3:45, carefully noting my actions in my diary. At 5:30 I couldn't stop myself, and snapped it back on. The local news made me feel nauseated and I quickly selected *Great Chefs* on public TV instead. I found it surprisingly hip. At 6:00 p.m. I went back for the Channel 4 news and stayed for Brokaw, then went to Dan Rather. By 7:30 p.m. I was feeling somewhat alienated and turned it off, wanting to keep a good distance from Cosby (I didn't need him/he didn't need me). I took care of some correspondence, but at 10:45 p.m. I suddenly felt I was missing something and rushed to the set for the last segment of 20/20, and then stayed tuned for the *Channel 7 News*. As I watched, I became aware of the tension in my body. I felt tempted to quit, but hung in there through Johnny's monologue, when I snapped it off in a cold sweat. The end of my first day as a Nielsen Family, I signed off at a quarter to twelve.

Day Two, Friday, I didn't go near the set at all, not wanting to repeat yesterday's programs.

Day Three on Saturday night, Paul came over and wanted to watch *Golden Girls* because a friend of his had a cameo role. For Paul, I had to write "Visitor," and then his approximate age and his sex. We talked a lot during the show and I turned off the set as soon as it was over. There was no *Saturday Night Live* because of a sports special, and there was no Ted Koppel either, so I signed off.

Day Four on Sunday, I rested, and read Creating *Alternative Futures: The End of Economics* by Hazel Henderson. She had written about how the private manipulation of information-gathering is disastrous for public decision-making in the same way the Nielsen ratings have been for the quality of television, and how "these methods tend to screen out of consideration new or random ideas, which are a vital component of an innovative society."

Day Five on Monday, I got home late and in a fit at missing the news, I gorged myself with *The Newlywed Game* at 7:30 p.m., and then *TV's Bloopers and Practical Jokes* at 8 p.m. At nine I watched *Kate and Allie*. Kate and Allie were nice, conservative, 38-year-old roommates. They were good-hearted and laughed a lot. In this episode, they made a big deal over Kate going out with a black man. At the end, it turned out they were not bigoted after all. Then I really did it. I stayed tuned for *Newhart*. My first time. And my last. At 10 p.m., I switched over to Channel 18 where I sometimes watched *Bilingual Jackpot Bingo*, which was produced by one of my old students from Goddard College. I caught the end of *Maharishi TV.* They were talking about how TM (Transcendental Meditation) can slow down, and actually reverse, the aging process. But the tape was too slow and static, and I turned off the set, signed off in my viewing diary and listened to Sally Jessie Raphael on the radio until I fell asleep.

On Day Six I watched the network news but quickly turned off the set before prime time.

By Wednesday, Day Seven, I had no interest in any of the usual fare, and was horrified by the repetitive nature of my previous viewing habits, so on this, the seventh day, I only watched *NBC News*, which looked suspiciously like last night's.

This must be something like Smoke Enders, I thought, leafing through my completed viewing diary. On the last page, "Please," it said, "use the space below to comment about local programming, such as news, and list favorite programs that you missed watching."

And I commented: "TV in general is very disappointing and I can hardly find anything to watch even though I want to. And about 'local programming,' such as the 'news' (unless you mean *Eye on L.A.* or something), the news is reactionary and disturbing. Still, I continue to wander in the channels, searching for the relevant, the heartening." I wrote that, and I signed it, and I sent it in.

At the end of the survey week, relieved of my viewing diary, I found myself again in front of the set. Steven Speilberg was feeling out of sorts. He had been locked out of the Oscars. I watched the awards alone with the shades drawn. Most notable moments: Jane Fonda's double, looking all cute and Barbie-like in a sequined strapless (it couldn't really have been Jane, could it?), Audrey Hepburn's standing ovation, Don Ameche's standing ovation, Geraldine Page's standing ovation, and everyone being so well-behaved. Later, on *Barbara Walters' Oscar Night Special* she chatted with the President Reagans about movies. The Reagans were in favor of less sex and more violence in the movies. Ronnie liked Rambo. I would never know stuff like that without TV.

171

Chapter Thirteen:
Aunt Betty's Secret
and the New Right

WHEN I WAS SEVEN, my dad took me with him on a business trip to New York. It was just the two of us. We rode the train overnight from Detroit. We had dinner in the diner at a beautifully set table with stiff white linen tablecloths and napkins and the scenery going backwards out the window. After dinner we retired to our roomette, a cleverly constructed space with stainless steel plumbing that popped out when needed, and where the seats turned into beds at night. I was cozy in my upper berth all cuddled in with the window curtains open, watching the passing night. Clack clack occasional flashes of landscape. Ding ding ding we rolled slowly through the little towns and then the miles of black night and the lonely whistle.

We arrived at Grand Central Station at seven a.m. We were going to stay with my Aunt Betty. She was one of my dad's sisters (he had nine). Betty Lipton lived on West 90th Street right near Riverside Park. She worked at Altman's Department Store on Fifth Avenue in the rare books department. She dealt in literary treasures, autographs, documents, and maps. She dealt in books with gold edges. I was excited because the following day we were going to pick her up at Altman's and then we were going to the Empire State Building. And after that my cousin, Jimmy Lipton, who was an actor, was going to take us all to Chinatown for dinner.

I was curled up in Aunt Betty's bedroom with the reassuring sounds of the grown-ups laughing and talking in the living room. I had the light on so I could look around at all her stuff. She had books and pictures and knick-knacks, and as my eyes scanned the room, I spotted a large heavy piece of paper rolled-up like art work of some kind leaning against the wall at the corner of her desk. I hopped out of bed

172

and went over to it. I rolled the rubber band down the paper, and I don't even want to tell you what I saw when I pulled it open. I mean this was a shocking, disgusting picture. I couldn't imagine why Aunt Betty would have such a thing. She obviously kept it rolled up for a reason. It was a picture of a man with hardly any clothes on. He had only a ragged piece of cloth covering him. And, here was the disgusting part, he was nailed onto two pieces of wood. His arms were outstretched and there was a nail pounded through each of his hands. His feet were crossed so that one long thick nail went through both of them. There was a lot of blood. And if that wasn't bad enough, there were other people below him with spears stabbing at him while he was nailed there and his eyes were rolling around in his head. There were gouges in his chest and thighs. I had never seen anything so horrible in my life. I was dizzy and nauseated. My heart was pounding but I stayed calm. I rolled the picture back up, stretched the rubber band around it and tried to remember the exact angle that it had been placed. I went back to bed but I didn't sleep. I wasn't going to tell anyone what I saw because I was pretty sure I wasn't supposed to see it. And I didn't want my aunt Betty to think I was snooping. Plus, I thought she wouldn't have wanted anyone to know she had it.

So I kept Aunt Betty's secret, and for the most part never ventured into Christian symbolism or anything Christian for that matter. But now, it could no longer be ignored. What was the state of American culture that in 1987, a charming smiling nodding Christian folk-Nazi like Pat Robertson could make a serious run for the Presidency? What was Pat's agenda? Who were his constituents? What was his strategy? Perhaps some of my fascination came from the fact that Pat Robertson and I were both in the television business. While I was building *Lanesville TV, Probably America's Smallest TV Station,* Pat was building the *Christian Broadcasting Network* (CBN). Of course, he was a little better at fundraising than I was. But then, he had the buzz word, "God." He owned the God word and it was pre-sold. He didn't have to explain anything. Viewers just sent the money. Now he had the fourth largest television network in the world. He also had relief centers around the world in the private sector, called "Operation

173

Blessing," and broadcast operations in Central and South America, the Caribbean, Asia, Africa, and Europe.

Now Pat Robertson was attempting to organize a potentially significant voting block in the Pentecostal and Charismatic churches. Along with God, Pat Robertson had the drama of healings and possessions, he had speaking-in-tongues and prophecy, and these things were attractive to a large public. Significantly, Pat Robertson's legal foundation had recently won the Alabama school textbook case. Judge W. Brevard Hand became the leading activist for the far right when he upheld the fundamentalist Christian plaintiffs who declared that "secular humanism" was a religion and banned more than 40 state-approved books that he ruled promoted "godless doctrine."

What was the climate in this country that made Pat Robertson possible? No one had ever been able to crack the veneer of Pat Robertson. And even though I had a good and definite contact within his organization, who had promised access to the campaign, it did not mean that we could get alone time or sit down time with Pat or even ask him a single question, much less have him reveal anything whatsoever about himself. If I had the chance, I was ready with my short list.

ARE THERE PROPHETS OR POLITICIANS today who get direct revelations from God?

Your Voice of Hope TV station in South Lebanon beams anti-Arab, anti-Muslim messages and supports Israeli take-over of Arab lands. Is this a Christian thing to do?

Knowing that you and other evangelists believe every Jew will either be killed or converted to Christ, why should Jews collaborate with you?

What about the level at which you do business globally with your relief centers and broadcast operations? The only other industries that deal at that level globally, are dealing in arms, oil, and drugs. You must often find yourself in the company of international business people, military generals, spies, thieves … Pat?

But let me tell you, there was no one in Los Angeles that year who was interested in putting up any money for this story. How about an

174

independent thinker? Trying my last best hope for funding I got in touch with musician/composer Frank Zappa, who had been outspoken about the Christian Right. Gail Zappa, Frank's wife, answered the phone and began talking to me about the 1967 Summer of Love. I'm not sure why she told me this, but in a startling parenthetical moment she said "There was no Summer of Love! There was the war, and there was the government that made sure that young people stayed stoned and didn't vote." She told me this without my asking.

Then Frank got on the line and said, "There's no way you can do a documentary on Pat Robertson." Frank said the Robertson people were obviously lying to me about access and that Public TV was lying when they said they would play it. He asked me how I was getting such great access. Before I could answer, he said, "You must be blowing him." Frank called me a "girl" twice and indicated that I could never pull off the kind of production I was suggesting. Then he said his phone was being tapped and indicated that the religious right was after him.

"You're a fool," he said to me in closing. And when there was silence he added, "I guess I'm not telling you what you want to hear." Most people don't.

Haiku on the Campaign Trail:
I bleeding gently
into a slender tampon
shoot Pat Robertson

Filmmaker/videomaker Wendy Apple and I decided to go ahead, even without the money, and get as much footage as we could of the Pat Robertson campaign of 1988. Our first location was in Orange County at the "Americans for Robertson Gala Dinner," a huge fundraiser featuring Pat Robertson himself. Wendy and I were looking like the straight media with our Beta rig, camera crew, and high heels. We moved among the festive crowd, wanting to sop up as much of this culture as we could.

We were trolling for people who wanted to talk, when I spotted a kindly looking gentleman in a minister's collar smiling broadly at me.

175

This was the Reverend Harald Bredesen. I introduced myself and I asked him how well he knew Pat Robertson. He said, "How well do I know him? Back in 1958, young Pat Robertson was my student assistant!" Reverend Bredesen leaned in close to me with his eyes flashing, and whispered, "Just think if the people in that stuffy old church really knew what was going on behind those stone walls and double-locked doors. Wouldn't they have a fit!"

"What were you doing?" I asked.

"We used to pray in tongues," the Reverend said enticingly. I asked him to pray some for us now, but it was time for dinner to be served. After the chicken I engaged him once more. He was seated at the head table next to Pat and Dee Dee Robertson, Dean and Laurie Jones, Paul and Jan Crouch of Trinity Broadcasting; Rhonda Fleming and her husband Ted Mann; actress Charlene Tilton, Mr. and Mrs. Rosie Greer (the footballer turned minister), and Lee Coppack, the heavyweight fundraiser who did the money pitch for the campaign before dessert.

The printed program for the event described Reverend Bredesen as a "Pentecostal" and said he'd been a member of the board of directors of Pat Robertson's Christian Broadcasting Network since 1962.

"Why are you so involved in politics?" I asked him.

"Who needs Christ more than these world leaders surrounded as they are by people who tell them what they think they want to hear? You reach a world leader, you reach not only him, but those who have their eyes on him. This has been God's call in my life. I'm convinced it's God's call." And then Reverend Bredesen added, "I was sort of thrust into politics when Pat Boone invited me to Governor Reagan's home. And that day we received a prophecy that Reagan was going to be President of the United States. This was in 1971."

The reverend looked dreamily heavenward and said, "I converted Pat Boone on a hillside overlooking Beverly Hills a few years ago." I flashed the Reverend a big smile. Reverend Bredesen wanted to be friends. He said he'd like to get together with me privately and "climb Prayer Mountain."

"Where's that?" I asked. He laughed. "Oh, I get it," I said. "It's a concept, right?"

I asked Reverend Bredesen to get in touch with Pat Boone so Wendy and I could tape them talking about all this politics and religion. We made plans to videotape with them a couple of weeks later in a park near Pat Boone's home in Beverly Hills. I picked up the Reverend out in Chatsworth at Jane Boeckmann's home, where he was a house guest. Bert Boeckmann, Jane's husband, owned the Galpin Ford dealership in the valley, and they lived in a huge new gated house way way out in the boonies (turn left on Minnie Ha Ha Drive). The Boeckmanns were Co-Chairmen, along with Mr. and Mrs. Barry Hon, for the "Americans for Robertson Gala Dinner" where I met Reverend Bredesen.

Reverend Bredesen dozed and prayed alternately as I drove him from the Boeckmann's in my Honda to meet Wendy and the crew at the park in Beverly Hills. Somewhere en route the reverend asked me if I planned to go to Heaven. I glanced over at him. He seemed sincerely interested. I decided to continue to be upfront with him about where I was in terms of religion. "What moxie to think that there is something special planned for you after you die." He smiled knowingly and closed his eyes. I continued. "But okay, suppose you, with all the data that you have stored in your brain, suppose that yes, there you are, the actual you, up in heaven all day. Does your obscurely buzzing consciousness live alone, or do you hang out with your old friends and family? What do you do all day? Can you remember what you used to do back when you were alive? How long will this heaven scene go on? Is Bob Marley there? Marilyn?" There was silence for a good while as we sped along the 405. "Reverend Bredesen?" He had dozed off. Just as well.

Pat Boone and the Reverend were genuinely delighted to see one another and began conversing animatedly for our camera while sitting on a park bench.

Pat Boone was clearly wistful when he said, "Do you remember why our mutual friend George Otis thought we ought to get together?"

"Well, George Otis and I were out for a walk one day and he said, 'I've taken on Pat Boone for a financial consultation as well as a means of reaching him spiritually.'"

177

"And I knew Otis was a terrific business doctor," said Pat.

"He was the general manager of Lear Industries, wasn't he?" asked Reverend Bradesen.

"That's right," Pat said, "and I really was looking to him for some investment advice, but he seemed to be plugged into something spiritually that was beyond my experience. He wasn't fooling me. I knew he wanted to advise me spiritually and I wanted that and his business expertise."

"Where does Ronald Reagan fit in?" I asked, always interested in stories about a sitting president.

"Ronald Reagan and I have been friends since we had little kids in school together in Bel Air," said Pat Boone. "He was just an actor and doing his stuff for GE. And we used to talk about political things around the fire after a school function, and he and Nancy and Shirl and I have been quite good friends. I used to come home from those meetings saying, 'I wish a guy like Ronald Reagan would run for office. I mean, he's so articulate, He'd make a great congressman.'"

They both laughed.

"A Senator, maybe," said Pat, "but now he was Governor. So we went by, and you were there," he nodded to Reverend Bredesen on the park bench beside him, "and George Otis, and Shirley and I, and Herb. I don't remember if there was somebody else, one or two people. We went by and had a pleasant meeting in the late afternoon in the sunshine over at the governor's mansion. He was very cordial, and of course, Nancy, and before we got ready to leave, somebody suggested that we just have a word of prayer. And Reagan, of course, was very happy to join us in prayer. I think Nancy left the room and so we joined hands in a circle and we began to pray and suddenly, the prayer was interrupted, if you remember, and there was a strong word of prophecy, if I remember properly, it came through George Otis."

"That's right," said Reverend Bredesen.

"And he said 'Your father is pleased with you.' Do you remember exactly what he said that day?"

"Something to the effect that if he would walk in the ways of the Lord, that God was going to put him in the White House," said Reverend Bredesen.

"He mentioned the address, 1600 Pennsylvania Avenue, and of course we recognized it," said Pat, "and it was so strong and so unexpected by George or by any of us, and we praised the Lord and thanked him for the prophetic word. And we opened our eyes, and I'll never forget it, I looked immediately of course at Ronald Reagan. I didn't think he had ever been involved in a circle or a prayer like this or heard such a prophetic word like this, and really, I remember his gaze being sort of glassy."

"And his arms dropped!" said the Reverend.

"Well, yeah, he was standing between you and George, and there was an electricity that flowed in this circle, and this word came so positively and so strong that I think we were all somewhat shaken by it. Certainly, he was and I was. And then after that we felt surely this was going to happen. This is from God, you know. I called Ronald Reagan the night after the election when the results were in and I said, 'Do you remember that prayer time back in Sacramento that afternoon?' And he said, 'I sure do.' And I said, 'It was right on, wasn't it?' And he said 'It was right on.'"

Pat and the Reverend laughed.

Reverend Bredesen turned to Pat Boone and said, "You know, that story has an interesting sequel. Two years later, I was a dinner guest of Leonard Streilitz who was the Chairman of the United Jewish Appeal, and over dinner he asked,'Harald, how well do you know Pat Boone?' I said, 'Why do you ask?' And he said, 'Do you think he would he be willing to have the Israeli ambassador as his guest in his home? Then we would invite in Jewish money men, and the ambassador could give them the pitch for Israel.' And I said, 'I'm sure he would,' and when I checked with you, you were only too happy to."

"Um hum."

"And I said to Streilitz, 'If you want to know how well I know Pat Boone, let's get into his story.' This was when you were going broke with that ball team. And so we got to the part where we laid hands on you and prayed for a massive immediate financial miracle and within twenty-four hours, a total stranger appeared from Washington D.C. and purchased the Oakland Oaks for two and a half million dollars, and he

179

burst in, and he said, 'Don't tell me who that total stranger was who purchased the Oakland Oaks from Pat Boone. I'll tell you who it was,' and I said, 'Who was it?' 'Earl Forman!' Streilitz said. And I said, 'How in the world did you know?' 'Because I bought the Oakland Oaks from *him* for two and a half million dollars, and will you please pray that someone will buy them from *me* for two and a half million dollars?'"

They laughed.

"Now, not that many people buy the Oakland Oaks for two and a half million dollars," said the Reverend.

"No. No."

"You know, Pat," the Reverend said, modulating his tone, "God has done so much for us, let's just praise him and worship him right now."

"Oh, gladly."

As Wendy and I stood there, camera rolling, we were treated to forty-five seconds of pure prayer, such a perfect duet in the cutest little language I have ever heard. It was lilting and had none of the harsh sounds of say, Hebrew or English. A soft friendly language. There they were, the two of them, arm in arm, with outer arms raised high to the Lord.

"A loyo a robliatta catilia a tata callayenda ala palua a ka cinia a capatatta la tichi ayatta ratta a luchi ola aya lata."

And Wendy and I mirrored them, arm in arm, smiling broadly, sharing one perfect heavenly blissful moment of getting the shot.

They ended together, a good sign for any band. The spell was broken only when Pat looked over to us and asked, "Now, did you want a walking shot?"

Later, I sat on Pat Boone's doorstep for nearly an hour until he finally came out and signed a release for me.

Chapter Fourteen:
The Wilton North Report

REVEREND BREDESEN AND PAT BOONE were a hit in the underground video world of Los Angeles. Wendy and I played our speaking in tongues tape at several folding-chair gallery venues like EZTV in Hollywood and I had a showing at the American Film Institute.

Whether by chance or not, both Wendy and I had landed jobs as field directors on the new late night show on the very new Fox TV called *The Wilton North Report*. I had shown the producers a reel of Lanesville TV and they hired me. I was amazed. Paul was also working on the show as a writer and an on-air commentator.

The natural event happened at 7:42 a.m. just as I was picking Paul up to drive us to work at Fox. Waiting by the stairs to his apartment I heard a grinding sound, a low rattle of aluminum, like someone trying to get the automatic garage door to go up and it was jammed. Then I realized the sound was coming from all the garage doors in the alley. The vibration built up in intensity. Wow, my equilibrium. Looking up, I saw the phone poles and the power wires were swaying violently, but there was no wind. I leaned against the side of the building but it was moving with me. People began pouring out of their houses in their pajamas, some with towels wrapped around them. The earthquake had hit. My first big one. I was thrilled. Six-point-one. In a moment or two Paul appeared at his door, two stories up on the precarious wooden landing at the top of the stairway. He was carrying a small trampoline which he had planned to move into his office at the studio. "Sorry about that," he said. "I didn't mean to jump so hard."

Then again at four in the morning, 3 days later, ooh, ooh, ooh, I scrambled away from the window near my bed. An aftershock! Five-point-five. "It's going to crack off," my mom warned over the phone.

"I'm glad I got here before it does," I said. And I was, because I finally had a great job working on *The Wilton North Report*. This new show would be taking the place of Arsenio Hall, who had been taking the place of Joan Rivers. It was going to be a mock news show with a lot of wit. I went out every day with my camera crew to shoot the stories I was assigned, and I could also pitch them story ideas of my own.

The Wilton North Report was named after the building we worked in, which in turn had been named after the street the studio was on. The producer of the show was Barry Sand, who had been hired away from *The David Letterman Show*. It was going to be so great. Five nights a week, live. A sort of humorous look at the day's news using clips and, we hoped, loaded with irony. I would have a juicy salary every week, working on a show that would feature (as I saw it), my little videos. Instead, if you believe the critics, *The Wilton North Report* was the absolutely worst show that had ever been on TV. With Barry Sand at the helm, after only three months of employment, and three weeks on the air, *The Wilton North Report* was dead.

"A feast for geeks," proclaimed the *San Francisco Chronicle.* It was suggested that Barry Sand's show appealed to people who found Muzak just too darned entertaining. The only thing critic Tom Shales liked was a little short documentary I had made about a retirement party for a man who had worked for thirty years at the gas company. ("One thing about Bob, he loved ketchup," said a co-worker.) But for the most part Wilton North was described as being "for seriously maladjusted adolescent males who fry bugs under magnifying glasses." Blame was laid specifically on the two ex-drive-time DJs from Sacramento whom Barry hired as hosts. These guys were perfectly plain, totally honk-honk radio personalities, very nice but dreadfully banal. We all tried to tell Barry it was a mistake to hire them, but he wouldn't listen.

The story goes that Barry had seen what happened at Letterman where the talent took control of the show and the producers ended up working for the star. Barry didn't want that to happen here, to him. It was his contention that the show should be the star, not the host. He wanted it to be *Barry Sand's Wilton-North Report.* So he searched far and wide for the blandest, most replaceable, yet professional, hosts they could find. Paul suggested the new comedian, Ellen DeGeneres for host. Barry said she was "too dykey." "Well, how about Richard Belzer?"

"Too reptilian," countered Barry. "Chris Rock?" "Too raw." Well, how about *Wilton North* Staff writer Conan O'Brien? "Unprofessional."

Now that Barry had hired the drive-time radio guys, my job ended up being to go out and shoot little videos that would suit the hosts, or even feature them. Now the stories were like, the lady who was married to her dog, and the couple who had a toaster that was possessed by Satan. They didn't buy my idea of following the Pat Robertson Presidential Campaign for the laughs. On January 5, 1988 *The Wilton North Report* was canceled. Many years later *The Daily Show* on *Comedy Central* would take the format and run with it.

I BEGAN TO NOTICE THE PAIN while I was at Fox, but I refused to search for the source while I was in production. But now that the show was canceled, I felt for the place with my fingers. I knew what it was. I continued in my state of knowing and denial for two more months and in March, the pain was such that I finally decided to share my predicament with Paul. I had no medical insurance, and that was my biggest problem. Paul and I did most of our talking when we were in the car. Now I was about to tell him. We pulled into the parking lot after a ride from Hollywood during which I was unable to bring up the subject. Now I figured I'd better say something fast, because he was opening the door to get out. I said, "Can we talk about something?"

"Of course."

"I can feel this tumor in my back near where it was last time and I'm afraid to see a doctor because I have no health insurance and no money for health insurance, and what if I go to a doctor and they call it a pre-existing condition and it won't be covered by any subsequent medical insurance?"

Paul was calm and sweet. He reassured me. He said he'd help me figure out what to do. We embraced in the car. Later the same day he came over and he showed me his Writers Guild health insurance plan, which would be going into effect on April 1st. It was all free and clear for himself and a spouse. He told me I could be his spouse and that would take care of all my medical. "We could get married. Not just for the medical," he said, "for real."

We agreed to keep our separate residences and get married at City Hall on April Fool's Day. Rita and my sister Linda came with us. Then we found a surgeon at Cedars Sinai, and I lived through it. This time they didn't have to saw off any of my bones, so it was only excruciatingly painful instead of deathly, agonizingly, unendingly painful.

Recovering again, standing in the unemployment line in Santa Monica, I thought I knew a little about pain and adversity. That is, until my next gig. Now I was a location director for a new daytime strip show (and by strip show, I mean five days a week) called *From the Heart*. How this one worked was that we re-enacted these horrendous heart-wrenching stories, using the actual people who lived them. I would go out with a script based on pre-interviews with the subjects. And then go into the editing room and hook together the story using the interviews and the re-enactments, then lay in some voice-over. I asked only questions that would elicit the exact response for the script. For example, at the interview I would ask: "As you were lying in the hospital, your spine shattered by a thief's bullet, what did the doctor say to you?"

The most wrenching story I directed began, "I never let the twins go out at night unless I drove them. Then one night I was sick and the worst nightmare a mother can have, came true." We cut to the re-enactment. Fern and her husband Virgil are asleep. The clock says four a.m. Piercing sound of telephone. Fern answers the phone. She freezes. The look on her face spells disaster. "Virgil, it's Kimani. He's been shot." Then the host of the show says, "Meet Fern Stamps. One year ago Fern and her husband Virgil had their worst nightmare come true as gang violence touched their close-knit and happy family with the random murder of one of their 15-year-old twin boys. How this family survived the tragedy is today's story on *From the Heart*."

On location at Fern and Virgil's home, I asked Kwame if he would play the part of his dead brother Kimani, and also the part of himself. I had them playing football with each other. Kwame had to play both parts. First throwing the football, and then as his dead brother, catching it. It was abstract. It had to be. It was only a matter of changing shirts.

Chapter Fifteen:
Ian

RITA XANTHOUDAKIS and Freddie Stafford got married at city hall where Paul and I did, so we knew which building and which room to take them to. In attendance were Freddie's teenaged daughter Justine, twenty-year-old son Ian, and our friend Stanley Young. Stanley drove us all to city hall in his big van. We blasted out "Goin' to the Chapel" on booming speakers and videotaped our jolly ride. Later, at Rita and Freddie's home in Mar Vista, we had a big joyous wedding party. Rita was a radiant bride in slinky red silk. Justine did a Spanish dance on the hardwood floor. Ian offered a toast.

Some months passed. Freddie got the call about one in the morning. "You'd better come here right away," his daughter Justine said. "Ian is dead." Freddie felt faint, dizzy, nauseated. "Rita!" he screamed. Rita knew something terrible had happened. Murder.

It was the worst ride to Glendale. Justine and her mom, Sharon, were there at the hospital, waiting. They had already looked at Ian, so Freddie went in alone. Ian was lying in the bed with a blue sheet over his head. A nurse came in and pulled it back some for Freddie to see. Freddie touched Ian. Freddie kissed his cheek. Only two days ago, Freddie and Rita had taken Ian out to dinner to celebrate his twenty-second birthday. Rita had given him a nice shirt. He was wearing it when he was shot. Freddie felt sick. He sank to his knees and wept. A doctor said some comforting words to Freddie. "He didn't suffer," he told Freddie. Then why was his body so twisted, so contorted, if not from pain, shock, surprise?

The sun didn't shine on the day of Ian's funeral. The night before, there was a sickly green aura around the mortuary where he was lying. Freddie and Rita stood in front of Ian in his casket. Pale Freddie. "He's so still." Freddie put his hands on Ian's. "Goodbye, son," he said. Rita reached over the top of the casket and brought the netted fabric over Ian's face like a bride. We left the mortuary and walked out onto South Central Avenue in the heart of Glendale. On the fence across the driveway, a group of gang members taunted the mourners. Wendy and Jody and I walked past them as we crossed the dark parking lot to our car. We pulled out onto South Central Avenue, and a police car fell in pace behind us. The police car followed us down the side street and pulled us over. Another police car approached us from the other direction. They turned their red lights on us. The cop told us he wanted to make sure we were okay. He said they had stopped two cars with guns in them that night, right around the mortuary. They told us a short cut home and we took it.

It was several weeks before they had the suspect in custody for the murder of Ian. His name was Johnny Sanchez. It was Johnny Sanchez who killed Ian. Rita found out. Although they had a sharp young prosecutor, Rita was the private detective who brought the case together. She knocked on the doors. Hugged the mothers. Asked for their help. Rita's information was that Johnny Sanchez had already shot two people 20 minutes before he killed Ian. He shot two boys sitting in a car. One of them died too. But they didn't think they'd be able to hold Johnny because they didn't have a positive identification. The witnesses wouldn't testify. They were afraid of Johnny Sanchez, who himself had the nerve to come over to Ian's friend Tom's house and threaten him. Tom was with Ian when he was killed. Rita was getting to be friends with Tom and his mother and his brother.

Rita asked Tom, Ian's friend, to please tell Freddie what happened that night, because Freddie needed to know. So Tom sat down with Freddie and told him. He said that on that night, he had called Ian to ask him to help a friend of theirs who was having a bad trip, PCP, maybe. And he called Ian because he knew Ian could calm the guy down and help him. So Ian came out and met them on the corner. Freddie imagined the scene. He knew every movement, every motion that Ian would have made. Of course he did. Ian was his son. He imagined the van pulling around the corner and the two young men getting out and confronting Ian and his friends. And all this only a few blocks from his home. One of them, Johnny Sanchez, pulled a gun.

186

"Where you from?" he said to Ian. Ian raised his hands and stepped back slightly. "I'm from nowhere," Ian said, putting his hand up and stepping back, afraid, but trying to calm the guy with the gun.

It was that instant, that Johnny Sanchez stuck his gun in Ian's stomach and pulled the trigger. Ian's stomach was blown through him. Then Sanchez pointed his gun at Ian's friend Tom. He tried to fire, but the gun jammed. Johnny tried and tried to fire his gun. Ian stood up holding his wound and tried to run but he fell. And Johnny Sanchez got in the van and drove away. And Tom came back and found Ian on the ground and ran to him and held Ian's head in his arms. And Ian said, "Why me?" and he died. And Tom closed Ian's eyes for him. And Johnny Sanchez was on the loose. He was on the loose the night we were at the mortuary. And maybe that was Johnny with the rest of his gang who shouted taunts at us as we drove away.

THE TRIAL OF JOHNNY SANCHEZ took two days. There was no jury. Both sides agreed to let the judge decide. The Sanchez family was there. Mr. and Mrs. Sanchez, Jimmy Sanchez, Johnny's twin brother, his sisters, and other relatives were there. They sat on one side of the aisle, and, Freddie and Rita, Paul and Jody and I sat on the other side. The energetic young prosecutor's proud mom and dad were in court to watch their son perform. They sat on our side, right in front of me. The prosecutor's dad thought he was presenting a good case. His mom thought he should have worn a suit instead of a sports jacket. He had a solid case against Johnny Sanchez, with a witness (Ian's friend Tom), who for sure was going to have to move far away from the 'hood, and fast, after the trial.

Johnny Sanchez had a flashy, not-very-well prepared lawyer, and the judge found Johnny guilty. Mrs. Sanchez broke down in sobs. So did we all. Mrs. Sanchez begged. "No, please no." Johnny was taken away. The sheriff's escort walked us down through the back steps and into a special elevator to make sure we didn't have to ride the elevators in the front lobby with the Sanchez family.

One month later Johnny Sanchez was sentenced, and Freddie read his victim's impact statement before the court:

"… Johnny Sanchez didn't know Ian, though it is ironic to think they must have seen each other in school, and maybe even played ball together in Little League or Pony League. Johnny Sanchez had to have known Ian and his companions weren't gang members. They didn't fit the 'profile', but he killed Ian anyway, and he tried to kill the other two boys as well. Hence Ian's last words, 'Why me?'

"For a long time I wanted to die myself. Up until last month, when Johnny Sanchez was finally convicted, I was filled with rage; rage in court when I was face to face with Ian's murderer, rage in the streets when I drove past Johnny Sanchez's brothers and his homeboys, and rage when I thought of Justine and Sharon, their lives now filled with so much agony and pain. At times my rage was so great I felt I would risk anything to avenge my son and my family. I prayed that Johnny Sanchez would be convicted and sent away forever so that I wouldn't have to satisfy my rage.

"Now, are there any circumstances that mitigate the guilt of Johnny Sanchez? I expect we shall hear a few during the customary plea for mercy. From what I can tell, Johnny Sanchez's parents are hard working, and law abiding, and have demonstrated their concern for him by their continued presence here at his side. Perhaps there is some sociological excuse for this crime, or a racial excuse for the verdict. Mr. Jacke [Johnny Sanchez's lawyer], you will recall, prior to exclaiming that his client was the victim of a miscarriage of justice and then storming out of the court, made some reference in his closing argument to 'Beverly Hills.' I have wondered why Mr. Jacke felt it necessary to covertly insert the notion of class or racial exclusivity into these proceedings. Perhaps he believes that this crime, or this verdict, is the fruit of social distinctions?

"Well, I would like to state here, for the record, we are not from Beverly Hills. I drive an 8-year-old domestic automobile, live in a rented apartment, and work 56 hours a week over a hot machine. Besides, what does any of that have to do with murder? The fact is, Johnny Sanchez chose of his own free will to take the life of a fellow human being. We who survive must suffer the consequences of Johnny Sanchez's choices, and so must he.

188

"Johnny Sanchez shows no sign of remorse. His tears over the verdict were merely the result of this reflecting on the prospect before him. Furthermore, there are a number of principles in this case—other members of the 'Notorious 187 Crew'—who have gotten off free. So be it. As for Johnny Sanchez, the shooter, he has committed the severest crime that man can commit. Let the severest penalty be applied. Let the penalty here be a message to all those gangbangers in Frogtown, Toonerville, and the Avenues gangs who will surely hear of it. And let that message be this: We are a society ruled by law, and the price for life is life."

Chapter Sixteen:
The Nineties

Roll over, Mike Wallace, and tell Morley Safer the news: *The 90s* is here, and it stands in relation to traditional TV magazine shows like *60 Minutes* and *20/20,* as Chuck Berry did to Bing Crosby.
—*Minneapolis StarTribune*

WHEN TOM WEINBERG WENT TO Miami Beach for TVTV in 1972 to pull the production together for the coverage of the political conventions, he earned himself a nickname, "Score." For years we all called him Score, because in just a few days he had gone to Miami, arranged for the rental of the big house on the canals, and gotten press credentials for thirty of us for the Democratic National Convention. By the time the 1990s came around, Tom had produced hundreds of programs, mostly for public television in Chicago, and had developed a long and warm relationship with Bill Kirby of the MacArthur Foundation. Tom got Bill Kirby excited about the concept of an alternative TV network delivered via satellite. So now it seemed the MacArthur Foundation was going to fund *The 90s.* Tom, as the Executive Producer of *The 90s* would be using the weekly hour as an example of what the primetime program block might look like.

I was always amazed when anything having to do with video worked out right, but it now appeared that this concept, this network, this activist, co-operative, democratic, independent, global, local, video network was beginning again. This time it would originate in Chicago.

During the first season, *The 90s* was seen in only a few markets, mostly on public television usually late at night. Then, the second season, we were on 120 more public TV stations, and some in prime time.

As head of west coast operations, I hired my friend and fellow video shooter Judith Binder to work on the show with me. Judith was a happy and energetic person. Nothing was ever a problem for Judith. She expected things, and they came, like parking spots. Not that she would take handicapped spots, but red lines she considered "iffy." Judith would lunge with jolly gusto for the biggest piece of cake on the plate then laugh resoundingly and triumphantly when she got it. She already had a load of outrageous videotapes she had shot with several L.A. artists. People seemed to naturally open up to Judith. They showed her things. For example, the beautiful young artist, who upon meeting Judith, took her directly into the ladies room, hopped up on the sink and with her fingers spread herself apart to show her clit-piercing to the camera.

Immediately, Judith and I were working, shooting and editing and coordinating assignments. Tom supplied us with a beautiful brand new Sony editing system, which we installed in the downstairs bedroom of the house on Clubhouse Avenue. We were doing theme shows.

The main office of *The 90s* in Chicago sent a list of the show themes and deadlines to video journalists around the globe. TV, Culture, Drugs, Wars, Architecture & Design, Earth & the Environment, Relationships & Sexuality, Love & Marriage, Kids, Schools & Learning, Fun & Games, Invasions & Revolutions, Money ... there was no end to the possibilities. And each video journalist had a unique approach to the subject. Fascinating and unpredictable material arrived from all over. Our systems were working smoothly and we were putting out fabulous media product.

Our field producer in Los Angeles was Jody Procter, a true Renaissance man. From a long line of Boston Procters, he had come to California for the Summer of Love and by now had funneled his gush of thoughts and ideas and words into twelve unpublished novels. Now he was writing this thirteenth novel about a guy who had written twelve unpublished novels. In the seventies, Jody Procter was a performance artist with Doug Hall. They called themselves *T.R. Uthco*. They collaborated on a lot of projects with *Ant Farm,* including "The Eternal Frame," a re-enactment of the assassination of John F. Kennedy, video-taped on location in Dallas.

Now, along with writing novels, rollerblading and courting despair, Jody was researching all the themes for *The 90s,* and setting up production shoots. First we went down to San Diego where Habitat for Humanity was building 26 houses for needy families. Jody Procter took all of his carpentry tools along with him and began raising the walls of a couple of houses, eventually working right next to former president Jimmy Carter. Most media people left the site after the morning press conference, but we stayed until the sun went down so Jody could finish the day's building. "Where are ya from," Jimmy Carter asked Jody. "I'm originally from Boston but I came to California for the Summer of Love," Jody replied. "Hand me that hammer," said the President.

Jody Procter also took us on a personal video tour of the Los Angeles city dump. We drove up there together on a grey day that threatened rain. The scale was huge at the Los Angeles city dump. It was a staggering expanse of garbage. White gulls soared above us. Thunderheads gathered above the silver mist. Our guide Jody Procter had clearly been to the dump before. He knew his way around the dump like the artist that he was. As we walked along the ridge, he said to the camera, "I wonder if we can climb up to the periphery for the view." We scrambled up to the rise and there it was. It was garbage from horizon to horizon. It was magnificent.

"Oh, yeah! This is great." Jody Procter took a deep, satisfied breath. "This is really just standing on garbage mountain. And the crows are down there," he said pointing below us, "and over there— the freeway." The camera lingered on the scene. "And over there is all Bob Hope's land." We strolled for a while when Jody spotted a discarded blue velveteen parlor chair in the midst of the garbage and debris. He took a seat in it, and reminisced for the camera.

"When I come to the dump, I always look for things like people's desk drawers, and photographs. I used to look for photographs and then I realized that there were dumpsters outside of photo labs which are probably loaded with treasures.

"And one day, I was in San Francisco, and I stopped at my local photo lab dumpster and I found all these photographs of Jonestown, of these dead bodies. They were photographs taken by a TV cameraman who had flown in with the first group of people to look at the dead bodies. And I knew that, because I had seen him on the news the night before. I had about sixty of these photographs and I took them home, and then I had this feeling that the photographs had been that close to the negatives and that the negatives had actually been at Jonestown and that somehow they had been contaminated and I kept washing my hands all night long. Oh! Here comes the bulldozer!"

Jody rose from the blue chair and moved out of the way. We watched as the blue divan and matching armchairs got turned over and buried. Gazing at the bulldozer, Jody said, "Look at the scoop on that thing!" He then turned his attention to the ground and said, "But it's these kinds of things, like this 'Sorry' card." He flicked the game card away through his fingers. "Sorry," he said. "Like see here? This is what I mean. I think this is somebody's office file. Oh, look! Here are some tools. This was a building project. Look. Here's a perfectly good shoe," referring to a black boot with a buckle across the front. Jody shook his head. "Talk about the Sixties! And look, there's a whole roof. That can be somebody's house."

Nothing at the dump went unappreciated by Jody Procter. From the noble old five-piece living room set, to the dozens of tires being dumped out of a pickup truck. "You could build an entire house out of those tires. They would in Mexico."

IT WAS 1991 AND THE GULF WAR had begun. Jody Procter and I went over to Howard Rosenberg's house to watch TV with him. Howard Rosenberg was the television critic for the *Los Angeles Times* and he loved his job. He explained that writing about television meant you were writing about every subject, which, he posed, made him a decathlete among critics.

We found him at his desk, wearing a sweatshirt and shorts. Because he was on the phone when we got there, the four television sets in front of him were muted. He didn't mind at all that I left the camera running while he was talking to David Fanning of *Frontline*. When he got off the phone he said, *"Frontline* is one of the few places on public television that you can find anything with any balls."

We settled down with the remote control and started looking through the channels. I asked him about the shopping channels. Howard said, "Shopping channels! They're a real kick. I find myself watching them a lot." He loved Kathy Levin over on QVC. "She's incredible, she's amazing. She can sell anything. Do you know her? Kathy is like in another realm!"

Of course we ended up watching CNN and Howard said, "The amazing thing about this war coverage on CNN is that you have the feeling you can go to bed at night, and while you're sleeping, there's something on CNN that's live that's about the war. That war is going on live on CNN and you're sleeping in your bed. It's incredible." Howard flicked the remote.

"Here's one of my favorite channels. TBN, Trinity Broadcasting Network. TBN is just fascinating. And you can watch TBN for just about anything," he said, "because they're very topical, they're right on. And they'll talk to you about the war. I love to watch *Jews for Jesus*. That's one of my favorites, and some of the things they do are very compelling and very eloquent. It depends on your religious point of view, of course, because some of them are clearly propagandistic and full of proselytizing, but it's a fascinating world."

Howard continued, "Oh! *The Power Team*. Those are the guys who break the bats. Oh, he's amazing. Breaking bats for God. That's what I love."

"What do you think makes it so compelling?"

"Well, you know, it's interesting. They'll interpret the world according to Biblical scripture. It's really fascinating." We watched for awhile, then Howard began channel surfing again.

"It really is a drug, and it is addictive," he said. "And it's so easy because it requires very little on your part. You're a passive observer."

"But you're not a passive observer," I reminded him. "You're a television critic."

"In terms of being a television critic, if I were to pontificate, I would say that the purpose of my job is to elevate critical awareness. Just to get people to think about the television they watch." Howard flipped back to CNN at every opportunity because the war was on.

There it was. It had its own logo. *The Gulf War.* Howard said, "You see the war on television, but you do not see the war on television. I've seen people on television die before my eyes, and the scariest part is not so much seeing it. The scariest part is seeing it and not feeling anything."

In New York, Skip was shooting video outside the ABC Television Headquarters. A huge raucous demonstration was taking place, protesting the network's coverage of the Gulf War. People shaking their fists at the network headquarters and shouting "Shame! Shame!" Peter Jennings, who had stepped outside the studio to have a firsthand look at the scene, was instantly surrounded by protesters, and questioned about the networks' failure to report the war accurately and the lack of anti-war news. Someone in the crowd shouted to Jennings, "What are you doing here?" Jennings said he was trying to cover the story. "Accurately?" asked a woman who was wearing a papier-mâché television set around her head, with her face poking through the screen. Jennings replied, "I'll let you be the judge of that."

"You're not doing a very good job so far," she told him. "You'd never know there was an antiwar movement from watching the news!"

Betty Aberlin—who played the part of Lady Aberlin on *Mister Rogers' Neighborhood* was among the protesters outside ABC. "When people over the years ask what Mr. Rogers is about, I joke and say he's kind of like the flip side of Big Brother. And when I see our president George Bush [the first] playing Mr. Rogers with his talk of the 'darnedest search and destroy mission,' I must say the resemblance is a little too close for comfort." Behind her the protesters chanted to the network, "Shame, Shame! Tell the truth." Poet Allen Ginsberg tipped his Uncle Sam's hat to the camera on his way to the subway.

IN LOS ANGELES, PETER STRANGER, top executive at the Della Femina McNamee Advertising Agency, could not have been more charming and engaging to me. "I'm in charge of the west coast office of Della Femina McNamee, which is a New York-based company, which is again a part of a big European conglomerate," he beamed. "We're owned by EuroCom, the number one advertising network in Europe. In this office our biggest account is Joe Isuzu. We've had that account for ten years."

195

I asked him about their strategy for the Joe Isuzu campaign, which was extremely successful.

"I'm not sure if this was genius or dumb luck, but when we developed Joe Isuzu, we tapped into the nation's consciousness. There was a mood going on at the time, it was the Eighties, Wall Street was booming, 26-year-olds were earning $400,000 a year. It was sell, sell, sell and buy, buy, buy. And Joe Isuzu was a liar. But the interesting thing is that Joe Isuzu was the most honest car salesman out there, because he was lying. Because he was a parody, the truth was always there. And what he did was, he mocked the chest-beating that was coming from the standard auto manufacturer. Joe Isuzu came along and he acknowledged the intelligence of the viewer and … people fell in love with him. He was adored, he became fashionable. The word 'Joe Isuzu' has been used by two presidents and one presidential aspirant in network speeches. Even Lee Iacocca, in a network television commercial that ran for three months, said, 'And I'm no Joe Isuzu.' I couldn't believe it. It was wonderful! Here was the president and chairman of Chrysler, using the name Isuzu in one of his commercials."

"What is your strategy for buying television time to play the commercials?"

"There is a real science in buying time. The demographics of the audience that watches TV have been studied and dissected both in terms of age, sex, household income, race, but also in terms of psychographics. What types of people are watching certain types of programming? So now we are in a position of knowing exactly who is watching *The Simpsons,* and who is watching football. As an example, if you're a brokerage house and you identify that you want to bring professional women into your business (I'm just making this up), but you want women with $50,000-plus in household income. You need women who are psychographically in tune with investment, and it has become a science on how to read them."

BACK IN THE EDITING ROOM in Venice, Judith and I searched for segues to hook the media show together. We decided to get some footage of changing channels on a TV screen. We set up and turned on the TV and,

196

as we began changing the channels, suddenly every channel on the television set was showing the same scene. The pictures were coming from Israel, where reporters were frantically putting on gas masks with an ear out for the whistling sound of the scud missiles from Saddam Hussein. Every channel was showing the same pictures and telling the same story. Except QVC, the shopping channel, where Kathy Levin was actually selling the U.S. flag for the bargain price of $10. Kathy, where's your gas mask? Come on, get with the program, girl!

Chapter Seventeen:
Camnet,
the Camcorder Network

"They have toured the Nixon Library, hung out with anti-nuke protesters in the Nevada desert, and aired previously unseen outtakes from Elvis's 1968 comeback special. They have caught up with writer Paul Bowles in Tangiers and journeyed to Amsterdam to cover *High Times* magazine's official 1994 Cannabis Cup, a smoke-out where so much dope was consumed that one gets a contact high just watching the footage."

—Wired Magazine

JOHN SCHWARTZ WAS a "spectrum junkie," always searching for un-owned television frequencies that hadn't been claimed by anyone. And he found one. It was an allocation for a noncommercial television station in Colorado that had never been issued by the FCC. It was licensed to somewhere between Denver and Boulder and it didn't exist. John filed all the papers and figured out how to get the station and license for KBDI (later known as The Beedy Eye). There were some major Washington hassles, but he managed to get control of the frequency and KBDI television was set to go. John was set to broadcast but he had no programming. So he called Tom Weinberg in Chicago. On the day before the launch John went to Chicago, and he and Tom searched through hundreds of Tom's old videotapes packed them up and they got on a plane to Colorado. They had enough video to do programming for about two weeks straight, or for eight weekends. So there it was.

Then John began looking at microwave TV. There were two kinds of microwave TV—the commercial, used for pay-TV, and the noncommercial, used by schools and churches and for educational purposes. Of course, the commercial channels were much more valuable. John and Tom became partners and went after and secured licenses in several cities for these noncommercial microwave channels known as "ITFS" for "instructional television fixed station."

The nonprofit they started was called the Instructional Telecommunications Foundation (ITF). The first deal they made was in Philadelphia where they leased their channels for more than $100,000 and were able to use that money to help pay the initial costs for *The 90s*. All along, Tom and John saw this ITF and channel-leasing thing as a way to pay for their programming. They were committed to new forms and new distribution and using the money they got to pay for independent programming.

When a deal came along for leasing the channels for "wireless cable" in the Denver area, John set up the Denver local ITF foundation without Tom and began dealing with the people at TCI, John Malone's Telecommunications, Inc. At that time TCI was in the process of upgrading their systems in places like Baltimore and California. They wanted John's excess capacity, so the deal was, instead of taking cash from TCI, John worked it out that they would supply a leased channel on each of those systems, which John would then program. The deal was good for three years.

So now John had eight channels in eight cities. Eight big cities, like Detroit and Baltimore and Los Angeles. Being a thrifty sort, John figured out how to run his itinerant network on the cheap by playing only two hours of programming a week on a continuous loop. He was taking two hours of *The 90s* a week and playing them over and over continuously, twenty-four hours a day. He bought two video decks for each of the eight studio locations. When one deck begins to rewind, it triggers the other to play. He hired a kid in each city to come in once a week and change the cassettes.

Although the channel was playing the same two hours twenty-four hours a day, it was working out because everyone who received cable saw *The 90s* channel, if only when channel-surfing. And if viewers hadn't seen it yet that week they always stopped to watch. It stood out instantly from the other channels. It looked different. *The 90s* channel was pretty cheesy, but it was definitely on the dial.

When *The 90s* show was canceled by PBS, that meant there would be no more programming for *The 90s* channel. So there was John Schwartz with eight channels and no programming. Judith and I still had the editing equipment and all of our systems working and we thought we could generate two hours a week. It wouldn't cost us much to put out two hours of new video a week as long as Tom let us keep the editing equipment. Tom was generous to let us keep the equipment for the duration of our contract with John. So, *CamNet, The Camcorder Network,* was born. All our video journalists from The 90s were up for it.

The deal we made with John Schwartz was that for the last two weeks of each month, only *CamNet* would be seen on *The 90s* channel in all eight cities. *CamNet.* Twenty-four hours a day. I signed a nine-month contract with John to deliver four hours of program per month which would play the last two weeks of each month. We gave them the programs for free, and they gave us back eight minutes per hour which we could sell to advertisers. So we tried it. We had nine months to make CamNet a household word.

CAMNET WAS NOW THE NEW HOME of the great video journalist and ecological warrior, Jay April. Jay had been a student of ours at Goddard College and had subsequently worked in the television industry and understood about ad availabilities, and affidavits, and all the business savvy we would need to start dealing with advertisers. And, Jay was a nice guy with an engaging personality, open and smiling. People liked to talk to his camera. He was perfect in every way except for one thing. The one thing about Jay was that he was always late. I'm not talking a half-hour once in awhile. I'm talking about days, sometimes weeks. He would just disappear. He always had a good excuse, though. "There's a hole in the ozone, Nancy. Isn't that more important?" But when he did show up, Jay invariably had something to show us. Jay would blow in with a videotape he made with Adam Trombly, the physicist who founded Project Earth with Buckminster Fuller. There was Adam, sitting on a porch swing in front of his home in Colorado, talking about

Anthrax and TB in the Persian Gulf. Trombly explained to Jay why no veteran of the Gulf War can give blood. "There were biological lines all along Saddam Hussein's border," he said. "When we penetrated the lines, we blew the biological lines up. There was a short-acting retrovirus that was created in Maryland by former government employees who formed a biological warfare company, and they sold it to Saddam Hussein. We, the American Congress, the American people, allowed the sale of biological weapons to Saddam Hussein because he was our friend, right?" Jay always came back with startling information.

Jay was livid, almost sputtering when he heard the news. A species had become extinct a few miles south of us in Palos Verdes. Although Jay was furious, his voice was friendly and engaging from behind his camera when he arrived at the location.

"Are you aware that this park is the last known habitat of the Palos Verdes blue butterfly?" he asked a young mother pushing a baby carriage.

"No, I'm not. That's interesting," she said, smiling.

"Yeah. They bulldozed the last known habitat to build this park."

"Oh, thanks for the information," the woman nodded. Jay tried talking to a couple watching a softball game from a row of bleachers.

"And there are no more?" asked the woman, when Jay told them that the butterflies were now extinct.

"There are no more," Jay told her sadly. "As a matter of fact, in 1984, the mayor of Palos Verdes violated the Endangered Species Act and built this park."

"Is this park now an endangered species?" she inquired.

"No. It's too late now. The butterfly is extinct."

"Sorry to hear that."

"If that issue was before the voters today, let's say, you know, butterfly versus baseball, what do you think would happen?" Jay asked the couple.

This time, the man answered. "I don't think its butterfly versus baseball, I think its butterfly versus the people who live in this area. I think it's unfortunate that there are species that are being lost, but I don't think we can keep every species there is."

"It's called evolution!" the woman added. This drove Jay nuts. He turned, camera rolling and stomped directly out onto the ball field and stood next to the center fielder during play. "You know, you're playing on what used to be the habitat of the Palos Verdes blue butterfly."

"Yeah?" said the ballplayer.

"Yeah," said Jay, "they went extinct because they built this park."

"No kidding," said the ballplayer.

"Yeah," said Jay, and laughed dejectedly. "Another sacrifice for baseball."

The ballplayer caught a grounder and threw it to first base. "Nice play," said Jay.

As Jay was leaving, the man sitting in the bleachers added one more thing. "I think species sort of just come and go," he said. And the woman chimed in, "But baseball is forever." They both laughed their cigarette-laughs into Jay's camera. "Now the park is here," the man continued, "and I think people have more appreciation for the park than they would have for butterflies."

Jay had taken on a painful mission but he was determined to save the earth. Jay was on the front lines with Earth First, and the Rainforest Action Network, and Greenpeace. So it was Jay, our prize video journalist, who turned out to be the big story when *CamNet* was featured in the *Wall Street Journal*.

LOS ANGELES—CAMERAMAN JAY APRIL sinks ankle-deep into a three-story-high compost heap, believed to be the largest in the Western world, and trains his camcorder on the heap's long-haired, bearded owner, who speaks only in rhyme ...

There we were. July 30, 1992 on the front page of the Market-place section of the *Wall Street Journal*. With those ink drawings they have. One of me and one of Judith. We were each holding a camcorder. They pulled a quote from me and put it in a box next to my picture: "Process is product. I have a high tolerance for raw tape."

Mark Robichaux told us right off that he was the youngest reporter at the *Wall Street Journal* and proud of it. A friend of his saw

CamNet on his cable system and told Mark he ought to do a story about it. Mark pitched it to his editor and they actually sent him out to Venice.

Mark came to Venice to spend a week with *CamNet*. He arrived wearing a blazer, a white shirt and a tie. He had gotten lost trying to find the house on Clubhouse Avenue. Judith had to go out to Pacific Avenue and wave him in. He was very polite. By the end of the week Mark was wearing a work shirt, jeans, and his boots were dusty and crusted with compost. He was rosy-cheeked and relaxed. One of the best scenes in Jay's video at Zeke's Heap, the world's largest compost pile in Altadena, was when he asked Mark from the *Wall Street Journal* to put his hand inside a scooped out portion of the steaming seventeen-foot-high compost pile. Mark reached into the rich dark hole. He was in up to his elbow when he turned to the camera and nodded appreciatively. "That's one hot hole!"

"Think of television as food," Jay told the *Wall Street Journal*. "We've been eating the same meat and potatoes served up by the networks since the 1950s. Now people are cooking more exotic dishes at home." Mark described Jay as a "militant environmentalist who slept in a giant green tent in his living room." That was Jay.

Now, since we had appeared in the *Wall Street Journal*, *CamNet* was instantly catapulted onto the media food chain. We were inundated by the press. It's amazing how powerful the *Wall Street Journal* is. *TV Guide* picked up the story in November, calling us "America's first all-camcorder channel, showing life on the fringe." In *Rolling Stone* in December, Jon Katz wrote, "The peoples' news will make journalists out of all of us and plug us back into the political system in ways that would have had the radicals who founded the nation's media dancing in their cobbled streets." Yes, we had a model working, but if you pulled back the curtain on this little TV network, there was simply Judith and me up to our knees in video cassettes.

BABARA BROWNELL, MOTHER, ACTRESS, teacher, singer, housewife, and active citizen, lived in North Hollywood and got *The 90s* Channel on Channel 18. Barbara's teenage kids turned her on to *CamNet*. She watched one show, went out and bought a camcorder and called us to get some instruction. It took a month or so before she began to catch on to the shooting style. "Tell the story by showing it to us," Judith advised. And Barbara did. She took her camera everywhere. Since she volunteered her time at the food pantry of a local church, she met a lot of people who were in dire circumstances and consequently recorded a true and honest glimpse of modern living in the San Fernando Valley. Barbara videotaped Anna, who lived in her van with her two young sons. "It cost me all my money," Anna told her, speaking of her vehicle. "I worked for six years and the company I worked for changed hands so I didn't have a job." She pulled open the door to her van with pride. "There's a little auto-potty in there and a tiny sink, too."

"So you lost your job?" said Barbara.

"Yeah, and I lost my big house. My whole philosophy is changed now, and we live better in a way now than we did before. The kids get to go play and they're still secure. Kids are born gypsies." Brave Anna smiled optimistically at Barbara's camera.

Judith was off to spend the day with The Nude Handyman. She hadn't met him yet but she had spoken to him on the phone. About The Nude Handyman, not everyone may want his services, but if you do and you are a lady (Ladies Only), The Nude Handyman will come to your house, strip down to only a gold chain and sun glasses and re-do the caulking around your sink, if that's what you need. Judith made a plan to meet The Nude Handyman on the corner across from Canter's Deli on Fairfax, and then go with him in his car to his job. "You'll recognize me. I'll have the camcorder," she told him.

When she arrived on the corner, she saw a man a few feet away and he gave her a little wave and a nod. He walked up to her and Judith gave him her best smile and said, "Hi. Are you my Nude Handyman?" He wasn't. When the handyman did show up, Judith climbed into his car. The handyman's two clients that day were given the extra option of oiling him up before he began working on their kitchen pipes. They did. Then they watched his ass from the breakfast room table while they snacked on fruit. "This is great, isn't it Sally?"

BY THE SUMMER OF 1992, Judith and I were filling our ad minutes with public service announcements but still wanted to have some interesting coverage of the coming political elections, and we needed to deliver four hours of video each month to *The 90s* Channel.

Our good fortune, Beth Lapides! An astute and outrageous standup comic/commentator/artist, Beth was going to New York anyway to launch her new media campaign for the job of First Lady. "Pick her and pay her," was Beth's campaign slogan. Good idea. She was going to campaign for the position of First Lady using the Clinton convention as a backdrop.

It was Bill Clinton's convention all the way and Beth was done up for the event. Her hair, in a very high French twist, was two-toned. It was platinum blonde in a modified Woody Woodpecker in the front, and a black twist in the back. She had seams up the back of her opera hose, and a keen eye on the proceedings. In the din and the frenzy, Beth moved in closer to the camera, speaking confidentially and intimately in a low voice. "I feel like I need to be close because I have some personal things to say."

Our audience of *CamNet*ians leaned closer to the screen when Beth confided in them. "I want to be the right distance for this because it's overwhelmingly alienating inside the hall right now," she said. "People cheering about God and saving America, and I just feel very lonely here at this convention. There's a lot of delegates, there's a lot of balloons, it's like one of those birthday parties you went to when you were a kid and everyone was having such a good time and why do you feel so lonely? It's very, very kind of mass, kind of, 'What about people who are different?'

"We're lionizing Clinton, just as we are Mario Cuomo here tonight, who, may I point out, brought up God many times in his keynote speech. You know, Church and State, Church and State, let's remember they must be separate for very good reasons. I actually am for some kind of spirituality in schools but you can't have God because, you know, what about the people who believe in the Goddess? And then at that point, what about the secular humanists? So, you gotta pray to the *New York Times* also. And so at that point why not just throw in

Elvis? You want to be right but you don't want to be holier than thou."
Beth walked toward the concession stand.

"There's a lot of bad food here. See that Bud sign? There's just a lot of really bad food. There are a lot of hot dogs. The smell of sauerkraut in this place is overwhelming. You don't realize when you see it on TV how bad the smell is. We're standing here next to Beverage Express but there is nothing healthy to eat here.

"You can get lost in this place, it's a maze, you get hungry, you get thirsty and the food is awful and I think that very much symbolizes how hungry Americans are for some real food. How hungry I am now for something nutritious to eat is how hungry America is for something good. And I wanna have hope that Clinton can do it, but right now in this hall I am not feeling that is so true."

Poet/performance-artist/tattoo-enthusiast Nicole Panter took the CamNet camcorder to Houston for the George Bush Republican National Convention in '92. Nicole brought back two videos that you didn't see on the networks. The first was an interview with a thirteen-year-old boy who was attending the convention with his delegate parents. Nicole cornered the kid in a stairwell in the hotel and interviewed him. The kid had his hand on the doorknob the whole time he spoke.

"Can you explain what 'family values' are?"

"Oh." (He laughs a little because he knows Republicans are talking a lot about family values) "Well, a family value is like, say, your dad died and he had a ring. And he passed it on to you, and then you passed it on to your kid. That would be a family value." With this, the kid makes a speedy exit down the stairwell.

Outside of the Astrodome, Nicole found a few dozen pale teens gathered, holding signs that said QUEER YOUTH EXIST. GET USED TO IT! A thin boy with a small voice took the megaphone and addressed the crowd.

"Hello, um, I'm Tommy," he said, slowly gaining his confidence, "I'd like to address a few issues, first of which is the idea of abstinent teenagers. I had sex when I was in high school and it was good and I liked it. And we're saying to the people who say that teenagers have to have abstinence, 'Fuck you,' because it's fine that we have sex and it's good. (Applause) Secondly I want to address the topic of harassment in high school. In high school I was harassed daily. I got bashed in high school in the locker room. Teachers used to call me 'faggot' and no one was doing anything about it. The issues of gay and lesbian youth are completely ignored by teachers in high school and it's absolutely disgusting. Finally, I want to talk about the pigs in the Astrodome who continue to ignore this issue and to pretend that queer youth like me do not exist. In fact they know we exist but they'd rather we not, therefore they want to kill us, and the way that they're doing it is by saying that we shouldn't have safer sex education, that we shouldn't have positive role models. The president of the United States should stand up and say, 'Bashing gays and lesbian youth is wrong.' He won't say that. Therefore he is complicit and he is responsible for it. Fuck off, George Bush," Tommy concluded sweetly, as he raised his pale fist in the air.

MIKE RUPPERT ALWAYS spelled his name after he said it. R-U-P-P-E-R-T. That way the press would get it right. He was over-the-top with confidence and seemed to know everything about the 1992 Ross Perot campaign in Los Angeles. Here at the first big regional meeting at a hotel on the Wilshire corridor, the Perot people were on fire with enthusiasm. I asked Mike Ruppert about his own background.

"I was an LAPD narcotics detective. I ran across some CIA activity in terms of the drug trade years ago, and that's how I met Ross. So I'm experienced in dirty tricks of sorts and we know the Republicans have pulled out the stops in New York to keep us off the ballot." Turned out Mike Ruppert was working day and night on the Ross Perot campaign. "I studied Locke, Voltaire, Jefferson, Hamilton, all the founding fathers, and if it's true that all power comes from the people, all we have to do is remember that and nothing can stop us."

"Really? All the power comes from the people?" I asked.

"It's either true or it isn't," Mike said. "Remember what Yamamoto said after he bombed Pearl Harbor?"

"No."

"Yamamoto said, I'm afraid we have awakened a sleeping giant.'

207

Well, we're awakening again because conditions are intolerable and all that's happening with the Democrats and Republicans is that they are rearranging the deck chairs on the *Titanic*. Unless we make a fundamental change, of course, the ship is going down."

THE PEROT PEOPLE WERE FUN and easy to videotape. They were sincere, friendly, open, and many of them, unlike Mike Ruppert, were totally naive politically. The Perot people were beginners and were sharing their ideas about how to get their candidate elected. Bella was well into her sixties and spangled in red white and blue with a sequin-billed cap that said Perot on it. "… and go find the women's groups," she advised. "They have nothing to do. They'll talk about it with you."

Bill, a Vietnam veteran from Santa Clarita, said, "If you blitz your area with tables, everybody will see them. The people in California shop every day. So go to the stores and catch them." An oldster next to him chimed in, "And when you put that bumper sticker in the back window of your car, put your telephone number, too. I've gotten a flood of calls."

If there is a word for what the Perot people had, it was gusto. Old folks with gusto. I asked one of the volunteers about his political background. He said, "I've been almost everything. Once I was with the John Birch Society and then I joined the ACLU. I liked them both. I was a Democrat a few years ago, but with Jimmy Carter I couldn't tell where he stood."

"What about Ross Perot? Do you know where he stands?"

"I know where the candidates stand that I don't like. I don't know what Mr. Perot really is completely all about but that's okay. He's still good enough for me. I know it's an odd way to do it, but we're desperate."

An African American man in a Ross Perot T-shirt told me he had been "monitoring" Perot for ten years. He told me he sent Perot his last $5 when he heard he was going to run.

At the exact moment that Ross Perot suddenly dropped out of the presidential race, Barbara Brownell happened to be at the San Fernando Valley headquarters with her camcorder. Dumbstruck volunteers were standing agape, staring at the small television set propped on a folding chair. They watched him gesticulate. Macho men were crying real tears as Barbara walked with her camcorder through the storefront in Sherman Oaks. On a television set in the reception area, Ross Perot was squawking at them. This was all happening simultaneously with the Democratic convention in New York. Bill Clinton was being nominated on half of the screen while on the other half there was Ross Perot live, speaking to his stunned faithful. "Now that the Democratic party has revitalized itself, I have concluded we cannot win in November, and that the election will be decided in the House of Representatives. So, to the volunteers, I'll always look back at this with the fondest memories."

Estelle, a Sherman Oaks volunteer, shook her head unbelievingly. Even though Estelle was a grandmother, this was her first political campaign. She loved Ross and was willing to work continuously to get him elected and so were her girlfriends. She had never been so involved and excited. Now she was devastated. "The only thing I can think of is that maybe his family was threatened or then maybe it just might be another maneuver in the campaign. He can't mean he wants us to stop," reasoned Estelle. Barbara commiserated with her from behind the camera and then threaded her way through the chaotic crowd of dazed workers and television crews, and into the back office.

Mike Ruppert was at the desk, surrounded by co-workers, and his eyes were beginning to well up. Mike looked into Barbara's camera as she came up to him. "Film at eleven?" he asked her sadly and sardonically. Then he said, "Mike Ruppert, R-U-P-P-E-R-T, former press liaison for the Los Angeles County Perot Petition Committee."

"Are you feeling particularly disillusioned this morning?" Barbara asked.

"How could I not? If any volunteer who's put in sixty to seventy hours seven days a week can tell you they aren't crushed, aren't heartbroken, aren't angry, then they're still in shock."

"Did you have any hint that this was going to happen?"

"The only things we knew were that those of us in key positions

209

in the campaign had been seeing things for the past five or six weeks that did not make sense. They just didn't get the fact that Dallas [Perot's Headquarters] was still taking this to be a headlong effort. The dissatisfaction in this office, I mean, we've taken calls in this office from Oklahoma, Colorado, New York, Houston, people saying 'What's going on?' It just didn't make sense. Some volunteers were locked out of offices. Key promotional plans were not being followed through with. Enormous opportunities were just dropping into a dark hole."

Mike looked totally exhausted. His sadness was palpable. "My personal feeling is that … ." He stopped, and holding back his tears, he swallowed. "My personal feeling is that there could have been a better way to tell so many people who have worked so hard that this was not gonna fly. There are a lot of people who are walking out of here, and I hope Dallas (Perot headquarters) is watching, I hope Dallas is listening, there are a lot of people who won't get on camera, who won't get quoted, who are out smashing trash cans, who are crying, who are angry and hurt, who feel betrayed."

Perot still took nineteen percent of the votes, handing the election to Bill Clinton on a platter.

NOW THAT THE ELECTIONS WERE OVER and the results were in, we all began to adjust to a new administration. We had a new young president. Our president. Surely happy days were finally here again.

"Hey, an omen. Look. A fan letter for *CamNet*." Judith opened the letter, read it and gasped. Then she began laughing hysterically. "It's from one of our viewers! Listen to this," she said, and read aloud to me.

To Whom it May or May Not Concern:

I was appalled at your recent airing the week of August 10th here in Scottsdale, Arizona, of a young woman performing an abortion while perched on a billboard platform. I find this to be totally unacceptable viewing and barbaric photojournalism. Your station is a disgrace to those in the industry who try to convey tasteful coverage on many diverse subjects. I believe that you have gone beyond the boundaries of decency and hope that others will respond to this clarion call for sanity to return to the media. You have lost on both counts. Although my community is forced because of leased public access space to presently carry your station, I look forward to its removal at a future date.

Outraged,

Carolyn C. Lagrand

Scottsdale, AZ

The letter was copied to the mayor of Scottsdale and the general manager of TCI Cable. The videotape in question, to me as the program editor, was rich in culture, charm, humor and tension. First you see a wide shot of upper Broadway in Manhattan. Pan up above the street to a huge billboard with an image of a wire hanger on it. Then you see a small figure of a woman climbing down a metal ladder from the roof of the building. She edges herself along the ledge in front of the billboard several stories up, and nude under her red silk kimono which is flapping in the wind. A few pedestrians on the street stop and look up. As they stare at her, she whips off her robe, and standing naked, she takes a wire hanger and simulates the act of pushing it up inside her, and a huge gush of simulated blood splashes out onto the billboard behind her and onto the street below as she screams. It's over in a flash. A few seconds.

Dave Channon, from behind the camcorder, talked to the people on the street the moment the act was over, and it was clear that no one really knew what it was about. Dave prompted them: "A hanger? And blood? What do you think that means?" A man on the street said, "It's an abortion thing, right?" The woman next to him said, "With a hanger? They still do that? Because they can go over to the Margaret Sanger over on 3rd Avenue."

In a few minutes, the artist herself appeared on the sidewalk below her billboard, which now had the image of a hanger with blood splattered on it. Enjoying a Marlboro, and breathlessly exhilarated from her performance, she said, "I'm Alise Milikin. I'm a performance artist. New York based. Abortion is not the government's right to decide. It's my right to decide what to do with my body. The government doesn't own my art, the government doesn't own my body—so hands off!" She took a deep drag on her cigarette.

Dave asked her "Were you scared up there?"

"No, I wasn't. I wasn't because I'm doing this for a reason. If it's a little shocking, that's good. You have to suffer a little bit for art because you have to suffer a lot in life."

Maybe you can imagine how much John Malone and TCI (Telecommunications Inc.) hated having *CamNet* playing continuously on eight of its channels. They were bothered enough that in October 1992, TCI commissioned Talmey-Drake Research, a national public opinion and market research firm in Boulder, Colorado, to conduct a survey about programming on cable television, aimed at getting some good hard numbers. *CamNet* programming was a particular focus of the survey. Of those surveyed, 83% had seen the *CamNet* programming and 68% regularly or occasionally watched it. When asked if they would prefer other services not currently provided instead of *CamNet* programming, *CamNet* fared quite well. Of those surveyed, 34% preferred *CamNet* over The Sci-Fi Channel; 26% preferred *CamNet* over *E!;* 33% preferred *CamNet* over *Court TV;* 15% preferred *CamNet* over *The Learning Channel;* and 33% preferred *CamNet* over *The Cartoon Channel.*

When asked about the possibility of offering CamNet programming as a separate pay service, meaning that the subscriber would have to pay an extra dollar or two a month, in addition to what is paid for basic cable service in order to receive it, 18% responded that they would definitely or probably subscribe. Of course TCI could easily put an entirely different spin on the numbers, but they still couldn't get rid of us until the contract expired.

Rolling Stone featured *CamNet* among the "Ten Things in 1993 That Didn't Suck" in their year-end edition. We were number 2 on the list. HBO was number 1, and Court TV was number 3. Number 4 was Howard Stern. But despite our cheap ad rates, CamNet still had only a few advertisers and we often played public service announcements, in many of our available ad spots. Although we were attracting a lot of attention, adding to our roster of video journalists, and covering stories that were seen nowhere else, we were going broke in the process.

Karen Dola picked up on us in *Rolling Stone* and arrived for her

212

meeting with Judith and me promptly at 1 p.m. in Venice. Karen worked for a new show called *Real TV* which was going to be distributed by Paramount five days a week starting in September. Needless to say, she was voracious. Karen was one of several producers out gathering footage for *Real TV.* What she wanted was "video driven material."

"What do you mean?

"Well", she said, "for example, I just got an incredible piece of video of a man who jumped out of an airplane with his video camera but forgot to put on his parachute. You hear him say 'Oh, no!' and then you actually see him recording his own death."

"Oh," I said, "we don't have anything like that."

She said she noticed on our tape index that we had a story about Hannibal the elephant who recently died at the Los Angeles Zoo. She wanted to know if we had the actual death on tape.

"No, only the aftermath."

Karen was uncovering a lot of material for *Real TV.* She had made a deal not only with the FBI for their old video, but also the CIA, the DEA, and the Border Patrol. She said she was looking mostly for "shock" but they also wanted to end each show with something "warm and fuzzy." Karen thought maybe we had something like that. I told her that wasn't how I would describe our programming, but perhaps we could find something for them.

Karen told her executives she would like to "tie us up" anyway, even if we weren't shocking because she figured that someone was bound to buy *CamNet* and it might as well be them. She asked about our impending coverage of the political conventions. She wanted to have first look. Judith said she would have to come up with some cash to have that happen.

ENTER PRODUCER MICHAEL LAMBERT. He used to be in charge of syndication at Fox. He wasn't a big mogul like some of the guys he started out with, but he had a track record in television syndication. Remember *Studs*? (*Studs* was a lot like *The Dating Game,* but without the class.) So, one of Lambert's development companies, called Partner Stations Network, had put together a group of independent television stations

213

across the country and made a little network out of them that would play programs that Lambert produced. (What an idea!)

Partner Stations Network sent Judith and me a deal memo to produce *CamNet* as five-days-a-week syndication to distribute over their little network. Now we began negotiations. Through all of our negotiations, we never met Michael Lambert. He had Jake and Adam handle us. We met Jake and Adam in their strangely empty offices in a strangely empty building on Olympic, barely inside Beverly Hills. In what would have been the reception area at the PSN offices, Jake and Adam had a little basketball court set up but the baskets were only about four feet off the ground so it was a little easier for them to score. They had pictures of clowns painted on velvet lining the walls of their conference room. Meant to be ironic? I didn't know.

Gary Herman and George Merlis had brought Judith and me to Partner Stations Network, as they had brought us to CBS and Fox and Castle Rock and a half-dozen other places before this. The deal was that we were partners with Gary and George on any show or series we sold with them. We sort of trusted them. After all, Gary did hire me for my first Hollywood job as a field director on *The Wilton-North Report* at Fox. It wasn't Gary's fault or mine either that the show was a disaster.

George and Gary had been pals for years even though to my mind they were not much alike. George had been the executive producer of *Entertainment Tonight* and *Good Morning America* and *The Home Show.* He always dressed in blazers and ties. Gary used to be in network news in the Middle East and he was more the safari-jacket sweater type with a beard that was turning white.

After the first meeting with PSN, we hadn't been able to come to an agreement. This deadlock lasted from February through June. Is this normal? They wanted our little *CamNet,* in the "forever in perpetuity in the universe" way, then they would hire us back (maybe) at a small salary to produce our own show for them. They would be willing to give us fifteen percent of the net. We told them, "Sure, it would be one thing if we had come to you with an idea, but we came to you with a completely developed program. We are, after all, *CamNet! The Camcorder Network!* And we've played 24 hours a day for two weeks of the month on ten United Artists cable systems that are owned by TCI and we have market research proving that people watch our channel. We're America's First All Camcorder Channel and we must have more of a joint venture with PSN." Jake said he'll talk to Michael Lambert about sweetening the pot. We consulted an attorney.

Renee Golden, Gary's lawyer, said she wanted to talk about it in person. She said to come at 3 p.m. We went out to Renee's place in West Hollywood. The first thing you noticed when you entered Renee's house were the carefully pinned, mounted, and framed rare and grotesque insect specimens covering the walls in the foyer. I've seen butterflies this way but not bugs. These treasures, we found out, had been left to her by a dead uncle.

Seated in her office, she advised us that we would do better by throwing *CamNet* in a drawer and waiting tables than doing a deal based on the offer from Jake and Adam at PSN. "I can't, in good conscience, let us get screwed so royally," she said. She explained that if *CamNet* didn't work out for them that it would have cost them practically nothing. But if it hit, then we would be totally screwed. We'd get nothing. They'd get everything. "Things like that just don't happen to my clients," she boasted. "I have some pride even if you don't."

Then Renee called Jake and Adam at PSN, to tell them that unless they could come up with a partnership arrangement of some kind, we would be talking to other people about the project. But Jake was busy on another line, and Renee made the secretary say that he would call when he got off the phone. We waited around for the call back, and Renee gave us tea and snacks and said that she wouldn't charge us for this part.

At some point I reached down to my briefcase that was leaning against the side of my chair. As I opened it to get a copy of the deal contract, a huge brown cockroach jumped out of one of my folders and skittered across Renee's Oriental carpet. I decided not to say anything. It wouldn't occur to anyone that the bug came from my house, I thought. I hoped it would just disappear, but suddenly Renee looked down and screamed, and a hubbub ensued and Renee rushed to get her astonishingly-handy bug exterminator, a sort of small vacuum-type affair with some dead bugs already in the clear cylinder attached to the nozzle. She chased my cockroach around the room but it escaped under the floorboard. I was vastly relieved. We all talked excitedly about whether it was a roach or a beetle or a water bug. Gary said back east they call them something else. We decided not to wait for Jake to call back even though it would have been enjoyable to hear Renee yell at him for treating us so badly. As if he was ever gonna call.

I HAD NEVER SEEN A COCKROACH until I moved to Christopher Street in the Sixties. On Christopher Street in the beginning, we had to sleep in shifts to protect each other from the thousands and thousands of cockroaches that lived inside the walls of our apartment. We might never have known they were there, except one day my sister Linda happened to see one on the wall and watched it go through a little crack in the molding. So, being curious, she pulled back the molding a little. She screamed in horror. There they were, racing past like cars on a super highway. Thousands and thousands and thousands (did I mention thousands) of them. We soon found out that calling the exterminator was a poor idea on Christopher Street because if you sprayed your apartment, all the roaches moved next door to your neighbor's apartment. It took about ten seconds for the Italian lady next door to start screaming at us through the wall. I didn't know exactly what she was saying but it must have been that we should never ever do that again. Eventually things settled down between the roaches and us. I read somewhere that roaches have families.

"Guess what?" I said to Judith as we left Renee's house and escaped down the driveway, "That roach jumped out of my briefcase." Judith laughed heartily for a good twenty seconds. I read somewhere that twenty seconds of hearty laughter is as beneficial as twenty minutes on a rowing machine, so the day hadn't been a total loss.

Jake finally did call Renee and said he was "ready to deal." He offered safeguards and royalties and other stuff, but Renee wasn't that interested. He said that they would have to put a lot of money into the development of *CamNet*. Renee laughed at him and said that *CamNet* was already developed. "*CamNet* has been on television for two years already," she told him. "You meant to say 'tweak,' not 'develop.'" Jake said. "Look, come back to me with a firm proposal and we'll talk."

Renee wanted to wait a couple of days and then ask for a lot. But somehow Renee wasn't effective. When Renee's office finally faxed the (allegedly) negotiated contract from PSN to us, we were shocked to find that not one of the points that we had asked for in June had been addressed at all. All these months and we receive the exact same contract as the first one! How could this be happening? Sadly, I had to tell Renee and George and Gary that we would not ever possibly agree. George was livid and said that if Judith and I were not willing to give up 100% of our ownership, then we had an unsellable product. George chastised me for going back on my word to them that we would accept the offer. George and Gary were so fiercely angry they couldn't even speak. They sputtered and hung up. They didn't call back. They were permanently pissed because for them it would be an okay deal. All they would have had to do was get us the meeting (which they had already done) and they would collect 40% of our new company and we would have to deliver all this programming while working for this company at a small salary with a 5% raise after 2 years. But fortunately for us, we were still free.

Associated Press called after seeing the *Wired* article before it even hit the stands, and *Columbia Journalism Review,* and a media journal from Tokyo. Even Keith Espanos, Executive Producer of the *Channel 9 News,* called. He had been watching our channel. He told Judith that he loved our stuff and had shown our tapes to his camera operators at Channel 9 as an example of what he liked. He was trying to train them not to be so stiff. Judith said that he'd better come up with an idea where we could make some money. "How about buying a *CamNet* minute for your news each day, something like that."

"Yeah, well, I love the stuff but most of it I couldn't use. It would all have to pass our codes."

"Codes?"

"For language and nudity."

"What?" I still didn't understand how they could play their news programs, which are a major assault on the senses, and not be able to

217

play *CamNet,* which really is sweet, especially butted up against their daily bombardment of local news. Over on MTV at 7 p.m. you could see a cartoon featuring characters with nipple rings, performing weird and masochistic acts, but Channel 9 couldn't play *CamNet* at the Cannabis Cup.

Chapter Eighteen:
How to File for Bankruptcy

AS A YOUNG WOMAN, at the end of the 19th century, my great-grandmother, living in Dayton, Ohio, used to go down to the train yard and watch the oranges being unloaded from the trains not far from her home. And she noticed that the bruised oranges were tossed aside to be discarded. So she asked the people at the railroad yard if she could have the bruised fruit and they said, "Sure, take it away."

So she got a basket, loaded it up with the bruised oranges and took them over to the Old Soldiers Home where these guys from the Civil War were sitting on the porch, and she gave them a good price for the ripe fresh fruit. Her pennies started adding up and pretty soon she opened her own stall at the market, branched out into other produce, and according to my Aunt Ruth, became "a merchandising force to be reckoned with." And my Aunt Ruth also became a merchandiser of children's clothes in Detroit with similar success. But that was food and clothing. Maybe I should try selling video by the yard or the pound.

Sarah Teasdale was born in Lanesville and lived with the Videofreex for her first years. Now Sarah had graduated from college and was moving to Los Angeles to be a third grade teacher in Pasadena through Teach For America. She took me on a tour of the house she and two other teachers had rented over in Hollywood, which I videotaped to send to Carol and Parry, and then we went to lunch at the Beachwood Cafe. In the restaurant, Sarah asked me if I could cosign her car loan. I laughed. I explained to her about show business and my credit rating. "The bottom line is that I just don't qualify." She asked me how I could live if I had no money.

You know, bankruptcy is a wonderful thing, and the USA is a great country to have such a fine plan for its desperate citizens. Paul, who was basically in the same financial condition, and I, decided to file together. Together we were going to wipe out our debts, get court

219

protection from our creditors and make a new start. The last thing I bought with my credit card was the Fourth National Edition of *How to File for Bankruptcy* put out by the Nolo Press Self-Help Law. We filled in every blank in the forms in the book, which took about a week, and then took our papers downtown to the courthouse.

On Friday, the 21st of July 1995, when we got home from the Bankruptcy Court, the phone was ringing. It was Cindy from the Bank of New York. Had I sent the check? Would I be sending it?

"Cindy," I said, "It's over. It's all over. I filed. This morning. I just got home."

"Oh, okay," said Cindy, "What Chapter?"

"What?"

"What Chapter did you file?"

"Oh. Chapter Seven."

"And the name of your attorney?"

"No attorney."

"Yourself," she says.

"Yes."

"Okay, I guess that's all I need to know. Bye."

"Bye, Cindy."

Chapter Nineteen:
Chicago Revisited

DURING THE DEMOCRATIC CONVENTION of 1996 Paul was doing midnight shows at the Mercury theater in Chicago. The press was all over Paul, since this was the first time he and the Democrats had been back to Chicago since '68 with the Yippies.

Now it was very civilized in Chicago and we even rode on the free delegates bus that went from the hotels to the convention center. The only thing even slightly reminiscent happened one evening aboard that very same delegates bus. A steely-eyed Chicago police officer pushed my own camera into my eye as I was taking his picture. He left me a little bruise. "No pictures!"

"Okay, okay," I said.

"I used to bust drug dealers. I get a lot of death threats," he told me as an explanation for not wanting to be videotaped. I guessed he was trying to impress me by covering my lens with his hand while he spoke. Like no one ever thought of that before. Then he ordered me to erase my tape before he would let me get off the bus, which he had been riding 14 hours a day to protect it and the riders from bombs. I forwarded to an unrecorded section of videotape and showed him that there was nothing on it, but I didn't erase.

In Chicago, as a member of the press I was given a 5.5 oz. package of "Democrats in 96! Kraft Macaroni & Cheese" as a free gift with my media credentials. The convention floor was packed for the nomination of Bill Clinton for his second term. Each person there was crushed against someone else's body while simultaneously speaking to each other on cell phones. It was hilarious. I believe that 1996 was the first total cell phone convention. Arianna Huffington, the then-conservative wag, was there on the convention floor reporting for *Comedy Central* with Al Franken on the left. Surreal.

In the Human Rights Campaign's hospitality suite at the Hyatt

Regency, I recorded Chastity Bono saying that in private, her father Sonny was all for same-sex marriage.

At the official protest area across the street from the Hilton I met three elderly Albanian gentlemen cheering in a crowd of 200 people for a John Belushi postage stamp. "He's from where we're from," they said.

"Give him a damn stamp! Give him a damn stamp!" the crowd roared. And then some tumblers entertained. The event was produced by Richard Roeper, Roger Ebert's co-movie-reviewer.

The Chicago Counter-Convention-anarchist-nose-ring-tattoo-crowd was alleging that the cops had been continuously raiding their loft on Carroll Street and gassing them and trashing their equipment. I have been to the Carroll Street loft. Talk about politically correct—in their loft they had two large painted portraits of O.J Simpson idealized as a revolutionary hero, hanging as a backdrop on their stage. I felt their paranoia.

Dave Dellinger, 81, activist and member of the *Chicago 8*, and Andrew Hoffman, thirty-something son of Abbie, finally got arrested after trying for three days. They got together and burned a flag, but they couldn't get arrested. Not blocking a bus route either. At last Dellinger and Hoffman figured out what was illegal. After being refused admission to Representative Carol Mosley Braun's office with seventeen other protesters, they blocked access to a metal detector. Bingo! Busted! No press ever mentioned why Dellinger and Hoffman wanted to be noticed. I know Dave wanted to free certain federal prisoners. And Andrew ran a clean-needle program in Boston. These were issues that certainly needed attention but they didn't get any.

Chapter Twenty:
Quick Gig with the Greatest

MUHAMMED ALI WAS LIKE the Buddha up at the Sports Placement Agency on Sunset and Doheny, Penthouse 2. His presence was huge, peaceful and almighty. As Ali entered the office, he came directly up to my camera. He stared into it. I stared back. He held out his hand to me. Slow motion, I beheld him. I reached out. He felt both soft and hard. He gazed into my eyes. What was that feeling? Was it awe? I don't know. I am not given to awe. I had no interest in prize-fighting. Ali gave one of those little punches into my lens. I did not flinch. I had no fear of Ali. He was here to sign serigraphs of himself made by artist Steve Holland. The signed serigraphs were going to be sold in galleries.

No cameras allowed. Only I would be watching Ali continuously through my viewfinder. He signed each piece of art with a pen of gold ink, and I could hear the steady scratching of his signature clearly in my headset as I videotaped him.

Steve's original six-foot oil painting of Ali in the ring was hanging on the wall to Ali's left. Ali sat with his back to a picture window with the smoggy expanse of Los Angeles shimmering behind him. The serigraphs were printed on canvas and were 47x32. Each one looked like an original oil painting. A tiny assembly-line kept a new print in front of Ali and then moved the signed work away.

Now Mr. Fingerhut, the publisher, arrived with his wife and two young daughters to witness the signing. They came in from Minneapolis, but Mr. Fingerhut must have gotten the surfer-printed baggie beach trousers he was wearing in Venice. Everyone was happy and awed. Janelle, Steve the artist's wife, kept things moving. Harlan the agent let a couple of guys from the office down the hall come in to meet Ali. They each had a cardboard camera. The Fingerhut girls, six and ten, gave Ali little gifts. They gave him prayer beads and a miniature carved wooden shoe. Ali put his finger through the little shoe. He smiled. He put his face to theirs. Not exactly a kiss, but a touching. He did his magic trick for the girls. The red silk was poked into the palm of one hand with the other hand. The other hand opened, and presto, it had disappeared. Amazement. He did it again. Further amazement. Then Ali revealed the trick. A fake thumb. Then appreciation. I recalled that on *Sixty Minutes* Ali's wife told Ed Bradley that Muhammad wants to go to Heaven, and that you can't play tricks on people and still go to heaven. Muslim heaven, that is. So that's why he always shows people how it was done after he tricks them. Most magicians, as we know, discourage the practice.

Scratch scratch, slowly, kindly Ali signed his name as the sun moved across the table in front of him. He never spoke. His right hand was steady and each signature was perfect. Golden.

At first Steve the artist said I would only be able to tape for a few minutes, but the tape-counter in my viewfinder read 57 minutes when I handed the cassette over to him. Goodbye, little videotape. They are going to take you back to Minnesota and make a five or seven minute promo and verification tape to send along to the galleries that are dealing this art product of Muhammad Ali. I had the feeling they wouldn't take any of my beautiful audio ("Hey, you're a nice guy," said 10-year-old Christine Fingerhut to Muhammad Ali). They'll take a wide medium and close-up maybe.

Chapter Twenty-one:
Whee!

WOW! IT'S THE WORLD HEMP EXPO and Extravaganja known as *"Whee!"*
We're out in the boonies a little north of Eugene, Oregon. In the heat of
summer, thousands of people from all over the country forming an
instant city rising up from a dusty rutted old corn field. A suddenly
bustling metropolis ringed by tiny steaming kitchens, head shops, cars,
pop tents, campers, arts and crafts, and port-a-potties. Yes, there are
hippies. Hippies galore.

Whee is the brainchild of Steve Hager, editor of *High Times*
magazine, who was prowling the premises of his whiz-bang-quick-city
like a lean and wiry godfather wearing his traditional skin-tight leather
trousers and four-gallon hat. I rode the perimeter with Steve and his
field marshal after the last band played on the first night. It was one
o'clock in the morning, but the cars were still streaming in through
the north gate. Steve wanted to make sure the latecomers were
being taken care of courteously and that no one would be turned
away. This was where the money was collected, so everything had to
be copasetic.

We posed as tired travelers and queued up with the vehicles at
the gate to see what the vibe was. And while we were waiting, Steve lit up
a big doobie and the vibe seemed to be really good. All the way down
the line. But the gate staff was exhausted. Steve walkie-talkied back to
the base for some relief and some food. Steve's walkie-talkie code was
420. He was 420. Get it? In case you don't, "four-twenty" is code for it
being time to smoke a joint. No one is sure exactly where "four-twenty"
came from. Some say that it's a police code for a drug bust and others
say that's not true. Some say that its 4:20 the time. You know, like, tea
time could be at four-twenty. When I attended the Cannabis Cup in
Amsterdam, where the year's best pot is tested and rated, 4:20 was
officially celebrated twice daily in the lobby of each of the delegates'

hotels. Some even wore "4:19—Load" T-shirts ("load" meaning "put the pot in the pipe").

By the second evening of the Whee! festival, the organically developing streets and avenues were well tramped into the landscape, and animated life emerged. Children romped and tumbled in the twilight, spinning red and green neon wands, chasing each other through the throngs of hippies strolling chatting twirling tripping shopping eating—all the while from the big stage and the huge speakers, the reggae bands blasted from noon to midnight—bahm ba ba bahm ba ba—smoke it legalize it peace and revolution. This was the Woodstock generation thirty years later.

Trixie Garcia, the twenty-something daughter of original Merry Prankster Mountain Girl and the Grateful Dead's Jerry Garcia, painted the faces of little girls for free or for a dollar. Sunshine Kesey, the twenty-something daughter of Mountain Girl and novelist Ken Kesey displayed her glass sculptures which reflected pinwheels in the eyes of passersby. Novelist Ken Kesey himself made a grand entrance in the Merry Pranksters' psychedelic school bus called "Further," seated on top of the touring relic like a sweating, red-faced pasha nestled in a customized luggage rack, shaded by ribbons and banners.

Kesey and the Pranksters presented an elaborate satirical performance on the main stage—a powerful rage against guns, prompted by the recent high school shooting in Springfield, Oregon, a few miles from Kesey's own home. He decided it wasn't guns that were the trouble but ammunition. Without ammo, guns would be okay. "Let us have no law that will infringe on the right of the bozos to have guns," Kesey shouted, prancing across the stage. He urged his audience to think. "They want you not to think!" Whee! understood. We were not a gun-totin' crowd. For us it was bong, not bang!

As an extra added attraction at Whee!, Stephen and Ina May Gaskin had arrived from The Farm in Tennessee. Back in the sixties, Stephen Gaskin taught creative writing at San Francisco State University. He would hold court at his Monday Night Class, and tons of students and newly-stoned hippies would come and sit at his feet to listen to him philosophize. Sometimes a thousand people would show up to discuss

226

politics, religion, acid, sex, and love. Eventually, Gaskin led busloads of these young people from Haight-Ashbury to Tennessee where they started their own sort of city-state called The Farm, which is still going strong today. This night at Whee!, Gaskin, a lanky gray-haired sixty-something hippie with an ancient tattoo on his arm that says "U.S. Marine Corps," would be doing his talk on the main stage. Gaskin was running for president. He was campaigning against activist Ralph Nader for the Green Party nomination. And after only a couple of days at Whee! I was thinking that a Gaskin presidency might have been a fine change of pace for America.

Ina May Gaskin, would-be first lady, is a midwife. Many babies have been born at The Farm in Tennessee and Ina May delivered plenty of them. She is a well-known expert when it comes to childbirth. She even has a birthing technique named after her. It's called the "Gaskin Maneuver." When a baby is twisted the wrong way to come out, Ina May reasoned that if you get into a doggie position the baby pops out (but I exaggerate). "Traditionally," Ina May said, "doctors have left women lying on their backs for hours suffering while they try to pry the baby out. Basically, the problem is that most doctors don't like midwives getting into their business." Midwifery is an extremely politicized and emotional subject, but Ina May was beginning to get the respect she deserves and was on her way to Minneapolis after the Whee! festival to talk to a group of doctors about how babies are born. "They have no idea how it happens," she said. Ina May came to the Whee! festival for the fun of it, but when she saw so many young families and mothers with babies in attendance she decided to address the pulsating throng of vacationing hippies. Ina May was a shining image on the big stage, with her salt-and-pepper braids and bright pink hemp dress that she sewed herself. She was urging these young women to breast-feed their children, her soft voice booming sweetly through the reggae-sized speakers. "We have nipple phobia in this country. We have to get over that."

The *High Times* Cannabis Cup Band played Ina May off the stage as the dashing emcee, Fantuzzi, introduced the Zen Tricksters. I found myself a shaded space under some Indian bedspreads tied to poles,

227

took a toke from a giant joint passed to me by a friendly stranger and drifted back into the rhythm, forgetting that the smile on my face was still illegal.

BACK IN LOS ANGELES at the pro-Prop 215 rally to legalize medical marijuana, I was accused by the hippies as being a narc. A narc? One of the beach hippies confronted me with his camcorder blazing right in the middle of the rally at the Federal Building in Westwood, and said that I had been pointed out by the juggler down on Venice Beach. Seems the juggler told everyone that I fingered people who were "selling" on the beach, and got them busted. "That's hilarious," I told him, never turning off my camera, "because I think you're a cop. And I think the juggler's a cop too." So this beach hippie with the camcorder asked me my name and to see some ID. "What's this for?" he asked me, pointing to my camera. I gave him my card. Then I told him that the guy speaking on the stage behind him was my husband Paul, and he would vouch for me. He turned around and saw the counter-culture's own Paul Krassner on stage and got all flustered and apologetic. He turned off his camera, I didn't. I won. But only by playing the Paul card, so it didn't really count. Now this guy started blabbering about his name and where he's from and how he met Paul once. Then another camcorder shooter, who had been tipped off that something was up, came over with his camera running, and said, "Are you one?" I said, "No. Are you one?" He said "No." He thought he might have a scoop.

Later, some federal cops hassled some vendors for the cameras, and a fine time was had by all. Dennis Peron, who had started the Cannabis Buyers Club in San Francisco and co-authored Prop 215 for Medical Marijuana, was there and was feeling pretty confident that the proposition was going to pass. And why not? Prop 215 was certainly the only reason I was going to the polls that year. For Medical Marijuana, not Bill Clinton. I wasn't going to be fooled twice, so on election day, I walked over to the Westminster School and voted Peace and Freedom all the way, and Yes on Prop 215. No one reported on how many votes my candidates, both women, received, but Proposition 215 passed handily and now it was okay, if not legal, to use marijuana for medical reasons in California. And about my being a boardwalk narc, on some steaming and intense days at the beach I have seen many scuffles erupt in the crowd. And suddenly every beach freak would be revealed to be an undercover cop, swinging into action. The biker would be a cop. So would the young woman in the bikini over there. And a couple of body-builders would be cops, and that Mexican guy would be one too. With the aid of helicopters and mounted police, arrests would be made. I had watched it happen many times.

Chapter Twenty-two:
Greetings from Cracktown

WAS IT A DREAM, or did I shoot video of Dan Rather sitting on a bench facing the boardwalk on Venice Beach right near my house? He was all ruddy and wind-blown, his hair was colored black, and his face was criss-crossed with Marlboro-man creases. He wore a clean white short-sleeved dress shirt that was tucked neatly into his belted blue slacks. He sat watching the passing scene and no one noticed him or made a fuss about him being the famous venerable old CBS television news anchorman, allowing himself to be so easily observed living his secret life.

Should I include Dan in this story? It's always tempting to use celebrity sightings, and it certainly shows what a weird and wonderful place Venice Beach is and how it's a comfortable fit for all kinds of folks. I waved to the old newscaster as I passed and, on a whim, I dangled in front of him a tiny trinket of wire and plastic that I had purchased from a vendor on the boardwalk. A small skeleton held together with twisted silver wire. I rolled the strand of metal between my fingers and made it do a little dance for Dan. "How cute is death?" I asked him rhetorically. He smiled slightly then tried to look away, but I quickly added, "Is anything cuter on the beach today than this tiny trinket of wire and plastic? Look how it dances in rhythm to the vibrations of my own movements. How cute is that? I am the puppet master. Death dances to my beat."

Dan nodded and smiled into my camera. His eyes twinkled in the sunlight. I took Dan's nod to be a fitting coda to this story. Perhaps simply a slow fade would work, I thought, as I continued on up the boardwalk, or a nice crane shot, a big wide happy ending, sort of a "life goes on" feeling, but no. Instead, I took the shortcut through the passageway behind the courtyard and my clatter awakened the sleeping man who was living on that stretch of cement between my house and the building next door. He was startled. I was flustered. I hurried past him and ran inside. It was our first direct encounter even though we had lived in this close proximity for several months. I knew that Roger the landlord was going to have the cops make a sweep of the property. Roger, who lives in Malibu, came by to fix the floodlight on the side of the house and saw the man sleeping in the sun and that's why he called the cops so fast.

It took me all day to gather the courage to talk to the man, but ultimately I went back there, gave him a small bag of groceries, and then I laid it out. "This isn't a good place for you anymore," I said. "The owner of the building is going to call the police." I kept a respectful distance. This man had survived on the streets of Venice for many years. In the early days he used to have a dog and keep a neat bedroll stashed in a doorway one cottage down the courtyard from mine. Back then, in the dog days, he and his pooch would be gone during the daylight hours doing who knows what, but probably strolling. Now the man was spending all day sitting staring or sleeping in the afternoon sun because the nights have been so cold and rainy and windy, how could he?

Along with the groceries, I gave the man a packet of information I had gathered for him on the Internet, listing all the services available for homeless people in Venice and Santa Monica. The irony wasn't lost on me that this information was listed where few homeless people would be able to access it unless they could get it together enough to go online at the public library. So I printed out the list of where to get showers, lockers, meals, doctors, shelter, lawyers, and training. The man is younger than he looks, He looks about sixty. Let's say he's a weather-beaten forty-five. He's tall and lanky, has white skin, thinning gray-blond hair, and red-rimmed blue eyes. He wears glasses so I know he can read the information I gave to him. I filed the pages neatly in a new folder along with a pen, some paper, envelopes, and seven quarters in case he might need a phone to make an appointment.

This meeting with the man is the first time he had ever looked up into my face. Usually, when he knows I can see him, he looks down or pretends he isn't there, and so do I. Yet, as unnerving as it has been to have this man always be there outside my kitchen window, always there standing or sitting or sleeping, it's the other men who come in the dark who really provided the critical mass for this recent shake-up with Roger the landlord and the police being called. The late-night men who smoke crack or maybe something even more far out because they are way way out there and sometimes one of them vomits in big splats and moans and sometimes one of them masturbates and shouts, "I'm going to eat out your pussy good, baby." The late-night men urinate on a little dying shrub growing next to the fence. The sweet little plant, whose lovely blossoms I used to enjoy as I rinsed my dishes in the sink, now glistens with piss on its browned and crinkling leaves.

After I handed the man the portable office, I told him he probably hadn't realized how many services were available for him, and I wanted to say I'm sorry about all of this but I didn't, and I wanted to say you'll be okay but I didn't, and I wanted to say look at all these possibilities I know you can make it, but I didn't. I stood there looking down at him sitting on his crate and was only able to take a step back and bow slightly. I told him that the police were coming and if he wanted to leave before they got here he should go now and he said, "Where should I go?" and I didn't know. Was I expecting him to quickly scan the long listings I had given him, circle the appropriate services and agencies, and now be running off to the phone booth to make appointments?

My first relationship with a street person was with the ragged man who used to sit on a box outside the Miramar Market, a little grocery store on the corner. In the beginning he would grumble and swear at me as I passed. For many months he sneered and muttered. He would sit on the walkway wrapped in a blanket, puttering around his box, going about his daily routine, eating, grooming, reading, writing, napping, and I ignored him as I walked past. He wanted it that way. Then one day I had to step sideways and by mistake I brushed against him in the narrow walkway. "Bring me some food!" he barked.

That's when I began shopping at the supermarket for the sort of groceries that make sense for someone who lives on the street without cooking or refrigeration facilities. I didn't know anything about this man, for sure. He hears voices, maybe. I never asked him his name

232

until one day I saw him sitting in the alley facing the garage wall, writing intently on a wrinkled page. "Are you a writer?" I asked him.

"My good wife dictates to me," he said.

"I see," I nodded. The next day he gave me a tin of Chantifrais Escargots de Bourgogne Preparation Francaise. "You take these," he said. "I haven't got a can opener."

"I'll bring you a can opener," I said.

"No, they are a delicacy. I'm not set up for them. They're not a part of my diet." He also gave me a 5-ounce can of Yeo's Singapore Curry Gravy. I gave him a loaf of bread, some turkey dogs in a can with a pull-off tab, and the same with the tuna, adding a pear, a six-pack of pudding, and some grape juice. He had very few teeth. I asked him his name and he hesitated. "Oh you can call me Junior," he said, "or Albert, if you want to be intimate."

That October, Junior started wearing a plastic pail on his head like a crown. He was a silent sentry wrapped in his army-green blanket at the market when I picked up my morning newspaper. "What are the headlines?" he asked me one day. "Closing Statements in the O.J. Case," I told him. He admitted having not followed the case very closely but did say that according to his calculations, O.J. should have been released more than a year ago. To make his point he cited the Charles Manson case and how Manson manipulated Squeaky Fromme by remote control. Then he said that he would read the newspaper and we could discuss the story later. He added that a friend of his had brought him a large lunch so I needn't worry that he would be hungry. Notably, soon after Junior's commentary, a jury in Los Angeles preserved our reasonable doubt and the catering truck arrived at O.J.'s house an hour before the verdict was even read. I recall that on the day after the verdict, the *Los Angeles Times* noted two things, though not in the same story. One, that it was Yom Kippur, and two, that O.J. was lounging by his pool.

On the following Saturday, October 7th, Junior advised me, "Always know the date. Don't take it for granted." Of course, for Junior it's important to know the date and also to know the name of the president because that's how the cops and other authorities test people

233

to see if they're sane. As he spoke, I realized that I actually didn't know the exact date. However, I believe I did know the month and year and who was president.

Anyway, the police arrived in short order for this man on the other side of my kitchen window. Four cops in two sets of two. They swaggered up the flowered walkway in their traditional LAPD shorts and blue shirts stretched tightly over heavy body armor, making them seem muscle-bound. All four officers were twenty-something and one was a woman. I told them right off that the man living outside my kitchen window was not dangerous and that he seemed very fragile to me. They asked me if he kept his belongings back there with him and I said yes because he did have a lot of stuff in trash bags piled up against the building.

"Look," I told them, "it's not this man so much as the nighttime men." One of the cops said he thought he knew one of the nighttime men who came here and he said "Ralph." The other cop added his last name and they asked me if he was Hispanic and I said I didn't know and that I had never seen him. "I only hear him vomit, not talk." All the police started laughing. "Yep, that's Ralph. I'll find him and take care of that too."

"When you say you'll take care of it, what exactly do you mean?"

"I'll tell him to leave. We're not going to beat him up," the cop said liltingly, as the foursome waddled off to confront the man.

It's strange, after all these months of the man being there, that now he's gone. He's gone, even though I still cringe away from the window out of habit each time I go into the kitchen, making sure I don't look out and see him by mistake. But he's gone. Who knows where he's gone? The cops had him gather up the belongings he wanted to keep and then watched as they had him put the rest of his stuff in the dumpster. They gave him the address of a place where he could go to for food and shelter, but the man prefers to live free.

When I get rich, will I move to a fortress? Will I drive into my residence like Batman, underground? Will I cover my windows with heavy canvas, baffled? Will I dig a moat? No possums will live under my house when I get rich. No vagrant will watch me heat the beans. When

234

I get rich I'll see about building some nice modern pods for the homeless where they can do as they please and doze in the noonday sun and eat ice cream and cookies and be safe from demons and neighbors and have self-cleaning kitchens and baths. And let's have prepaid cells, and groceries delivered. And I'd like visiting nurses when necessary, and wireless everything for everybody. Because—

> Thunder in Venice
> Happens once in a blue moon
> And bolts of lightning
> Crack again the night storm hardly ever.

Afterword

OH, WAIT! I want to say that at the time of this writing something is happening. And it's about media. And guess what? The whole world is watching. Really. It's global revolution live streaming. It's video shooters on the ground at protests around the world. They are a part of The 99 Percent who are occupying over a thousand cities at this writing. They'll probably be swept away, but they will be back, and whatever happens you can see it. I am monitoring Occupy Wall Street in NYC which began on Saturday, Sept 17, 2011, and is presently continuing into its fifth week.

Here it is, the new media revolution. And I have discovered it way out here, at the end of my rope, and it is beautiful.

Strangely, after all these years of working to free the media, I have to say, it's all so sudden! I wasn't expecting it. Only a few weeks ago, while considering an *Afterword* for this book, I had resigned myself to the fact that our good old video media revolution was history, and that it had been replaced by the new social media revolution and I was thinking that was enough. I was going to be content with a Facebook sort of world, or the YouTube community. Hi to all you brave single-mothers-by-choice, dogs who say "I love you," and the millions of kids in Asia. Go on, I would urge, Broadcast Yourself. You know, that was my idea in the first place. It was my plan exactly.

"Show me what democracy looks like," the occupiers chant. "This is what democracy looks like." Take a look at *livestream.com/ globalrevolution* as an example. Your friends are there, and your kids are there, and it might as well be you holding the camera whose feed you are watching on your screen right now. The shooting style is so familiar and intelligent. Wow! Yes, there I am, roving and roaming, never turning off the camera, cutting through the side streets, wandering the city, recording with no commentary, streaming unedited, and no news anchors or pundits. Do you like the revolution? It doesn't matter. The point is that it's happening, it's real, and you are there if you want to be. Cable news and other media are undoubtedly canned and

236

undeniably moribund in the face of live cameras in hundreds of cities. It is live streaming revolution just like we always wanted. It has happened. Viewer participants are constantly posting comments on the moving crawl alongside the streaming video. "Fox News is fake," someone says. Finally, they've got it. They've caught on. At the top left corner of the screen is the reminder that "Citizen Media is Not a Crime."

TO BE ADMITTED to the Video Data Bank at the School of the Art Institute of Chicago, you must present your driver's license to a uniformed woman behind a sleek counter to be copied. Then you must step back two paces and stand behind a line drawn on the floor and smile because that's where the guard snaps your picture. After that you are allowed to pass through the security gate and go to the elevators.

Upon arriving at the Video Data Bank, I am greeted warmly and escorted into a large room filled with shelves stacked with Videofreex tapes, neatly set up in numerical order exactly the way they were in our viewing room in Lanesville. Fifteen hundred of them, all there in the original boxes, with our original labels on the spines. There's my handwriting. Here is our earliest archive, safe and temperature controlled and waiting in line to be digitized. Okay, I Google Videofreex for old times' sake. Yes, we're there. We're all there.

Meanwhile, back at the global revolution, thousands of video-freex with all manner of devices are recording all the action as the cops threaten to close down the campsites and trap the protesters inside a cage of orange netting and cart them off to jail. I watch as push comes to shove. I watch it all live as the NYPD shouts "Back off! Get behind the barriers or you will be subject to arrest!" And the people? Well, the people hold their ground. Yes, the people hold their ground and the cops back off. In front of me, the phalanx of officers is ordered by their commander to take two steps back. The people hold their ground. The police step back. It won't always be this way, but it's amazing. Michael Moore, who has been on site often, asked a NYC police officer why the city is not taking a hard line, and the cop said "Mayor Bloomberg is afraid of YouTube." I rest my case.

Video days are back and they are roaring. So hold it steady, stay wide, and leave it on. Life is happening. The beginning is near.   *October, 2011*

Index

Page numbers in italics
signify photographs.

A

Aaron, Andy, *110*
Aaron, Jane, 81, 90
ABC Television Headquarters, 195
Aberlin, Betty (Lady Aberlin), 195
abortion, 150, 211
Accordion Institute, 32
ACLU, 208
"acquired cervical spinal
    stenosis,"152
Actors' Equity scale, 156
Admiral TV, 9
Advanced Formula Stress Tabs, 139
Agent Orange, 89
Agnew, Spiro, 65, 70
AIDS, 139
Alabama school textbook case, 174
Alanon, 167
Albany, 57
Albany Medical College, 78
Algeria, 42
Ali, Muhammed, 223, 224
All Things Chicago, *108*
alpha emitters, 81
Alternative Media Conference, *104*
Altman's Department Store, 172
Ameche, Don, 171
America, saving, 205
American Congress, 201
American Film Institute, 181
American Indian Movement
    (AIM), 46
"Americans for Robertson
    Gala Dinner," 175, 177
Amsterdam, 42, 198, 225
Ann Arbor, 55, 57
Ant Farm, 65, 191
Anthrax, 201
anti-Arab, 174
anti-Muslim, 174
Antioch College, 36

AP wire, 65
Appearing Nightly, 60
Apple, Wendy, 137, 175,
    180-181, 186
April, Jay, 123, 200-203
Aquarian and Conspiracy
    Book Store, 142
arts council grants, 46
ASCAP, 29-30, 32
Ashley Famous Talent Agency, 34
Asia, 236
Assassinationologist, 95
Associated Press, 217
Astrodome, 135, 206-207
"A Sunny Disposish," 50
Atkinson, David as "him," 157
Aunt Lois, 85
Aunt Ruth, 147, 219
Australian Jazz Quintet, 148
Avatar, 12

B

Bagley school, 79
Balsa wood, 43
Baltimore, 199
Bank of New York, 220
Bankruptcy Court, 220
Banner, Roxy, Hollywood 1984, *119*
Barbara Walters'
    Oscar Night Special, 171
Bart, Bruce, 97
Bart's Cowboy Show
    For Kids of All Ages, 47
Bayrak, Tosun, 29
Beachwood Café, 219
Beatles, The, 160
Bel Air, 178
Belushi, John, postage stamp, 222
Belzer, Richard, 182
Benjamin, Bobby, 57-58
Benjamin, David, 57-58

239

Benjamin, Elmer, 57, *103*
Benjamin, Gert, 58
Benjamin, Harriet, 57-59, *104, 106*
Benjamin, Johnny, 58
Benjamin, Louise, 58
Benjamin, Paul, 58
Benjamin, Scotty, 58, *103*
Benjamin, Todd, 58, *106,*
Benjamin, Willie, 57-59, *104, 106*
Benjamins, 61
Bernikow, Louise, 83,
Berry, Chuck, 190
beta emitters, 81
Beverage Express, 206
Beverly Hills, 168, 176
Bible, 92
Big Brother, 195
biker dudes, 143-144
Bilingual Jackpot Bingo, 170
Bill, a Vietnam veteran, 208
Binder, Judith, *123, 124,* 191,
    202-205, 210, 214, 216-217
biological weapons, 201
Black Panther Party, 101
Block brothers (H&R), 83
Bloomberg, Mayor, 237
Blue Calzone, 104
Blumberg, Skip, 8, 12, 35, 41,
    44-55, 56, 60, 67-70, 74, 78,
    90, *100, 105, 107,* 195
Blumberg, Skip, scrap book, *109*
Boekmann, Bert, Galpin Ford, 177
Boekmann, Jane, 177
Bohemians, 53
bone cancer, 146
Bono, Chastity, 222
Bono, Sonny, 222
Boone, Pat, 176-181
Boone, Shirley, 178
Border Patrol, 213
"Born on the Fourth of July," 72
Boston, 81, 90, 222

Bottner, Barbara, *122*
Boulder Colorado, 198
Bowles, Paul, 198
Brademus, Representative John, 74
Bradley, Ed, 224
Brandeis University, 15, 41
Braun, Representative
    Carol Mosley, 222
Bredesen, Reverend Harald, 176-180
Brill, Louis, 14
Brinkley, David, 69, 71
Broadcasting magazine, 2
Brokaw, Tom, 170
Brokenshaw, Jack, Australian
    Jazz Quintet, 148
Brooklyn's Children's Museum, 15
Brown, Harold, Momo's
    Cocktail Lounge, 148
Brown, Jerry, 78
Brownell, Barbara, 203-204, 208
Bruce, Lenny, 149
Buddha, 223
Buddhists, 141
Buddhists in dream, Venice, 136
Buffalo New York, 46
Bureau of Indian Affairs, 46
Burnett, Carol, 60
Bush, George Herbert Walker, 195
Bush, George, Republican
    National Convention 1992, 206

C

Cain, Alan, 6-7, 34, 141-143
Cain, Nancy , 61, 84, *100, 106,*
    116, 121
Cain, Nancy as Roxy Banner, *119*
Cain, Nancy , *107-108, 110,*
    111-114, 117, 120, 122-123, 126
Caldicott, Dr. Helen, 81-82
California, 42, 59, 199
"Camelot," 154

CamNet The Camcorder Network, *123*, 200, 202-203, 205-206, 210, 212-218

Canada, 55

Canarsie, Brooklyn, 60

Cannabis Buyers Club, 228

Cannabis Cup, 198, 218, 225

Canter's Deli on Fairfax, 204

carcinogenic substances, 81

Carey, Tobe, 91

Carmelites, 127

Carnegie Hall, child prodigy violin players, 153

Carroll Street, Chicago, 222

Carter, Jimmy, 77, 81, 208

Carter, Miss Genna (Dixie) 59

Carter, President Jimmy, 192

Castle Rock, 214

Catskills, 6, 45, 51, 61

Catstaneda, Carlos, 73

CBS, 1-2, 8, 10, 13-14, 17-19, 33, 35-36, 38, 41, *100*, 214, 230

CBS Headquarters aka Black Rock, 8, 11

Cedars Sinai, 184

Century City, 158, 162

Cesium-137, 81

Channel 18, 203

Channel 6, Woodstock Access TV, 90, 92-93, 96, 98

Channel 7 News, 170

Channon, Dave, 211-212

Chantifrais Escargots de Bourgogne Francaise, 233

Chapin, Harry, 95

Chaplin, Charlie, 54

Chappaquiddick Bridge, 6, 95

Charismatic Church, 174

Charlie Chan's Number One Son, 158

Chelsea Hotel, 53

Chicago Illinois, 198, 221

Chicago Counter-Convention-anarchist-nose-ring-tattoo, 222

Chicago 8, 15, 17, 32, *101,* 222

Chinatown, New York City, 172

chondrosarcoma, 79, 84

Christian Broadcasting Network (CBN), 173, 176

Christian Right, 175

Christian symbolism, 173

Christians, 92

Christmas Eve, 93

Christopher Street, Greenwich Village, 44, 216

Chrysler, 196

CIA, 63, 74, 207, 213

Circus Comes to Lanesville, 61

"Citizen Media is Not a Crime," 237

Citizens Party, 90

Civil War, 219

Clarke, Arthur C., 54

Clarke, Shirley, 47, 53, 54-55, *105*

clean-needle program, 222

Cleaver, Eldridge (Black Panther), 42

"climb Prayer Mountain," 176

Clinton, Bill, 209, 210

Clubhouse Avenue, 191, 203

CNN, 94

Cohen, Maxi, Democratic National Convention 1976, *110*

Colgate University, 15

Collins Avenue, 70

Colonel Sanders, 1972 Miami Political Convention, *107*

Colorado, 198, 200

Columbia Journalism Review, 217

Columbia University, 3, 82

Comedy Central, 183, 221

Commoner, Barry, 90

Communist Workers, 8

Community Decency Board, 94-95

Concord Hotel, 6

Congress, 74

Connecticut, 83

Connor, Russell, 61-62, *104*

Conspiracy Update, 95

Coppack, Lee, fundraiser, 76

cops, 1, 17, 22, 37, 50, 55, 69, 70,
    73, 93, 96, 156-158, 186, 207,
    221, 225, 228-229, 231-234, 237

Cornell University, 8

Cort, David, 14-16, 18-20, 32-37,
    44, 53, 55, 56, 90, *100, 103*

Cosby, Bill, 170

Costa Brava, 85

Costa, Teresa Marta, 97

Couzins, Michael, *107*

Cowan, Liza, 94

crack, 232

Cranbrook Episcopal Church, 146

Creating Alternative Futures:
    The End of Economics, 170

Creative Music Studio, 91

Crimmins, Mrs., 58

Cronkite, Walter, 69

Crosby, Bing, 190

Crouch, Paul and Jan,
    Trinity Broadcasting, 176

Cruise, Tom, 72

Crumb, R., 6

Cuomo, Mario, 205

Customs Inspectors, 56

Cyprus, 74,

D

Dali, Salvador, 43

Dallas Cowboys, 75

Dan White Case, San Francisco, 152

Dannon, Tony, 32

Darvon, 80

Dayton, Ohio, 219

DBCP pesticide, 89

Drug Enforcement Administration
    (DEA), 213

Debtors Anonymous, 163-168

Debtors Anonymous,
    fifteen questions, 165

Debtors Anonymous,
    Lord's Prayer,   166

DeGeneres, Ellen,   182

Della Femina McNamee
    Advertising Agency, 195

Dellinger, Dave, 222

democracy, 236

Democratic National Convention
    1968, 15

Democratic National Convention
    1972, 64, 77, 190

Democratic National Convention
    1976, *110*

Democratic National Convention
    1992, 209

Democratic National Convention
    1996, 221

Democratic Convention of Death, 17

Democrats, 64-65, 208

"Democrats in 96 !
    Kraft Macaroni & Cheese," 221

Denver Colorado, 198-199

Detroit Michigan, 55, 60, 81, 147,
    154, 156, 172, 199, 219,

Detroit News, After Dark column, 149

Detroit police, 156-157

Dial soap, 4-5

DJs from Sacramento, 182

Doberman Pinschers, 76

Dodge Dart four-door, 56

Dola, Karen, Real TV, 212, 213,

Donohue, 169

do-re-mi-files (aka solfeggio), 30

Douglas, Kirk, 168

Down and Out in Beverly Hills, 145

Downs, Hugh, 54

Downstairs at the Upstairs, 59

Dylan, Bob, 69

Dynasty, 160

242

E

e.e. cummings, 156-157
Eagleton, Senator Thomas, 64
Earth First, 202
earthquake, 6.1, Los Angeles, 181
Easter Sunday Grand Trample,
    Egg Hunt, One Mile Hike
    and Potluck Supper *121,* 168
Ebert, Roger, 222
Edgewood New York, 57
e.e. cummings, 157
Eileen E., 79-80, 146
Einstein, 82
El Topo, 34
Elgin Theater, 34,
Elvis's 1968 comeback special, 198
Empathy (Ecstasy), 151
Empire State Building, 172
Encyclopedia Britannica,
    158-160, 163
Endangered Species Act, 201
England, 42
Entertainment Tonight, 214
Espanos, Keith, Executive Producer,
    Channel 9 News, 217
Estelle—Sherman Oaks
    Ross Perot volunteer, 209
Eugene, Oregon, 225
EuroCom, 195
Everson Museum of Art, 55
Everything Anonymous, 166
Eye on L.A., 171
EZTV in Hollywood, 181

F

Facebook, 236
"faggot," 207
family values, 206
Fanning, David, *Frontline,* 193
Fantuzzi, 227

Farkle, Frank The Fist, 51-53
Farm, The, in Tennessee, 226, 227
Farmer Frank, 92
FBI, 213
FBI report, *112*
FCC, 49, 50, 198
Federal Building in Westwood, 228
Feldstein, Mary, *120,* 138, 158,
    163-164, 166-167
Fermi fast breeder, 81
Ferragamo shoes, 164
Festival of Life, 17
Fez, Morocco, 87
Fingerhut, Christine, 224
Fingerhut, Mr., 223
"First Aid #1," 16
"First Aid #2," 16
first-strike nuclear warheads, 91
Fisher Building, 148
5-Day Bicycle Race, *110*
Flakey Foont, 6
Fleischer, Mrs., 31
Fleming, Rhonda, 176
Florida, 83
Fonda, Jane, 171
Fontainebleu Hotel, 64
Ford, Betty, 84
Forman, Earl, 180
"four-twenty," 225
"Fox News is fake," 237
Fox TV, 181, 183, 214
France, 42
Franken, Al, 221
"Frankie and Johnnie," 157
Fred Hampton, *101*
Freex Tongue Group, *100*
Freihofer's cupcake, 52
Friedman, Bart, 34, 38, 41, 44,
    46-48, 50-51, 60-63, 70, 78,
    80-81, 85-86, 90, 129
Friedman, Bart, and Nancy Cain,
    Newark Airport sketch, 133-134

Friedman, Bart, taping Superbowl X, *100, 103, 105, 108*
Friedman, Bart, Democratic National Convention 1976, *110*
Friedman, Bart, Kingston, Jamaica,131
Friedman, Bart, Media Bus Studio, Woodstock, *111*
Frogtown, Toonerville, 189
From the Heart, 184
Fromme, Squeaky, 233
Fuller, Buckminster, 200
Fundamentalists, 166, 174
"Further," Merry Pranksters school bus," 226
Fusion magazine, 12

G

Gaberman, Phil, 149, 150, 154
Gaberman, Phil, Director of Guys and Dolls, *115,* 147
Garcia, Trixie, daughter of Jerry, 226
Gaskin, Stephen and Ina May, 226, 227
gay, 96
gay and lesbian youth, 207
gay porn movies, 93
General Electric, 91, 159, 178
General Motors Building, 148,
Georgia, 77
Gerald Ford's America, 73, 74
Ghostbusters, 75
Gigliotti, Davidson, 35-38, 40, 44, 48, 90, *100, 102*
Ginsberg, Allen 195
Ginsberg, Sam and Miriam, 45, 49, 62
Glendale, California, 185
Global Village, 35
God, 173-174, 180, 205
"God buzz word," 173

Goddard College, 77, *104,* 136, 171, 200
"godless doctrine, 174
"Goin' to the Chapel," 185
Gold, Joel, *110*
Golden Girls, 170
Golden, Renee, 215-217
Good Morning America, 214
Google, 237
Gorewitz, Shalom, *110*
Gotterer, Richard, 34
Goya, 87
Grand Central Station, 43, 172
Grateful Dead, 226
Great Chefs, 170
Great Fire of Malibu '85, 168
Great Peace March, 161-162
Greece, 74
Green Party, 227
Greenpeace, 202
Greer, Mr. and Mrs. Rosie, 176
Gregory, Dr. William, 156,158
Grey Advertising, 1
Griffin, Cy, 45-46,
Griffin, Janet, 46
Griffin, Jimmy, 45
Griffin, Tracy, 45
Griswald Avenue, 154
Grosse Pointe, Michigan, 50
Grossman, Linda, 10, 44, *114, 116,* 147, 184, 216
Gucci's, 168
Guernica, 87
Guerrilla Television, 64
Gulf Oil Corporation, 66
Gulf War, The 1991, 193,195
Gurdjieff, 3, 6
Guys and Dolls, 147

H

Habitat for Humanity, San Diego, 192

Hager, Steve, Editor,
  High Times magazine, 225
Haig, Alexander, 139
Haight-Ashbury, 227
Haines Falls, 52
Halback, Linda Jovin, 97, *111*
Hall, Arsenio, 181
Hall, Doug, 191
Hamilton, Alexander, 207
Hampton Beach, 129, 130
Hanalei, 88
Hand, Judge W. Brevard, 174
Hannibal the elephant, 213
harassment in high school, 207
Hare Krishnas, 143, 144
Harlem, 8, 42
Harlem, new city dream, 130
Harp, Rush, 95, *111*
Harpo Marx, 47
Hart Island, 42
Hart, Gary, 139
hashish, 86-87
Hawaii, 89
Hayden, Tom, 32
Headley, Mr., 160
Hearst, Patty, 80
heaven, 177
Hells Angels, 49
Henderson, Hazel, 170
Hepburn, Audrey, 171
Herman, Gary, 214-217
High Times Cannabis Cup Band, 227
High Times magazine, 198, 225
"him," 156-157
Hiroshima, 91
"Ho Ho Ho Chi Minh
  the NLF is gonna win," 18
Hoffman, Abbie, 15-16, 19-20,
  32-34, 50, *101, 222*
Hoffman, Andrew, 222
Hog Farm/Movement City,
  15, 47-48

Hogan's Heroes, 49
Holland Stevens Portrait Studio, 154
Holland, Janelle, 223
Holland, Steve, 223
Hollywood, 145, 219
Hollywood, new-age/neo-pagan/
  voodoo store, 135
Holmes, Ernie, 76
homeless, 231, 235
homophobia, 94
homosexuality, 94
Hon, Mr. and Mrs. Barry, 177
Hooker, Dwight, 154, 155
Hope, Bob, 163, 192
Horn and Hardart's, 43
Hornbeck, Mescal, 94
Hospital for Joint Diseases,
  New York, 152,
House of Representatives, 209
Hsieh, Tehching,
  performance artist, 129
Hudson River, 6
Huffington, Arianna, 221
Human Rights Campaign, 221
Hunter Mountain, 45, 52
Hunter New York, 60
Hunter-Tannersville Rescue Squad, 51
Hussein, Saddam, 197, 201
Hyatt Regency, 221-222

I

Iacocca, Lee, 196
IBM, 46
Instructional Telecommunications
  Foundation, 199
Intellectual Free For All, 96
Internet, 231
Iodine-131, 81
Israel, 179, 196
Israeli ambassador, 179
Israeli take-over of Arab lands, 174

Isuzu, Joe, 195, 196
"ITFS," instructional television
  fixed station, 199

J

J.P., 49-50
Jacke, Mr., 188
Jackie Gleason Convention Center, 66
Jackson, Jesse, 139
Jake and Adam, PSN, 214-215
Jamal—Rita Xanthoudakis' cat,
  136, 139
Jay, Ricky, 34
Jefferson, Thomas, 207
Jefferson Avenue, Detroit Michigan, 56
Jennings, Peter, 195
Jesus, 92,
Jews, 137, 194
Jews for Jesus, 92, 194
John Birch Society, 208
Johnson, Jeanne, 153
Jones, Dean and Laurie, 176
Jonestown Murders, 95
Jonestown photographs, 192-193
Junior aka Albert, 233
Junior's Delicatessen, 145

K

Kahn, Miss Madeline, 59
Kansas City, 83
Kate and Allie, 170
Katz, Jon, 203
Kauai, 88
KBDI (The Beedy Eye), 198
Ke'e Beach, 88
Kelly, Peter, 34
Kelman, Scott, 150
Kennedy, Chuck, 33-35, 41-44,
  49, 55, 81, 90, *100, 105*
Kennedy, Chuck, *106-107*

Kennedy, John F., President,
  killed, 142
Kennedy, Rhea, 90
Kennedy, Robert, killed, 142
Kennedy, Teddy, 95
Kent State University, 35
Kenwood Restaurant
  and Lounge, 149
Kesey, Ken, 226
Kesey, Sunshine, 226
Kiker, Doug, 70-73, 107
King Arthur's Deli, 60
King George of England, 57
King of Prussia, 91
King, Martin Luther, killed, 142
Kingston New York muscle gym,
  45, 131
Kirby, Bill, MacArthur
  Foundation, 190
Koch, Howard and Ann, 90
Kopechne, Mary Jo, 95
Koppel, Ted, 170
Korsts, Anda, *107*
Kovic, Ron. 70-72
Kozlow, Uncle Richard, 85
Krassner, George, 153
Krassner, Holly, 153
Krassner, Ida, 153
Krassner, Marge, 153
Krassner, Paul, *121, 122, 126,*
  150-152, 153, 158, 181-183,
  185, 187, 219, 228
Kria yoga, 141
KSCI-TV, 160
Kweskin, Jim, 13

L

La Barbara, Joan, 140
L A Weekly, 168
Los Angeles Zoo, 213
Lagrand, Carolyn C., 210-211

246

Lambert, Michael, 213-217
land grant, 57
Lanesville, 39-45, 48-49, 57, 59-62,
    64, 77-78, 80, 90, *103, 105,*
    219, 237
Lanesville TV logo, *110*
Lanesville TV—Probably America's
    Smallest TV Station, 49, 51, 59,
    61-63, 75, *106,* 173
LAPD, 234
LAPD narcotics detective, 207
Lapides, Beth *125,* 205
Lark cigarettes, 42-43
laser, 54
Las Meninas, 87
"Latrine,"
    aka "The Shit House Tapes," 16
Lauper, Cyndi, 144
Lawrence, Jon, 146
Lear Industries, 178
Leary, Rosemary, 42
Leary, Timothy, 42
Lennon, John, 55
Lehrer, Tom, 147
lesbian, 94, 96
Letterman, David, 130
Levin, Kathy, *QVC,* 194, 197
LifeCycle, YMCA, Santa Monica, 140
Lily's poodle skirt, 60
Lipton, Aunt Betty, 172-173
Lipton, Jimmy, 172
livestream.com/globalrevolution,
    236
Locke, John, 207
Logue, Joan, *107*
London Fog trench coat, 7
Long Island Expressway, 95
Lord, Chip, 66, 71-72, *107*
Lorenz, Hugette, Queen Goddesses,
    wife of Robert, 139
Lorenz, Robert, *Technology
    of Change*, 139

Los Alamos, 129, 130
Los Angeles, 46, 174, 199, 202,
    207, 219, 223
Los Angeles city dump, 192
Los Angeles County
    Perot Petition Committee, 209
Los Angeles Times, 233
Los Angeles Times interview
    with Paul Krassner, 151
LSD, 4, 32
Lucy Ricardo's kitchen, 160
Lyman, Mel, 12-14

M

MacArthur Foundation, 190
Machaver, Harvey, 152
Madison Square Garden, 141, 160
Madrid, 85, 87
Maharaj-ji, Astrodome levitation, 135
Maharishi, 141, 160
Maharishi TV, 171
Mailer, Norman, 32
Maletta, Lou, 93, 96
Malibu, 168, 231
Malibu Alanon, 168
Malone, John, 199, 212
Manhattan Cable, *110*
Manhattan Transfer, 50
Manistee on Lake Michigan, 155-156
Mann, Andy, *107*
Mann, Ted, 176
Manson, Charles, 233
Maple Tree Farm, 39-40, 42, 45,
    47, 60, 90, *102, 105, 112*
Mar Vista, 185
Marilyn, Susan Milano's
    production partner, 129
Markey's Seafood Restaurant, 130
Marlboro, 211
Marley, Bob, 177
Marpet, Bill, *110*

Marquez, Hudson, 64, *107*
Marx Brothers style movie, 47, *105*
Maryknoll nun, 127
Maryland, 64, 201
May Company, Los Angeles, 143
May Day Video Collective, 36, 38
Mayor Moscone, 152
Mazursky, Paul, *Down and Out in Beverly Hills*, 145
McCartney, Paul, 39
McCloskey, Pete, 70
McGovern, George, 62, 64-65
"me," 157
Meals on Wheels, 92
Media Bus Archives, *103, 105*
Media Bus Inc., 35, 47, 55, 61, 77, 90, *102, 111,* 132
medical marijuana, 228
Medina, 86
Men in Film, 93, 96-97
Men Who Love Trucks, 96
Mercury Theater, Chicago, 221
Merlis, George, 214, 217
Merry Pranksters, 226
Merv Griffin Show, 139
Miami 1972 Political Convention, *107*
Miami Beach, 64-65, 76, 190
Michels, Doug, 66
microwave TV, 198
Middle East, 74
midwifery, 227,
Milano, Susan, 129
Milikin, Alise, 211-212
militant environmentalist, 203
Milk, Harvey, 152,
Milky the Clown, 9, *113*
Milky's Movie Party, 9, *113*
Miller, Martha, *107*
Milton, Joanna, *110*
Minneapolis, Minnesota, 223-224, 227
Minneapolis Star Tribune, 190

Minority Report, 96
Miramar Market, 232
Mister Rogers' Neighborhood, 160, 195
Mitchell, husband of Linda Montano, 127
Mobilization to End the War in Vietnam, 17
Momo's Cocktail Lounge, *117,* 148, 155, 156
Mondale, Walter, 78, 139
Monroe, Marilyn, 177
Monroe, Robert, 96, 97
Montano, Linda, 127-128,
Moore, Michael, 237
Morey, T.L. (Tom), 66, *121*
Morocco, 85, 127
Morris and Max, Shirley Clarke's dogs, 53
"Mr. Natural," 6
MTV, 218
Mudd, Roger, 68, 74
Murray, Bill, 75-76,
Museum and Television exhibit, 41
Museum of Science and Technology, 37
Mushroom, the dog, 39
Muslim heaven, 224
My Sister Eileen, 147

N

Na Pali Coast, 88
Nader, Ralph, 227
Nafzger, Lester, 96-97
National Football League, 76
National Gallery, 37
Native American rights, 45
Native Americans, 46
NBC, 159
NBC News, 66, 70, 72, 171
New Jersey, 45

Newman, Judy *107*
New Paltz, New York, 90
New York City, 38, 53, 59, 61, 77
New York Daily News, 58
New York Mets, 8
New York State, 42-43, 46, 55,
   82, 90, 172, 207
New York State Council on the Arts,
   40, *104*
New York State Thruway, 46, 55
New York Times, 205
New York University, 141
New York Yankees, 9
Newhart, 170
Newman, Jim *107*
Newsom, Ginny, *121*
Nielsen TV Viewing Survey, 169-170
Nielsen, Art, Jr., 169
Night Owl Show, 96
Nikon, 155
Nixon Library, 98
Nixon, Pat, 67
Nixon, President Richard M.,
   9, 36, 62-63, 65, 70-73
Nixons, official portrait, 75
Nolo Press Self-Help Law, 220
Nolte, Nick, *Down and Out*
   in Beverly Hills, 145
North Hollywood, 203
Northern Ireland, 73
Northwood Inn, *116*
"Notorious 187 Crew," 189
Nude Handyman, The, *124,* 204
NYPD, 237
NYU Film School, 137

O

Oakland Oaks, 179-180
Oberon, the parrot, 44
O'Brien, Conan, 183
Occupy Wall Street in NYC, 236

Ohio National Guard, 35
Old Soldiers Home, 219
O'Leary, Dr., 152-153
Oliveros, Paulene, 128
Olympic Arts Festival, 140
Ono, Yoko, 55
Ontario, Canada, 55
Operation Blessing, 174
Orange Bowl, 76
Orange County, California,
   168, 175
Oregon 47
Oscars, 171
Otis, George, 177-178
Overeaters Anonymous, 167

P

Page, Geraldine, 171
Paik, Nam June, 1, 41
Paley, William S., CBS Chairman,
   11, 63
Palm Island, Florida, 76
Palos Verdes, California, 201
Palos Verdes blue butterfly, 202-203
Panter, Nicole, 206
Paramount Studios, 144
Paraquat, 89
Paris, 43
Partner Stations Network
   (PSN), 213-215
Pasadena, California, 219
Pasteur School, 146
"Paul Bunyan," 51
Paul Mendoza, 149
PBS, 200
PCP, 186
Peace and Freedom Party, 228
Pearl Harbor bombing, 207
Pemberthy, Bev, 157
Pennsylvania Turnpike, 55
Pentagon, 89

Pentecostal Churches, 174,176
Peoples Video Theater, 35
Peron, Dennis, 228,
Perot, Ross, 208,
Perot Headquarters, Dallas, 210,
Perot, Ross, 1992 campaign,
    207-210,
Persian Gulf, 201
Philadelphia, Pennsylvania, 199
Phil Gaberman Trio,
    Detroit 1963, *117,* 148
Phillips, Chyna, 144
Phillips, Lynn, 137
Phillips, Michelle 144-145
Phoenicia, New York, 62, 90
Phoenix House, 42-43,
Physicians for
    Social Responsibility, 161
Picasso, Pablo, 87
Pin Ball Parlor, 96
Pine Tree Drive, 65
Pittsburgh Steelers, 75-76
Plainfield, Vermont, 77
Plato's Retreat, 139
Plowshares 8, 91,
Pluto, God of Hell, 82
Plutonium, 81
Poland, 42
Powers, Dr., 78
Prado, The Museo del, 87
Prague, Czechoslovakia, 42
Prime Time America, 63
Prince Street loft,
    29, 35, 38, 41, *100*
Princeville, Kauai, Hawaii, 88
Procter, Jody, 21, 191-193
Project Earth, 200
Proposition 215, 228
Pro-Peace offices, 161
Prosperity meeting, 168
psychographics, 196,
Public TV, 175, 193,

Q

QVC, 194, 197

R

Rabbi Kelley, 50
Radical Software, 64
Radio City Musical Hall, 6-7
Rain Shop, Kauai, 88
Raindance Corporation, 35, 64
Rainforest Action Network, 202
Ramaiah, Yogi, *118,* 141-143
Rambo, 171
Ramis, Harold, 75
Rancho Mirage, California, 84
Rapage, Louie, 144, 145
Ratcliff, Curtis 15-16, 35, 44,
    46-47, *100, 105*
Ratcliff, Curtis and Cy, wedding of,
    46-47, *105*
Rather, Dan, 67, 170, 230
RCA portable TV, 12 inch, 169
Reagan, Nancy, 178,
Reagan, Ronald, 139,
Reagan, Ronald, Governor, 176-179
Reagan, Ronald, President, 160-171
Republican National Committee, 74
Republican National Convention 1972,
    64, 66, 69, 73-74, *107-108*
Republicans, 65, 67, 70, 73, 75,
    207-208
Restocraft Mattresses, 9
Rhinebeck, New York, 78,
Rip Van Winkle, 51
Rivers, Joan, 59, 181
Robertson, Dee Dee, 176
Robertson, Pat, 173-176, 183
Robichaux, Mark, 202-203
Rob, interviewer,
    Great Peace March, 161
Rochester, New York, 46

Rock of Gibraltar, 86
Rock, Chris, 183
Rodeo Drive, Beverly Hills,
   California, 168
Rosenberg, Howard, 193-195,
Roeper, Richard, 222
Roger the landlord, 231-232
Rogers and Hart songs, 147
Rolano, Bobby, 158-160
Rolling Stone magazine, 13, 203, 212,
Rose Art Museum, 41
Rose Café, Venice, California, 141
Rosebud Reservation, 45-46
Rosh Hashanah, 151
Route 214, New York, 48, 50
Route 28, New York, 95
Rowan and Martin's Laugh-In, 60
Roxbury, Massachusetts, 12
Rucker, Allen, 64, *107*
Ruppert, Mike, 207-210
Rush, Molly, 91

S

Saarinen, Eero, 11
Safer, Morley, 190,
Saks 5th Avenue, New York, 148
Sally Jessie Raphael
   radio show, 171
salted-peanut effect, 168
"San Antonio Rose," 146
San Fernando Valley, 204, 208-209
San Francisco, 228
San Francisco State University, 226
San Franciso Chronicle, 182
Sanchez, Jimmy, 187
Sanchez, Johnny, 186-189
Sanchez, Mr. and Mrs., 187
Sand, Barry, 182,183
Sanger, Margaret, 211
"Satin Doll," 148
Santa Monica, 168, 184, 231

Saturday Night Live, 170
Saugerties, New York, 90, 97, 130
Sawkill River, 93
Schenectady, New York, 46
Schmidt, Douglas, 90
Schneider, Ira, *107*
School of the Art Institute
   of Chicago, 237
Schreier, Curtis, 66, *107*
Schwartz, John, 198-200
"Score," nickname for
   Tom Weinberg, 190
"secular humanism," 174
Seabrook Nuclear Power Station,
   129-130
Second City, 2
Secret Service, 72
secular humanists, 205
Selective Service Board, 16
Separate Tables, 147
Seth, L.A. Buddhist, 143
Seven Mile Road, New York, 149
Sevilla, 85
Shales, Tom, 182
Shamberg, Michael, 64, 69, 71,
   74, *107*, 131
Sharon, mother of Justine and Ian,
   185, 188
Sholom, Alan, *105*
Shoprite, 45
Shriver, Sargent, 64
Sibert, Jody, 65, 71-72, *107*,
   121-122, 135, 139-140, 186-187
Sibert, Kit, *121*
Sibert-Procter, Tara, *121*,
Simon and Garfunkle,
   "Mrs. Robinson," 142
Simpson, O.J., 222, 233
Simpson, Ruth, 96
60 Minutes, 190, 224
Sklar, Robert, 63
Slings and Arrows, 149

"Smile of Sunshine"
   photo contest, 9, *113*
Smoke Enders, 171
Social Ecology, 77
Soho, New York, 29, *100*
Soltes, Elon, *108, 110,* 135, 139,
Somma, Robert, 12
Sony Porta-pak, 15
South Africa, 160
South Central Avenue, Glendale,
California, 186
South Dakota, 45
Spaghetti City Video Manual, 99
Spain 85
speaking-in-tongues, 174
"spectrum junkie," 98
Speilberg, Steven, 171
Spider-Man, 54
Spike, Harold Brown's bulldog, 148
Sports Placement Agency, 223
Springfield, Oregon, 226
Stafford, Freddie, *121,* 140, 143,
   160, 163, 185-189
Stafford, Ian, *121,* 185-189
Stafford, Justine, 185, 188
Stamps Family, 184
Stanley, Yoga instructor, 168
Stanton, Dr. Frank, 2, 11
Starr, Ringo, 55
Steal This Book, 33
Stein, Seymour, 34
Steve Christiansen, *107*
Stone, Oliver, 72
Stony Clove Valley,
   New York, 48, 57
Straits of Gibraltar, 86
Stranger, Peter, 195
Streilitz, Leonard, 179-180
Strontium-90, 81
Studs, 213
Subject to Change aka
   "The Now Project," 16, *100, 101*

Subotnik, Morton,
   Olympic Arts Festival, 140
"Summer of Love," 175, 192
Superbowl X, 75, 76, *108*
Superior Court of Pennsylvania, 91
Swann, Lynn, 76
swastika, 97
Syracuse, New York, 46, 55
Syracuse University, 84

T

Tad's Steak House, 43
Taffy, Brittany Spaniel, 147
Talmey-Drake Research,
   Boulder, Colorado, 212
Tangier, 86, 87, 198
Tannersville, New York, 53, 60, 97
Tannersville-Haines Falls, 53
Tapanzee Bridge, New York, 6
Taxi, video installation,
   Women's Video Festival 129
Tuberculosis, 201
TCI Cable, Scottsdale, Arizona,
   211-212, 215
Teach For America, 219
Teasdale, Chloe and Emilia, 90
Teasdale, Parry, 15-17, 20, 33-35,
   37, 38, 40, 44 ,47, 49, 50, 55,
   60-62, 82, 90, *99, 100, 103,*
   104, 106, 219
Teasdale, Parry,
   Collection of, *106, 112*
Teasdale, Sarah, 47, 90,
   103, 106, 219
Technology of Change, 135
Telecommunications, Inc. (TCI), 199
Temple Beth El, 147
Temple Players, 147
Temple University, Pennsylvania, 6,
Ten Little Indians, 147
Texas, 66

The Bead Game, 34
The Big Chill, 131
The Boy Friend, 156
The Cool World, 53
The Connection, 53
The Daily Show, 183
The David Letterman Show, 182
"The Eternal Frame," 191
The Five Day Bicycle Race, 77
The Gary Moore Show, 60
The Home Show, 214,
The Lord of the Universe, 135
The Newlywed Game, 70
"the 99 percent," 236
The 90s Channel, 190-192,
   199-200, 203, 205
The Power Team, 194
The Republican Convention Drag, 69
The Simpsons, 196
The Smothers Brothers, 2
The Realist, 150
"The Runner," 92
The Threepenny Opera, 156
The Tonight Show
   with Johnny Carson, 140
The Velvet Trigger, 97, *111*
The White House, Washington, D.C.,
   65, 74, 84
The Wilton North Report,
   182, 183, 214
This Is Not Here, 55
This is Not the News, 91
Tilton, Charlene, 176
Time magazine, 60, 64
Tinker Street, New York, 90
Titanic, 208
Tokyo, media journal, 217
Tom, friend of Ian Stafford, 186-187
Tomlin, Miss Lily, 60-61
T.R. Uthco, 191
Transcendental Meditation, 160, 171
Transvestite-Madonna and Child, 127

"Travesty Night," 85
Trayna, John, *110*
Trinity Broadcasting Network
   (TBN), 176, 194
Trombly, Adam, 200
Trusso, Joe, 131-132
TRW, 166
Turkey, 74
TV Guide, 203
TV Horoscope Show, 160
TV's Bloopers
   and Practical Jokes, 170
TVTV (Top Value Television),
   64-66, 69, 71-76, *107-108,*
   131, 137, 190
TVTV scrapbook, *109*
"20/20," 170, 190
Twin Pines Milk, 9
245T Pesticide, 89

U

USC film school, 144
U.S. Customs, 55, 57
U.S. Marine Corps tattoo, 227
United Artists cable system, 215
United Freedom Front, Manhattan
   and South Africa, 132
United Jewish Appeal, 179
United States Army, 95
Universal Life Church, 47
University of Arizona, 147
Upstairs at the Downstairs, 3, 59
Utica, New York, 46

V

Valley Cablevision
   Arts Magazine, 140
Van Cleef & Arpels, 168
Van Gogh, 87
Van, Rocky, 51-53

Vanguard Playhouse, 156, 158
vegetarian, 43
Velázquez, 87
Velvet Peanut Butter, 9
Venice Beach, California,
    136, 161, 163, 196, 223,
    228, 230-231, 235
Vermont, *104*
"Video and Television Review" *104*
Video Data Bank, 237
Videofreex, 14, 16-17, 19, 33-36,
    38, 41, 43, 48, 55, 61-62, 74,
    100-102, 104, 131, 219, 237
Videofreex, book by Parry Teasdale,
    51, *104, 112*
Videofreex Library, *103*
Videotape Review, 61
Vidicon, 42
Viet Nam, 89
Vietnam Vets, 65, 71
Vietnam Vets Against The War, 38, 69
Volkswagen van, 1963, 142
Voltaire, 207
Vonnegut, Kurt, 2
Vontobel, Carol, 5, 7, 12, 35, 39,
    44, 47-48, 51, 55-56, 60-61,
    90 *100, 103, 106* 219

W

Wagner, Jane, 60,
Wagner, Robert, 168
Walden's bookstore
    at The Beverly Center, 159
Walkman headset,
    nuns wearing, 127, 129
Wall Street, 196
Wall Street Journal, 202-203
Wallace, Mike, 67-69, 190
Wallenboyd Theater,
    Los Angeles, California, 150
Walt, TV director WWJ-TV, 147

Walters, Barbara, 90
Waltham, Massachusetts, 41
Waltz, Butch, 83
Warner Brothers, Burbank, 145
Washington, DC, 35-37, 46, 74, 179
Watergate, 62
Wayburn, Leon, 9, *113, 115-116,* 148
Wayburn, Mil, *113, 116*
Wayburn, Tommy, 155-156
Wayne State University, 147
Weatherman, 20
Webcor reel-to-reel, 147
Weinberg, Tom, 64, *107-108,*
    110, 190, 198-200
West, Don, 1-3, 8, 9, 13-14,
    17, 19, *100*
Western Federal Savings Bank,
    Beverly Hills, 163
WGBH Boston, 13
Wilkes-Barre, Pennsylvania, 49
William Morris Agency, 6
Williams, Megan, 64
Willow, New York, 92
Wired magazine, 198, 217
Wirth, Dr. Carl, 79, 84
WJBK-TV, 10
Women's Video Festival, 129
Woodstock, New York,
    90, 92, 93, 98, 226
Woodstock Festival, 15, 48
Woodstock Nation, 21, 94
Woodstock Times, 90
Woodstock Town Board, 94
Woodstock Town Picnic, 91
Woodstock, Channel 6, *111*
Woodstock, Zen Center
    at Mount Tremper, 127
Woodstock's Talking Youth, 96
Woodward, Ann, 41-45, 47-48,
    90, *99, 100, 103*
World Hemp Expo and Extravaganza
    (*Whee!*), 225-227

254

World Series 1969, 9
Wright, Eric and Mary,
121, 168
Writers Guild, 183
WWJ-TV, 10

X

Xanthoudakis, Rita, *121, 122,*
135, 140-141, 143-144, 150,
160, 162-163, 169, 184-187

Y

Yablon, Marji, 90
Yamamoto, 207
Yeo's Singapore Curry Gravy, 233
YMCA, 46

YMCA in Santa Monica, 140
Yom Kippur, 233
Yonkers, 49
"You Can't Buy Bagels
in Huntington Woods," 147
Young, Stanley, *122,* 185
Your Voice of Hope TV Station
in South Lebanon, Ohio, 174
Youth International Party
(aka Yippies), 17, 19, 221
YouTube, 236, 237

Z

Zappa, Frank, 175
Zappa, Gail, 175
Zeke's Heap in Altadena, 203
Zen Tricksters, 227

Acknowledgment:

I want to express my appreciation
to
Joseph Cowles and Barbora Cowles
and everyone at
Event Horizon Press
for making this
a wonderful experience.